Doing Diversity Differently in a Culturally Complex World

ALSO AVAILABLE FROM BLOOMSBURY

Disposed to Learn: Schooling, Ethnicity and the Scholarly Habitus, Megan Watkins and Greg Noble

Multiculturalism and Education, Richard Race

The Promise and Practice of University Teacher Education: Insights from Aotearoa New Zealand, edited by Alexandra C. Gunn, Mary F. Hill, David A. G. Berg and Mavis Haigh

Developing Culturally and Historically Sensitive Teacher Education: Global Lessons from a Literacy Education Program, edited by Peter Smagorinsky, Yolanda Gayol Ramirez and Patricia Rosas Chávez

Reflective Teaching in Further, Adult and Vocational Education, Margaret Gregson and Sam Duncan

Identity, Culture and Belonging: Educating Young Children for a Changing World, Tony Eaude

Subject Literacy in Culturally Diverse Secondary Schools: Supporting EAL Learners, Esther Daborn, Sally Zacharias and Hazel Crichton

Navigating Trans and Complex Gender Identities, Jamison Green, Rhea Ashley Hoskin, Cris Mayo and sj Miller

Doing Diversity Differently in a Culturally Complex World

Critical Perspectives on Multicultural Education

**MEGAN WATKINS
AND
GREG NOBLE**

BLOOMSBURY ACADEMIC
LONDON • NEW YORK • OXFORD • NEW DELHI • SYDNEY

BLOOMSBURY ACADEMIC
Bloomsbury Publishing Plc
50 Bedford Square, London, WC1B 3DP, UK
1385 Broadway, New York, NY 10018, USA
29 Earlsfort Terrace, Dublin 2, Ireland

BLOOMSBURY, BLOOMSBURY ACADEMIC and the Diana logo are trademarks of
Bloomsbury Publishing Plc

First published in Great Britain 2021

Copyright © Megan Watkins and Greg Noble, 2021

Foreword: Fazal Rizvi, 2021

Megan Watkins and Greg Noble have asserted their right under the Copyright,
Designs and Patents Act, 1988, to be identified as Authors of this work.

Fazal Rivzi has asserted his right under the Copyright, Designs and Patents Act, 1988,
to be identified as Author of the Foreword to this work.

For legal purposes the Acknowledgements on p. xii constitute an extension of
this copyright page.

Cover image © Sanne Berg, Giulio Fornasar, PeopleImages,
VisionChina, Antonio Guillem, Dean Mitchell,
Style Photographs, M Image Photography / iStock

All rights reserved. No part of this publication may be reproduced or transmitted in any form or
by any means, electronic or mechanical, including photocopying, recording, or any information
storage or retrieval system, without prior permission in writing from the publishers.

Bloomsbury Publishing Plc does not have any control over, or responsibility for, any
third-party websites referred to or in this book. All internet addresses given in this book
were correct at the time of going to press. The author and publisher regret any
inconvenience caused if addresses have changed or sites have ceased to exist,
but can accept no responsibility for any such changes.

A catalogue record for this book is available from the British Library.

Library of Congress Cataloging-in-Publication Data

Names: Watkins, Megan, author. | Noble, Greg, author.
Title: Doing diversity differently in a culturally complex world: critical perspectives
on multicultural education / Megan Watkins and Greg Noble.
Description: London; New York: Bloomsbury Academic, 2021. | Includes bibliographical
references and index.
Identifiers: LCCN 2021017368 (print) | LCCN 2021017369 (ebook) | ISBN 9781350012998
(paperback) | ISBN 9781350013001 (hardback) | ISBN 9781350013018 (ebook) |
ISBN 9781350013025 (epub)
Subjects: LCSH: Multicultural education–Australia.
Classification: LCC LC1099.5.A8 W38 2021 (print) | LCC LC1099.5.A8 (ebook) |
DDC 370.1170994–dc23
LC record available at https://lccn.loc.gov/2021017368
LC ebook record available at https://lccn.loc.gov/2021017369

ISBN: HB: 978-1-3500-1300-1
PB: 978-1-3500-1299-8
ePDF: 978-1-3500-1-301-8
eBook: 978-1-3500-1-302-5

Typeset by Deanta Global Publishing Services, Chennai, India
Printed and bound in Great Britain

To find out more about our authors and books visit www.bloomsbury.com and
sign up for our newsletters.

For
Mary and Bill, you set us on this path,
Hanya, a tireless advocate for multicultural education,
this wouldn't have been possible without you,
and
Neroli, you were so much a part of this.

CONTENTS

List of Illustrations viii
Foreword ix
Acknowledgements xii
List of Abbreviations xiv

Introduction: Doing Diversity Differently 1

1 'Thinking' Multiculturalism and Multicultural Education 19
2 Questions of Identity and Culture 43
3 Grappling with Cultural Complexity: Knowledge Translation and Professional Learning 67
4 Lazy Multiculturalism: Civility, Celebration and the Limitations of Cultural Recognition 89
5 Engaging with Others: Constructing Educational Problems 113
6 From Inclusive Curriculum to Cultural Intelligence 139
7 Engaging with Cultural Complexity, Enhancing Professional Practice 171

Conclusion: Diversity Done Differently 191

Notes 205
References 208
Index 221

ILLUSTRATIONS

Figures

1 RMRME Project Action Research: Levels and modes of engagement 71
2 Remaking multicultural education 203

Table

1 Profile of RMRME Schools 16

FOREWORD

The main premise underlying this wonderfully researched and written book is that the dominant approaches to cultural diversity and multicultural education need to be radically reimagined. This is so because the experiences of diversity in schools and societies are no longer what they used to be. In the past, the notion of cultural diversity mostly referred to immigrant groups, focusing on issues of their ethnic origins and the challenges of their settlement into the mainstream community. What has now become clear, however, is that this logic of migration is at best limited, if not flawed. It does not sufficiently recognize the ways in which the processes of migration have changed over the years. Motivations that now drive migration are now much more diverse and complex. Increasingly it is not the individuals but ethnic and professional networks that drive migration. Over the past few decades, the number of skilled immigrants has grown rapidly. Dual and even multiple citizenships are now available to many immigrants. Nor does migration any longer involve an expectation of permanent detachment from the immigrant's country of origin.

Major developments in communication and transport technologies have enabled immigrants to remain in touch with their home communities in a whole range of new ways, on an on-going basis, in real time. Their ability to remain connected with friends and family around the world has allowed them to maintain and extend their transnational networks, take advantage of the cultural resources available to them, making it possible for them to develop a cosmopolitan imagination. The transnational experiences and networks have thus become a positive force, helpful in enriching cultural spaces, enhancing the possibilities of public diplomacy and becoming a source of economic productivity through cross-border trade, innovation and enterprise. In this way, it is mistaken to assume a tight relationship between the processes of migration and deficit notions of marginalization and disadvantage. That is not to say that many immigrants do not also experience considerable hardship. Refugees, in particular, are subject to unbearable levels of discrimination, even if they are able to remain transnationally connected. Harsh government policies often intensify their sense of marginalization, of belonging neither 'here' nor 'there'. The benefits of cosmopolitanism elude them, despite their determination to succeed, and the creativity they display in overcoming great odds.

What these observations suggest is that the diversity that now exists in schools and societies is much more complex, contingent and contradictory.

Experiences of diversity are themselves diverse, as are the ways in which differences are named and accorded significance. While some instances of difference are overlooked, others play a profound role in shaping social relations. The questions of why and how are, however, not easy to answer, since accounts of difference and diversity are always historically and politically constituted, and often contested. The processes of globalization have further complicated attempts to interpret and respond to the challenges of diversity. As levels of mobility not only of people but also of capital and finance and images, ideologies and information have increased, becoming more intense, so has the cultural politics of social institutions, cultural practices and even of identity and belongingness. Transnational mobility has given rise to issues of security, sustainability and adaptation to a world that increasingly involves complexity, contingency and uncertainty.

In light of these changes, Watkins and Noble use in this book a rich body of empirical data to show, convincingly in my view, how the traditional ways of addressing issues of diversity are no longer appropriate, if not mistaken. They rest on a logic of migration that does not adequately account for the contemporary experiences of superdiversity and transnational connectivity. This logic fails to take account of the dynamism of cultural change and the complexities of cultural identity and intercultural relations. The data presented in this book clearly demonstrates that a new approach to diversity is needed, which makes visible the intensity, and scope of global flows of persons, goods and ideas and symbols, on the one hand, and the anxieties about these flows, on the other. The romantic idea of multiculturalism, predicated on the liberal assumptions of tolerance, cultural maintenance and social cohesion, they argue, needs to be rethought, since it fails to take into account not only the dynamism of change but also the intricacies of power relations. Furthermore, it remains trapped within a set of nation-centric assumptions and is therefore unable to address issues of identity, culture and diversity under increasingly transnational conditions.

Diversity can no longer be viewed simply as a sum of fixed identities, frozen outside history and contemporary cultural relations, sidelining the facts of the growing levels of interactivity, both within and outside national spaces. Far too often, the traditional discourse of multiculturalism, which remains dominant in both schools and the wider society, embraces a notion of culture that is inherently naturalistic, conceptualized as an inherited way of life. This focus on way of life is reduced to cultural forms made most visible in language, habits and customs. This reduction both appeals to, and lends itself, to cultural essentialism, out of which grow stereotypes and prejudiced attitudes towards the others. This essentialism also implies that a society is fundamentally constituted by an uninterrupted accord between diverse cultures, and that through its consensual logic multiculturalism can accommodate differences in an impartial manner. The problem with this view, however, is that it does not only rest on the assumptions of essentialism but also presupposes that differences can somehow be accommodated within the prevailing structural norms, without disrupting them. It thus fails to recognize that identities and cultures are forged in histories and unequal relations of power.

This book amply demonstrates how schools and societies cannot afford to overlook the complexities inherent in understanding and addressing the complicated relationship between identity, culture and education. It shows the need to finally accept that our contemporary cultural condition is inherently complex, hybrid and dynamic. This does not mean that cultural traditions are not important, but that they need to be interpreted in new and creative ways, within the shifting contexts of interculturality that are continuously changing. While viewing cultural diversity in schools to be ubiquitous, organic and dynamic, Watkins and Noble do not, however, recommend abandoning the idea of multiculturalism but point to the importance of re-envisioning multicultural education that 'does diversity differently', helping students to engage with the relationalities of cultural difference in ways that are critical – but also productive.

Fazal Rizvi
The University of Melbourne

ACKNOWLEDGEMENTS

This book was only possible due to the willingness of many principals, teachers, parents and students in New South Wales (NSW) government schools: those teachers across NSW who took time during their busy day to respond to our survey and the school communities of the fourteen project schools who participated in interviews, observations, focus groups and professional learning. The generosity of those who offered their valuable, and often frank, insights into their experiences, perceptions and understandings was remarkable, and especially those teachers who undertook the action research. These projects involved a considerable commitment on top of their already weighty workloads, which is testament to these teachers' desire to effect change around multicultural education in their schools.

We also want to acknowledge our partner investigators on the *Rethinking Multiculturalism, Reassessing Multicultural Education* (RMRME) Project: Amanda Bourke, Nell Lynes and Eveline Mouglalis from the NSW Department of Education (DoE) and Robyn Mamouney from the NSW Institute of Teachers, now the NSW Education Standards Authority (NESA), with whom we worked closely on the design and implementation of the research and who provided invaluable input and advice. We've had a long and fruitful exchange with our colleagues in the NSW DoE through many projects, and we've always valued our open and challenging discussions.

Hanya Stefaniuk and Greg Maguire from the NSW DoE made significant contributions to the initial Australian Research Council (ARC) proposal for RMRME, offering guidance on both research design and conceptual framing. Of huge importance was the work of the NSW DoE Multicultural and EAL/D Education consultants – whom we can't name. These consultants worked closely with the researchers and with the schools, tirelessly helping with the design, implementation and evaluation of the schools' projects. Another teacher, whom we can name and who assisted us during the research and writing of this book, is Judith Kempthorne – a consummate professional! We always value her advice.

We would also like to thank our Western Sydney University (WSU) colleagues, especially Professor Kevin Dunn, our co-investigator, whose contribution was invaluable during the RMRME survey construction and statistical analysis. Many others at WSU have contributed: Helen Barcham, Simone Casey, Cheryl D'Cruz, Tulika Dubey, Garth Lean, Cameron McAuliffe, Kate Naidu and Virginia Piccone, who provided research assistance or administrative support during different stages of the project and writing of the book. Lucy Hopkins at Edith Cowan University also assisted with the data collection for this book and followed up on detail that was much needed. Neroli Colvin, a PhD student at the Institute for Culture and Society at WSU attached to the RMRME project and a dear friend, became an integral part of the project. Neroli completed her PhD following the project but tragically passed away before she could see the project to its fruition or indeed the impact of her own work. She is sorely missed.

We would especially like to thank Alison Baker, Evangeline Stanford and the team at Bloomsbury. Their support and patience have been greatly appreciated – this has been a much longer journey than any of us had anticipated!

We also want to acknowledge each of the following publications and thank the publishers for permission to reproduce sections from each of these within this book:

> Noble, G. (2017). 'Asian fails' and the Problem of Bad Korean Boys: Multiculturalism and the Construction of an Educational 'Problem'. *Journal of Ethnic and Migration Studies*, 43(14), 2456–71.
>
> Watkins, M. and Noble, G. (2016). Thinking beyond Recognition: Multiculturalism, Cultural Intelligence, and the Professional Capacities of Teachers. *Review of Education, Pedagogy, and Cultural Studies*, 38(1), 42–57.
>
> Watkins, M. (2018). Culture, Hybridity and Globalization: Rethinking Multicultural Education in Schools. In T. Ferfolja, C. Jones-Diaz and J. Ullman (Eds), *Understanding Sociological Theory for Educational Practice* (pp. 159–75). Cambridge: Cambridge University Press.
>
> Watkins, M. and Noble, G. (2019). Lazy Multiculturalism: Cultural Essentialism and the Persistence of the Multicultural Day in Australian Schools. *Ethnography and Education*, 14(3), 295–310.
>
> Watkins, M. (2016). Cultural Studies, Pedagogy and Reimagining Multicultural Education: Working with Teachers to Effect Change in Schools. In Hickey, A. (Ed.), *The Pedagogies of Cultural Studies* (pp. 133–48). London: Routledge.

Lastly, we would like to acknowledge the financial support of the ARC, WSU, the NSW DoE and NESA. NSW schools are now faced with increasing ethnic and linguistic diversity, as is the broader Australian community. The public funding of research is essential to ensure that we have the richest data for understanding the nature of this diversity, the theoretical tools for making sense of how it shapes our lives and the educational tools for addressing the needs that emerge from it. Good education needs good research. It is hoped the insights gleaned from this research will better prepare all teachers for the challenges this diversity poses, ensuring schools cater for the diverse needs of their communities and equipping students with the knowledge and skills they require to effectively navigate the complexities of the globalized world in which they live.

ABBREVIATIONS

ACARA   Australian Curriculum Assessment and Reporting Authority. Established in December 2008, ACARA is an independent authority responsible for the development of the Australian National Curriculum, national assessment programs and the collection of data for the MySchool website providing statistical and contextual information on Australian schools.

AITSL   Australian Institute for Teaching and School Leadership. This is the statutory body that is responsible for the accreditation of Initial Teacher Education programmes in Australia.

ARCO   Anti-Racism Contact Officer. Each school in NSW has a teacher who is a trained ARCO. Their role is to handle any complaints of racism and to promote anti-racism education in their school.

BOSTES   Board of Studies, Teaching and Educational Standards. BOSTES was incorporated in the former NSW Institute of Teachers and the Board of Studies. It is now known as NESA.

CALD   Culturally and linguistically diverse. This term has become all pervasive, but it is problematic for reasons we discuss in Chapter 2.

EAL/D   EAL/D is the term now used in Australian schools to refer to students whose first language is a language or dialect other than English and who require additional support to develop proficiency in Standard Australian English. It was formerly referred to as English as a second language or ESL, a term considered inaccurate as, for many students, English is actually their third or fourth language.

HSIE   Human Society and Its Environment. This is a Key Learning Area within the NSW Curriculum. It comprises subjects such as history and geography.

ICSEA   Index of Community Socio-educational Advantage. This is a scale used by ACARA based on the occupation and level of education of all parents in each Australian school. The median ICSEA score is 1,000 and values range from a low of 500 to a high of about 1,300.

KLA Key Learning Area

LBOTE Language Background Other Than English. This is the favoured term to refer to students who have a language background other than English in Australian schools. It replaces the older term NESB or Non-English-speaking background. Categorization in terms of language background is preferred over country of origin or ethnicity.

NESA New South Wales Education Standards Authority was founded in January 2017 replacing BOSTES.

INTRODUCTION
Doing Diversity Differently

This book, and the research informing it, derives from a number of different sources. It was findings from an earlier study into the differential achievement of students of Chinese, Pacific Islander and Anglo[1] backgrounds in Australian schools that led to this broader examination of multicultural education (Watkins & Noble, 2008). Among other things, this study found a tendency of many of the teachers we were working with to essentialize their students' ethnicity or, more precisely, that of the Chinese and Pacific Islander background students, assuming it was this that largely determined their academic performance – the impressive results that many of the Chinese background students achieved and the far lower achievement of those of Pacific Islander backgrounds. No such link was made between the Anglo-Australian students and their performance at school. Instead, 'Anglo' and 'Whiteness' operated as normative categories that masked these students' ethnicities leading teachers to foreground socio-economic status (SES) and/or individual family experience as more likely factors influencing their performance at school. We were interested in understanding what encouraged this way of thinking; how ethnicity was conceived as an attribute of being 'other than White' and, concomitantly, the lens through which many teachers came to make often misplaced judgements about their students' learning. It prompted us to consider the ways in which multiculturalism, and how it is realized in schools through various programmes of multicultural education, may have contributed to such understandings despite all its productive achievements; how efforts to be inclusive of ethnic difference through initiatives around cultural recognition and respect may have had the reverse effect, entrenching ethnic divides and a distinction between Anglo and 'Other'.

Our concerns were shared by our research partners in this earlier study from the former Multicultural Programs Unit (MPU) within the New South Wales (NSW) Department of Education (DoE). These colleagues were of a similar view that multicultural education needed to be rethought through an examination of how teachers approach the numerous initiatives in schools that are collectively referred to as multicultural education. In NSW, multicultural education encompasses a range of programmes: English as an Additional Language or Dialect (EAL/D),[2] community relations, intercultural understanding, culturally inclusive curriculum, anti-racism and support for refugee students, among other things. Some of these, such as those supporting EAL/D students and community relations, are specific to schools with concentrations of students with a language background other than English (LBOTE).[3] Others, namely intercultural understanding, culturally inclusive curriculum and anti-racism, must be implemented in all schools no matter what their population of LBOTE students, to foster an ethic of openness and acceptance of cultural diversity and an understanding of its impact within the broader community. There was a concern about teacher knowledge, how practitioners understood key terms such as 'ethnicity', 'culture' and 'multiculturalism', given that the meanings they attach to each of these have implications for how they approach multicultural education in their schools.

Once the study to investigate these issues commenced, it became apparent that there were teachers with similar reservations about current practices of multicultural education. As a principal in one school commented,

> when there is an emphasis on spaghetti and polka I begin to feel it's a pointless exercise. To me it is trivializing it. We've had multicultural lunches and we've had multicultural dances and we've had the kids come in dressed in multicultural costumes and we've had the multicultural concert, which is fine and all that's great, as long as it's coupled with more in-depth understanding.

Whether this principal is referring to student or teacher understanding here is unclear. What is certain is that student understanding is largely shaped by teacher knowledge. If students are to acquire the requisite conceptual resources to make sense of the cultural complexity of the world in which they live, their teachers need to be equipped with the necessary insight and skill to mediate this process. Critiques of multicultural education, as offering little more than a superficial celebration of ethnic difference, are not new. This principal's reference to an emphasis on 'spaghetti and polka' draws on how Kalantzis and Cope (1981) typified such approaches within an Australian context forty years ago. They argued then against the limited nature of such forms of cultural recognition and the reductive concept of culture – as static, homogenous and linked to discrete ethnic communities – that such events promote and which lacks any meaningful interrogation of racism or the means to counter the educational inequalities that many LBOTE students experience. Similar critiques are found elsewhere. In the UK, Troyna (1987, 1993) characterized them as the three Ss or 'saris, samosas and steel band' approaches and, in the United States, Nieto (1995) coined the phrase 'brown holidays and heroes' to refer to the tokenistic treatment of race within curricula and multicultural events in schools. Yet, despite these critiques, the popularity of such approaches continues.

With the exception of programmes that provide targeted support for English language provision and the initial orientation to schooling for recent migrants and refugees, multicultural education is often reduced to little more than these types of feel-good activities, what Ahmed (2012, p. 58) terms 'the lip-service model of diversity' and which we have characterized as forms of 'lazy multiculturalism' (Watkins & Noble, 2019). It is not simply that such approaches represent a lost opportunity in that the time and energy teachers devote to developing them could have been spent on more insightful examination of issues around cultural diversity; they actually warrant close scrutiny given the meanings they generate may run counter to the inclusionary logic of multiculturalism. While the abovementioned principal considered multicultural activities at her school were 'great' and simply needed to be supplemented with 'more in-depth understanding', such insight should lead to a questioning of these types of events or, at least, the ways in which they are often framed by essentialized notions of ethnicity and culture. Such approaches may attribute forms of identification to students which they may have little attachment to or which may have little relevance in addressing their educational needs. Casting a critical eye over such activities to determine their value in promoting the 'deeper level of understanding' that this principal is keen to encourage requires a particular orientation to knowledge. It requires that teachers grapple with notions of cultural complexity and forego the security of what has been established practice in this area; in other words, to understand that multicultural education may need to change.

Gaps in Teacher Knowledge

The fact that little headway has been made in relation to this, despite long-term critique from within academe, and to some extent within the teaching profession, requires some explanation. In his review of research into pre-service teachers' views of cultural diversity in the United States, Castro (2010) bemoans the dearth of any complex engagement with these issues, together with how many trainee teachers also lack any reflexivity about their own positionality given the predominantly White, Anglo nature of the nation's teaching profession and how this may impact upon their perspective on multicultural education. Similar findings are evident in Australia where various studies note the simplistic understandings of ethnic diversity that many pre-service teachers possess and the implications of this for student learning (Allard & Santoro, 2006; Mills, 2013; Santoro, 2013b, 2014). Such findings reflect poorly on initial teacher education, prompting calls for practitioners to be more effectively trained for working in ethnically diverse school environments.

These calls are framed in different ways. Premier and Miller (2010) stress the need for all teachers to be trained in EAL/D pedagogy given the number of students with these needs in mainstream classrooms. While this is valuable knowledge and would go some way towards improving the educational outcomes of LBOTE students, it does not directly address the gaps in conceptual understanding that teachers require for making sense of cultural complexity and its implications for schooling. To be fair, Premier and Miller indicate that the training they recommend needs to be supplemented with a grounding in 'multicultural issues', but their rationale for doing this is that it will allow teachers 'to become more empathetic towards CALD[4] students' and, through this, to better meet their needs (Premier & Miller, 2010, p. 38). Catering for the needs of LBOTE students, however, is only one aspect of multicultural education. Such a focus neglects its broader remit of ensuring all students acquire skills of intercultural understanding. The degree to which empathy assists the teaching of LBOTE students is also questionable (Boler, 1999; DeTurk, 2001; Zembylas & Papamichael, 2017). Coupled with the technical linguistic expertise to which Premier and Miller refer, teachers actually require the critical capacities to reflect upon their own positionality and to counter the kind of essentialism that often frames perceptions of ethnicity – meanings that are in turn transmitted to students. Rather than understanding in an empathetic sense, comprehending the cultural dynamism of the contemporary world and how it is realized within local contexts is reliant upon understanding as an intellectual task. This, however, is not always foregrounded in approaches to multicultural education within teacher training where pragmatic concerns of classroom practice are often given precedence.

Another example of the way in which teacher education should better prepare trainee teachers for such experiences is provided by Ladson-Billings (1999) who has long called for those entering the profession to spend time working in culturally diverse schools. Immersion in such contexts, however, does not always translate into reflexive practice around race and ethnicity. Concern over teachers' perceptions of ethnicity and its influence on student learning in some of the highly diverse school environments where we conducted a previous study prompted the research that informs this book. Such experience may prove beneficial, but it is more likely to be so if practitioners are armed with the appropriate conceptual tools for making sense of these empirical contexts – knowledge, for example, of the social constructedness of culture, ethnicity and race, prompting a questioning of the categories that are used to define students and the delimiting forms of identity they may engender (Appiah, 2018). Such knowledge has applicability for all educational contexts: schools that are highly ethnically and linguistically diverse and those that are not. The latter are often the most challenging for the teaching of multicultural education as their lack of diversity means such approaches may be given a low priority. It is in schools such as these that multicultural education may be most needed. This variance in how best to prepare practitioners for teaching multicultural education is also reflective of the different functions it performs in schools, from programmes to ensure access and equity for migrant and refugee students and their families to those encouraging better understanding and an ethic of inclusion for all students. Multicultural education has evolved to fulfil these different purposes, though what constitutes multicultural education in different national contexts can vary enormously, being dependent upon each nation's own particular history, political circumstances, ethnic make-up and patterns of immigration.

What Is Multicultural Education? Varying Perspectives

In Australia, where the research for this book was undertaken, multicultural education in schools can be traced back to 1969 and a pilot project for teaching EAL/D to the children of migrants (Inglis, 2009). Since then, multicultural education has expanded to include the numerous programmes already referred to, though EAL/D remains a core component. This expansion of multicultural education includes anti-racism, inclusive curriculum and intercultural understanding. It is an acknowledgement that increasing ethnic diversity poses numerous challenges and that living with difference requires certain skills and understandings that schools are well placed to develop. In Australia, this was necessitated by expansive migration programmes which, since the end of the Second World War, have seen the arrival of over seven million migrants. Today, 49 per cent of Australia's population of twenty-four million were either born overseas (28 per cent) or have at least one parent born overseas (21 per cent) (Australian Bureau of Statistics (ABS), 2017). While the largest groups of migrants are from the UK and New Zealand, in recent times, China and India have become the major source countries, and there has been a widening spread of nations including increasing numbers of refugees from Africa and the Middle East. The perception of Australia as a multicultural country is now firmly engrained within the national psyche (Markus, 2019). While not without its opponents, it is a perception that federal and state government policies of multiculturalism since the 1970s have actively encouraged, keen to expunge the nation's assimilationist past in favour of a diverse and more tolerant nation (Koleth, 2010).

As a settler-colonial country, Australia's cultural diversity is also characterized by its First Nations people, yet the dispossession of their land and ongoing inequalities wrought by British imperialism have never been resolved and remain issues that successive governments have failed to adequately address (Moreton-Robinson, 2015). Multicultural education in Australia, however, has tended to be quite distinct from Aboriginal education, and there is a clear political rationale for this. As the original inhabitants of the continent, Aboriginal Australians have a prior claim to the land and demand recognition as the First Peoples of Australia rather than to be subsumed within a category of being 'multicultural' that typically signifies migrant-derived diversity. Yet here, in effect, is part of the problem with multiculturalism and multicultural education. As both a descriptive category to refer to Australia's ethnic diversity and as policies designed to manage that diversity, 'multicultural' and 'multiculturalism' tend to denote the migrant Other, distinct from not only Australia's Indigenous population but also those of Anglo-Australian background. Despite its inclusionary rhetoric, multiculturalism, and how it is practised in schools, is rarely inclusive of all.

Curriculum initiatives at a federal level in Australia seem to have been designed to address this issue with a focus on intercultural understanding as a general capability now incorporated in the teaching of relevant subjects across the curriculum (ACARA, 2020a). Requiring all students to reflect upon their own cultural backgrounds, as well as those of others, this aspect of Australia's National Curriculum purports to equip students for 'living and working together in an interconnected world' (ACARA, 2020b). Its intention, therefore, is to be more broadly inclusive, to broach cultural divides and to foster intercultural engagement. To many, this is simply an aspect of multicultural education, whether or not it is effectively dealt with in schools, and so the relationship of intercultural understanding to the more established programmes of multicultural education, promoted by state education departments, is not entirely clear. Multicultural education is listed as one of the antecedents of intercultural understanding in material from the National Curriculum that is made available to teachers, along with language education and the disciplines of cultural studies, sociology, linguistics and anthropology (ACARA, 2013), but the omission of any further discussion of the relationship between the two, or indeed any mention of multiculturalism in any material associated with the initiative, suggests a shift away from the older paradigm of multicultural education. Critiques of multiculturalism, especially following 9/11, have led to similar curricula change in the UK (Race, 2014) and Europe (Catarci, 2015; Gundara, 2000) favouring intercultural or citizenship education over multicultural education, a move discussed in more detail later in the chapter. Yet multicultural education in Australia still has considerable currency. Whether intercultural understanding operates as a discrete initiative or is simply part of multicultural education's suite of programmes, it faces the same issue already discussed, that teachers need to be appropriately trained to ensure such approaches have the desired effect in schools.

Multicultural education is also of continued significance in other settler-colonial nations such as New Zealand and Canada. As with Australia, both these countries have populations derived from waves of migration, especially since the Second World War, overlaying that of their Indigenous peoples and colonial settlers. Multicultural education in both contexts is similarly tasked with addressing the challenges this diversity presents, though in New Zealand this sits alongside policies of biculturalism that recognize the Māori as New Zealand's original inhabitants and juxtaposes the Māori language with English as a medium of instruction in many schools (May, 2002). Canada, of course, has a long history of multicultural education. Recognized as the first country to endorse multiculturalism as government policy in 1971, Canadian education is said to be 'now thoroughly infused with multiculturalism' (Wright, 2011, p. 34). Moreover, not only does Quebec have an official policy of interculturalism that foregrounds the role of Francophone culture in the province, but Canada also has specific policies related to its Indigenous populations that generally lie outside the remit of multiculturalism. How multicultural education relates to these varying perspectives is not always clear, but, as in Australia, with policies of multiculturalism formulated primarily in response to migratory flows since the Second World War, it is this diversity which not only seems its prime focus but with which it is most associated in the public consciousness. As with multiculturalism more broadly, multicultural education has twin foci; its concern is for a specific type of diversity together with promoting an ethos intending to be inclusive of all. Its success in achieving the latter, however, may be precluded by its initial focus on a more constrained conception of diversity, or perhaps multiculturalism and multicultural education are simply being asked to do too much, far beyond their initial brief.

Multicultural education is practised more widely than in Australia, New Zealand and Canada. Despite its similar colonial-settler past and expansive migration from the late nineteenth century, the origins of multicultural education in the United States stem more from its civil rights movements of the 1950s and 1960s that were primarily directed towards countering the inequalities facing African Americans that derive from the nation's history of slavery and discriminatory race relations (Nieto, 2009). Such moves, prompting various educational reforms, served as an impetus for other groups to lobby for greater recognition within curricula and educational resourcing, first from a wider spread of ethnic groups and then to those marginalized in terms of gender, sexuality, faith and disability (Kirylo, 2017). As a result, multicultural education in the United States has a broader focus than that practised in Australia, Canada and New Zealand, though issues of ethnicity and race remain central to its agenda. Yet, despite this wider scope of multicultural education in the United States, it seems vexed by the same dilemma of reconciling how it deals with both a focus on specific groups and the broader orientation of engendering intercultural understanding among all students no matter what their ethnic background. James Banks, a key figure in the field, has remarked that 'When educators view multicultural education as the study of the "others", it is marginalized and held apart from mainstream educational reform' (Banks, 1993, p. 22). Yet the origins of multicultural education were very much framed by not only a study of the Others but of ensuring 'they' were appropriately resourced – dimensions of multicultural education that have continuing significance, but which are no longer its exclusive focus.

Many educators' difficulties in grasping the broader agenda of multicultural education may in fact relate to how it was initially conceived with an emphasis upon often reduced forms of recognition that assumed identity was simply a function of ethnicity or race. This is understandable given the context of the times in which the expression of forms of ethnic identification, beyond the norms of the White, Anglo mainstream, had been actively suppressed. The legacy of the identity politics that was influential in framing multicultural education, however, has been a persistent essentialism where, it could be argued, a focus on ethnic and racial difference has become its raison d'être. Multicultural education, therefore, has been complicit in the Othering that Banks critiques. Countering this, and re-purposing multicultural education, is a complex task. While it needs to maintain a strong advocacy role for those who are marginalized, it also needs to avoid essentializing this marginality. At the same time, while continuing to meet the needs of newly arrived migrants, multicultural education needs to embrace a broader agenda of ensuring all students develop capacities to interrogate their own positionality and to understand the cultural dynamics of the contemporary world.

To Banks, achieving this involves educators understanding what he sees as the five dimensions of multicultural education: the integration of content from a variety of cultural perspectives within a curriculum; an equitable pedagogy that facilitates the academic achievement of all students; an empowering school culture that counters structural inequality; programmes of prejudice reduction and; understanding how knowledge is constructed and the cultural assumptions that inform this process (Banks, 2009, p. 15). This is a comprehensive account of what multicultural education should entail, but it is the last dimension around knowledge construction – and deconstruction – which should be foundational, influencing the ways the other dimensions are approached. This should be a dimension that requires teachers to engage with ideas drawn from sociocultural theory, arming them with the appropriate conceptual tools so that when they are integrating content from different ethnic and or cultural perspectives, they can move beyond 'spaghetti and polka' and avoid the essentializing that such forms of multicultural education encourage. Such reductive understandings similarly imbue policies of multiculturalism. When ethnicity is conceived as primordial, and communities as discrete and bounded, it can easily feed conservative critiques of multiculturalism as engendering social fragmentation and the impossibility of broaching so-called ethnic divides.

Such critiques of multiculturalism have led to a move away from multicultural education in the UK and Europe though, with the exception of the Netherlands (Leeman, 2008), the latter has always favoured intercultural education with its emphasis on cross-cultural exchange rather than the multiplicity of discrete cultural groups (Allemann-Ghionda, 2009; Catarci, 2015; Gundara, 2000). Tomlinson (2009), for example, explains that the term 'multicultural education' is no longer referred to in curriculum initiatives in the UK. Race (2014) contests whether multicultural education was ever very influential within an English context, stressing that education policy was probably more focused on an integrationist agenda. Whatever the case, such critiques of multiculturalism have certainly had an impact in the UK with educational initiatives around cultural diversity highlighting Fundamental British Values and social cohesion within a new paradigm of citizenship education (Starkey, 2018; Weinberg & Flinders, 2018). A similar shift in emphasis is evident in Europe where approaches to intercultural education, which date back to the 1970s (Allemann-Ghionda, 2009), are also having to respond to the backlash against the perceived divisiveness of multiculturalism. This has resulted in the foregrounding of common national or European values (Veugelers et al., 2017), though the latter is also under attack as the UK's exit from the European Union and the rise of nationalist politics in Europe attest (Gusterson, 2017; Nicolaidis, 2020).

This change of direction has been more pronounced since 9/11, the rise of Islamic fundamentalism and the greater incidence of terrorist attacks which are often linked to increasing migration and ongoing refugee crises that many countries are unwilling or unprepared to accommodate. The resultant questioning of the viability of multiculturalism has repercussions for multicultural education and associated programmes related to issues of ethnic diversity and schooling. But while political agendas may change, the stark reality remains that many societies must now contend with increasing levels of ethnic, linguistic and religious diversity. In 2019, the number of international migrants worldwide reached 272 million, an increase of 51 million since 2010 (United Nations, 2019). This rapid acceleration and its varying impact are felt beyond the countries and regions already discussed. They attest to diversifying populations worldwide and an ever-increasing need for ensuring social inclusion and peaceful coexistence both within and across national boundaries. Schools are important sites where such foundational skills and understandings can be cultivated, but what this should entail is contested. As indicated, conservative critiques of multiculturalism have left their mark on educational policies and practices that are designed to address these issues. Key tenets of multiculturalism, such as cultural maintenance, are now considered questionable on the grounds that they limit migrants' integration within host nations and pose a threat to a cohesive sense of national identity and belonging, hence the emphasis on common values and citizenship education in some countries.

Yet critiques of multiculturalism are not the preserve of the political right. There are those such as Hage (1998, p. 209), on the left, who argue that the dominant form of multiculturalism is actually a variant of this 'assimilation fantasy'. He views the encouragement that migrants receive to retain their language and cultural traditions, and the banal celebration of this difference, as a mechanism for ensuring White domination that 'tames' ethnic groups. Conservative critiques of multiculturalism are an indication that this containment has been breached and that a neat demarcation between 'us' and 'them' is now being called into question, threatening the White hegemony that Hage claims multiculturalism was designed to safeguard. Conservative critiques of multiculturalism also reveal the hollow nature of much of the rhetoric that frames such public policy as being inclusive of all. Australia's 2011 multicultural policy, for example, declared that 'Multiculturalism is about all Australians and for all Australians' (Australian Government, 2011, p. 2). While this was a pleasing recommitment to multiculturalism by the government at the time, more recent conservative governments have been far less supportive. For White Australians, moreover, multiculturalism is still very much about 'the Others'. There may be broad acceptance of the multicultural nature of Australian society (Markus, 2019), but an 'us' and 'them' mentality still prevails, undermining multiculturalism's promise of a plural and inclusive society. This contradiction, inherent in multiculturalism, has long been recognized. Bullivant (1981), for example, referred to 'the pluralist dilemma'; competing logics of multiculturalism's recognition of the rights of ethnic communities, together with the universalizing claims of those of the nation. This is not only an issue for multiculturalism; it is of importance to multicultural education as it strikes at its core rationale of who and what multiculturalism is actually for. Is it about the recognition of the ethnic identities of students and their families and ensuring schools meet these students' educational needs, or is it about developing capacities to enable all students to bridge perceived cultural divides, foregrounding a broader civic identity attentive to a sense of the communal that is truly plural and equitable for all?

Multicultural Education in an Age of Superdiversity

The notion of 'plural' here requires some explanation. Within what we call a multicultural imaginary it has typically signified a plurality of discrete ethnic communities with individual identity defined in 'singular', group-based terms. With increasing globalization resulting in accelerated transnational flows of people, communication, information, goods and capital (Appadurai, 1996), such hermetic notions of community and identity are difficult to sustain. Terms such as 'superdiversity' (Vertovec, 2007) and 'hyperdiversity' (Noble, 2011) have been coined to not only refer to the widening spread of countries from which migrants now originate, and how globalization impacts upon these populations, but how it affects diasporic communities worldwide. Like nations as a whole, diasporas are continually diversifying through processes of intergenerational change, cultural adaptation and intermarriage resulting in hybrid identities. This is not to say that forms of ethnic group identification are no longer meaningful. Many attach great significance to these ancestral bonds which have ongoing resonance within people's lives, but we need to be careful of the meanings we assign such forms of identification. Moreover, rather than the single defining feature of individual subjectivity, ethnicity needs to be considered alongside class, gender, sexuality, age and religion. Any one of these may prove more significant, particularly for organizations like schools tasked with addressing individual students' needs. A focus on ethnicity, particularly when narrowly conceived, may simply obscure these. This is a view Vertovec (2010, p. 88) shares, explaining that in the UK, 'simple ethnicity-focused approaches to understanding and engaging various minority "communities" . . . as taken in many models and policies in conventional multiculturalism, are inadequate and often inappropriate for dealing with individual immigrants' needs or understanding the dynamics of their inclusion or exclusion'. Phillimore (2015), who applies these insights to the health sector in the UK, is also critical of the 'ethnicity focus' in the delivery of maternity services, suggesting it is inadequate for understanding the nature of need within contexts of superdiversity. Boccagni (2015, p. 614) offers a similar view in his account of superdiversity in the area of social work. He questions the relevance of ethnic group identification as the primary frame of reference for service delivery within the sector pointing out that 'different, less visible axes of identification' may prove more significant. We're suggesting here that the 'diversity' that arises from the copresence of ethnically defined groups is complicated by the intragroup variations within such 'groups', the complexity that arises from the hybridizing effects of intermarriage, etc., and by the complexities of a global world where we partake of elements of many cultural traditions in our daily lives.

Teachers, likewise, need to consider the challenges superdiversity pose and to rethink the way ethnic identification is understood, its role in relation to student learning, and the implications of this for how multicultural education is practised in schools. It should prompt an interrogation of approaches such as those designed to be 'culturally sensitive' or 'culturally responsive' to ensure that, despite the best intentions, they are not simply reinforcing cultural stereotypes and essentialized notions of ethnicity (Parkhouse et al., 2019; Schmeichel, 2012). Rychly and Graves (2012, p. 44), for example, conceive of culturally responsive pedagogy as 'teaching practices that attend to the specific cultural characteristics that make students different from one another and from the teacher'. By 'cultural characteristics' they mean 'values, traditions, language' together with 'communication, learning styles and relationship norms'. While it is important for teachers to ensure their pedagogy is responsive to their students' needs, to characterize these as 'culturally' derived in the sense intended here overstates the cohesiveness of culture, making little allowance for individual variation, pigeonholing students as representative of particular cultural types. Gay (2015) worryingly advocates a similar approach to that taken within business, suggesting that the segmented marketing techniques that target particular ethnic and social class groupings could be of relevance to education. While she posits the possibility of intragroup variation, making reference to globalization's impact on populations worldwide, she seems little convinced of its significance declaring, 'Whether this is true or not is not the issue' (Gay, 2015, p. 128). But, this is precisely the issue, as it draws attention to narrow demarcations of culture, ethnicity and race. How these are deployed within education and the understandings that teachers assign them have practical implications in classrooms. Gay, however, seems unwilling to question the substantive nature of these categories and so feels that each minority group 'demands and deserves different instructional strategies' (Gay, 2015, p. 135).

In contexts of superdiversity, where classrooms are often composed of students from many different ethnic backgrounds (Watkins, 2011), this is not only a logistic impossibility, but it also fails to account for the many students of mixed heritage and how teaching for them could be tailored in this way. More of a problem is the assumption that underpins such approaches, that a student's ethnic background is the chief determining factor in how they learn. The alternative to such approaches is not one of conformity to the dominant culture; it simply requires teachers to think in more complex ways as to the 'culture' they are being responsive to and to develop a form of 'cultural intelligence' (Ang, 2011) that allows them to better understand the nature of the world in which we now live. Without doing so, such differential teaching practice runs the risk of operating more like a form of pedagogic apartheid, streaming students on the basis of ethnicity or race. Multicultural education, therefore, needs to be alert to the ways in which superdiversity challenges how we understand conceptions of culture, ethnicity and race and to better grasp the hybrid forms of identification that may now be more characteristic of students' lives. Acknowledging hybridity does not entail discounting these categories, but it does require a different conceptual lens wherein they are no longer understood in essentialist terms. Maintaining a focus on these categories in this way also ensures teaching does not become colour blind (Dixson & Rousseau Anderson, 2018; Levine-Rasky, 2013) in the sense of masking racism and forms of structural inequality of which they are the root cause. Liberal forms of multiculturalism and their banal celebration of cultural difference are often critiqued for this reason (May, 2009), but a focus on cultural hybridity can be equally banal if such forms of discrimination remain unchecked.

Alternative Perspectives on Multicultural Education

These are some of the numerous challenges that multicultural education faces that others have sought to address. May (1999, 2009) and Sleeter (2012, 2018) are advocates of critical multiculturalism that derides the superficiality of liberal multiculturalism and its instantiation in schools in activities such as multicultural days. They stress the need for practices that disrupt the relations of power that help to maintain inequalities of ethnicity and race. Their approach to these issues is very much aligned with others that foreground a critical perspective within education such as critical race theory (Gillborn & Youdell, 2009; Ladson-Billings & Tate, 1995), critical pedagogy (Giroux, 2020; McLaren, 2015) and anti-racism education (Kailin, 2002; King and Chandler, 2016). With a reflexive take on these approaches, however, May and Sleeter (2010, p. 3) indicate they 'too often fail . . . to provide actual examples of transformed and/or emancipatory pedagogy and practice', which could explain the continued presence in schools of the approaches they critique, as teachers see the latter as much easier to implement. While May and Sleeter (2010) have sought to address this shortcoming, calling for a stronger focus on practical application, there remains an ongoing issue that the promotion of a critical race consciousness, more pronounced within critical race theory, may actually reinforce the category of race.

In response to these issues, others have embraced cosmopolitanism as the necessary antidote to multiculturalism's focus on the particular over the universal and a desire to foreground the global over the national (Donald, 2007). Attentive to critiques of cosmopolitanism as the preserve of global elites and as a vague liberal humanism lacking any groundedness in local concerns (Rizvi, 2014), there is a prizing of the cosmopolitan ethos of openness to others and acceptance of difference as having considerable utility within contexts of schooling (Reid & Sriprakash, 2012; Roxas et al., 2015). Rizvi (2014), for example, proffers a notion of 'cosmopolitan learning' as a way of examining the interconnectedness of the local and the global and the relationality of cultural flows that reconfigure the more narrow conceptions of identity and community that multiculturalism has tended to encourage – understandings that are often reproduced in schools though practices of multicultural education. The intent of cosmopolitan learning is to question such notions and instil in students a set of what Rizvi (2014) terms 'epistemic virtues' whereby students come to reflect upon their own situatedness in the world and their associations with others, no longer constrained by a national lens and fully cognizant of their relation to the global. In doing this, cosmopolitanism prompts a rethinking of notions of citizenship and citizenship education. In contrast to conservative critiques of multiculturalism that tend to tighten the parameters of what constitutes citizenship, cosmopolitanism broadens its scope. Cosmopolitan citizenship has the global community as its horizon and citizens' responsibilities exceeding those they have to the nation. Such ideas have influenced those wishing to reframe citizenship education, such as Osler and Starkey (2018), Sidhu and Dall'Alba (2012) and Guo (2014), who see the global orientation that cosmopolitanism offers as a bulwark against the ethnic nationalism that underlies the more constrained conceptions of citizenship that have surfaced in response to concerns over the perceived impact of increasing cultural diversity on social cohesion.

Rethinking Multiculturalism, Reassessing Multicultural Education

These various alternatives to multicultural education provide even further evidence that aspects of the approach need to change. They attest to a need for greater engagement with the ways in which globalization and transnational mobility impact upon populations, particularly those of high migrant-receiving nations, and whether multicultural education is equipping students with the requisite tools to make sense of this increasing cultural complexity. Teachers play a crucial role in relation to this, but, as discussed, little seems to have changed in the approach to multicultural education in response to these major demographic shifts, raising questions about teachers' professional learning that guides practice in this area. It was these concerns that became the focus of the research informing this book. First, the aim was to gauge teachers' understandings of multiculturalism, key concepts related to multicultural education and what they saw as the gaps in their knowledge that could assist them to improve how they approached its implementation in schools. Second, the research wanted to ascertain students' and parents' understandings of multiculturalism and what they saw as the role of multicultural education. Finally, the intention was to use this information in professional learning to support teachers to conduct action research that addressed areas of need around multicultural education in their schools and then to examine teachers' success in doing this – both their responsiveness to the training they received and how they applied these understandings in their schools. The study, titled *Rethinking Multiculturalism, Reassessing Multicultural Education* (RMRME), was funded through the Australian Research Council involving researchers from Western Sydney University[5] partnering representatives from the then MPU[6] within the NSW DoE and the former NSW Institute of Teachers,[7] which during the course of the project became the Board of Studies, Teaching and Educational Standards (BOSTES) and since then NESA. This was an important alliance as it brought together ourselves as academics working across the disciplines of sociology of education and cultural studies – and having conducted previous research into multiculturalism and aspects of cultural diversity and schooling – with the bodies responsible for the implementation of multicultural education in NSW government schools and teachers' professional learning.

The project adopted a model of engaged research (Third, 2016) involving cooperative design and implementation, with the three partners having a joint commitment to effect change in schools. The research involved three large data sets. First, there was data gleaned from a survey of NSW government teachers into their: cultural backgrounds; understandings and attitudes towards multiculturalism and multicultural education; professional learning experience and; needs and practices around multicultural education in schools (Watkins et al., 2016). The state education system in NSW is one of the largest in the world (NSW DoE, 2019, p. 1) and the electronic survey – the first of its kind in Australia to amass data on this topic – yielded 5,128 responses. This amounted to almost 10 per cent of the state's teaching population spread across 70 per cent of government schools, providing a comprehensive snapshot of multicultural education from an Australian perspective. Focus groups were also conducted with teachers, parents and students in the project's fourteen target schools to yield more detailed data on participants' cultural backgrounds and their understandings and attitudes towards multiculturalism and multicultural education (Noble & Watkins, 2014).

The last data set was acquired from a macro-analysis of action research projects that were conducted in the targeted schools (Watkins & Noble, 2014). At each of these sites, school-based research teams comprised of up to five members, including executive staff, classroom teachers and, in one case, parents, were interviewed at the beginning of the year in which the research was undertaken.[8] This occurred after their training, which was accredited by BOSTES and prior to their project commencing. A second interview was conducted following the completion of the project, each of which was presented at an end-of-year project symposium where schools submitted detailed reports of their findings. Each school's principal was also interviewed prior to, and on completion of, their school's project. Additional data was obtained from observations of the various initiatives that each school implemented over the course of the year as part of their action research. Partnering with the NSW DoE was invaluable during the action research phase of the project as they provided grants to schools to fund teaching relief for professional learning and for other aspects of each school's project implementation. The NSW DoE also supported schools through their Multicultural Education consultancy team[9] who received training from us, as the academic partners, to undertake this work. In a pilot project to RMRME, we had performed this role ourselves, visiting schools on a regular basis to assist them to design and implement their action research. This had posed something of a conflict of interest, however, in both assisting with the carriage of the project and researching its effectiveness. Instead, with RMRME, after the training, we took a step back from this role keen to examine how teachers applied the understandings they had acquired in rethinking their approach to multicultural education in the context of their own school.

In a broad sense, the project adopted a form of ethnography, but one which purists may not recognize. Our approach could be described as an 'ethnographic orientation' to the study of educational practice (Watkins & Noble, 2019). We were less interested in a conventional site-based ethnography and instead undertook ethnographies of two fields of practice. First, this involved an ethnography of the field of multicultural education. The schools,

TABLE 1 Profile of RMRME Schools

School*	School Type	Setting	Total Student Population	LBOTE Student Population (%)	Socio-Economic Status (ICSEA)**
Addington	Secondary	Urban	852	22	930
Barnett	Secondary	Rural	766	3	974
Beechton	Primary	Semi-rural	118	19	970
Binto Valley	Primary	Urban	268	25	1,199
Eaton Park	Secondary	Urban	1,109	59	1,138
Getty Rd	Primary	Urban	807	79	1,040
Graham's Point	Secondary	Urban	1,341	46	1,060
Harringvale	Secondary	Urban	967	83	1,066
Hingston Valley	Secondary	Urban	1,276	83	1,097
Pentonville	Secondary	Semi-rural	1,264	4	957
Smithton	Primary	Urban	527	70	1,067
Thurston	Primary	Urban	178	47	895
Wellington Heights	Primary	Urban	907	95	1,167
Wollami Lakes	Primary	Rural	380	27	924

* Pseudonyms are used for each of the schools.
** ICSEA is a value based on parents' occupation and level of education. See ACARA (2013). 1,000 is the median score. < 1,000 signifies a lower SES and > 1,000 a higher SES.

in this sense, were case studies within this broader focus. As Hage (2005) argues, there is no such thing as a truly 'multi-sited ethnography' because sites are not always easily separable. For us, and our partners, schools can also be seen as locations within a larger set of relations and discourses shaped by an institutional structuring and contested through competing visions of 'multicultural education'. Second, we were also interested in undertaking an ethnography of professional development, examining processes of professional learning and engagement, curriculum and programme construction and evaluation that teachers as professionals undertake but which tend to be invisible to other research approaches. Spread across fourteen schools, this meant there was a comparative dimension to understanding these processes essential for the overarching evaluation of RMRME.

From the beginning, the RMRME research team wanted to focus on how multicultural education was practised in a diverse range of schools, not simply those with concentrations of LBOTE students but those that were far less culturally diverse, with different socio-economic profiles and located in both urban and rural areas. The study also sought a balance of primary and high schools to investigate how teachers, across the school years of Kindergarten to Year 12, engaged with issues around ethnic diversity with not only their students but their broader school communities. Our partners in the NSW DoE held data on schools that helped identify the appropriate mix and, through their team of multicultural education/ EAL/D consultants who had regular contact with schools across the state, were able to suggest those with staff willing to commit to the training and to conducting a year-long research programme in their schools. Following discussions with principals and staff, together with those within the project research team, the fourteen schools shown in Table 1 were selected providing a good cross-section of schools within NSW, though with a greater number from within the Sydney metropolitan area given its greater concentrations of schools.

Doing Diversity Differently

This book draws upon this vast array of data. As with the RMRME project itself, its intention is not only to examine current understandings and attitudes towards multiculturalism and multicultural education held by teachers, students and parents but to act as a trigger for doing diversity differently; for rethinking how multicultural education is practised in schools. In many ways, the book troubles the very notion of 'cultural diversity' proffering instead a focus on 'cultural complexity' to acknowledge the entangled forms of identification that globalization exacerbates and that calls into question the settled understandings of ethnic identity and community long since associated with, and promoted by, polices of multiculturalism. Teachers were integral to this undertaking. It was through them that these ideas, with varying levels of success, were translated into practice. As educational practitioners, they shoulder a huge responsibility for making sense of the world for their students, a role poignantly described by Connell (2009, p. 224):

> Interpreting the world for others, and doing it well, requires not just a skill set but also a knowledge of how interpretation is done, of the cultural field in which it is done, and of the possibilities of interpretation that surround one's own. This requirement helps to define teaching as intellectual labour and teachers as a group of intellectual workers.

The extent to which teachers involved in the study saw their role in this way varied. Some were highly motivated to promote change in their school and others were resistant. The book documents what happened in each of these schools. It examines the success stories where teachers rose to the challenge of doing diversity differently by engaging with theory to enhance their professional practice and to then use this to modify their approach to multicultural education, and those where this knowledge was not so well applied and very little changed as a result. In all cases, lessons were learnt not only about multicultural education but about the 'professional cultures of teaching'. It is these insights which inform Chapters 4 to 7 where the action research projects are considered in terms of their overall approach and impact. These chapters are preceded by an examination, in Chapter 3, of the professional learning the teachers undertook that involved engagement with issues around globalization and its impact on culture and identity together with training into the theoretically informed approach to action research that the project adopted. The chapter explores teachers' differing reactions to this training which are suggestive of two distinct professional cultures: one with a narrow pragmatic focus in which professional learning serves a purely practical function and another with a broader intellectual orientation that recognizes the benefits of theory for rethinking practice. The book begins, however, with two chapters which not only 'set the scene' for the case studies but bring a broader focus to the field of multicultural education. Chapter 1 examines the ways multiculturalism and multicultural education are understood in the teaching profession, drawing on the state-wide survey and the focus groups with teachers, parents and students, exploring these findings in relation to what we call the competing 'logics of multiculturalism'. Chapter 2 extends this analysis by considering how questions of culture and identity – the central preoccupations of multiculturalism and multicultural education – play out in the profession and in school communities.

CHAPTER 1

'Thinking' Multiculturalism and Multicultural Education

There can be no analysis of multicultural education without discussion of the meanings of multiculturalism. Many studies have shown ongoing support for multiculturalism in Australia and elsewhere (Berry, 2013; Markus, 2019; Poushter, 2017). However, these studies also show a degree of confusion over what multiculturalism means, despite the term being part of political discourse for many decades (Dunn et al., 2004; Goot & Watson, 2005). This confusion has flowed into the field of education. As discussed in the Introduction, much has been written on the nature and consequences of 'multiculturalism', from both advocates and critics of various political persuasions, and in terms of policy applications and philosophical perspectives, in education and elsewhere. As the Introduction made clear, multiculturalism is not a single thing but involves an array of programmes and rationales, reflecting what we refer to as the diverse logics of multiculturalism. This complexity affects the choices practitioners make in institutions like schools.

The aim of this chapter, then, is to explore the ways multiculturalism is understood in schools. It draws on data from the state-wide survey of NSW teachers and focus groups in the fourteen project schools to consider what teachers, students and parents mean when they talk about multiculturalism and how this shapes the ways they perceive the goals of multicultural education. We do this not only to examine the competing understandings that typify multicultural discourse generally but to explore whether there are similarities and differences in perspectives between teachers as professionals and the wider school community of students and parents, and to make sense of the perceptual schemas that shape school practices. We argue that multiculturalism is most typically foregrounded across all groups as a descriptive fact of ethnic diversity *and* as a moral disposition towards exotic difference, which de-emphasizes the educational capacities students need to understand a culturally complex world and the professional capacities teachers need to help students do this.

The Logics of Multiculturalism

Considerable effort has been given over many years to unpack and debate the meaning(s) of multiculturalism: scholars have shown that there are variations between nations, shifts in meaning over time and contestation between groups about what multiculturalism is (Lentin & Titley, 2011; Schwarz, 2007). Research shows that while there is general public support for multiculturalism, it varies depending on context, and that there is also some ambivalence about multicultural policies and their effects on social cohesion (Ang et al., 2002; Markus, 2019). There are many sources of this confusion and ambivalence, but we want to focus here on several issues that are significant for examining perceptions of multiculturalism in school communities.

The first is the extent to which multiculturalism is used as both a descriptive term, which simply points to the 'fact' of ethnic diversity in many contemporary societies, born of migration programmes that have drawn migrants from many countries, and a prescriptive term, which refers to the set of policies which manage that diversity and foster a particular ethos around diversity (Kalantzis, 1988, pp. 91–2). Of course, the 'fact' of diversity deriving from migration does not guarantee the existence of a political strategy of 'multiculturalism' (Kenny & Lobo, 2014, p. 105), so we should avoid collapsing them. Moreover, migration itself doesn't constitute the diversity valorized in multiculturalism. A migration programme of only White British migrants, for example, would not make Australia 'multicultural'. Particular (exotic) differences matter more than others in constituting 'diversity'.

The second is that the ethnic diversity arising from migrant flows is significantly different to diversity arising from colonial occupation (Kymlicka, 1995). Multiculturalism is conventionally used to refer to the former but not the latter in settler-colonial nations like Australia, where Indigenous issues are separated. This raises the issue of what we mean by 'culture' in multiculturalism – whether we are referring to a whole way of life or an ancestral heritage, an issue we explore in Chapter 2. Arguably, while many migrants have brought aspects of their customs with them, Australia has only had a true plurality of cultures as whole 'ways of life' in terms of the fundamental difference between the historical modes of production of Indigenous populations and those who have arrived in waves of migration over the last two centuries (Castles et al., 1990, p. 124). These are complex conceptual issues, not just empirical questions, and yet they are rarely articulated in policy or interrogated in practice, educational or otherwise.

A third set of issues points to the coherence of multicultural policies. Even though some see multiculturalism as a unified policy with a single ethos, multiculturalism in practice 'describes a variety of political strategies and processes which are everywhere incomplete' (Hall, 2000, p. 210). Multiculturalism entails different policies, claims and modes of accommodation: forms of assistance, exemptions, internal and external constraints, self-government, relations of recognition and so on (Levy, 2000). While many commentators are primarily interested in the role of cultural rights in accommodating pluralism, following Kymlicka's (1995) group-based rights approach, there is another way of thinking about these diverse objectives and programmes.

Some scholars have argued that multiculturalism is just one mode of drawing migrants into the host society – in Australia it is typically contrasted with assimilation and integration (Jupp, 2011) – but multiculturalism itself entails different forms of 'inclusion'. These don't simply represent a messy 'patchwork of initiatives, rhetoric and aspirations' (Lentin & Titley, 2011, p. 2) but embody *competing logics*. These forms involve different orientations of purpose and practice which compel institutional responses in particular ways. From the early days of multiculturalism, a focus was on providing migrants with the assistance needed to settle. It was often attached to events, such as citizenship ceremonies, which are about symbolically binding the migrant to the nation and to certain rights and services. We call this a logic of *incorporation* – not in the sense that earlier policies required migrants to forego claims to the homeland but in the sense that migrants need to acquire particular resources (the dominant language, an understanding of political processes and social mores) to function in the host society. While 'incorporation' may retain, for some, the problematic idea of the 'mainstream', it frames the process of settlement in terms of equity and access to social services, shifting the responsibility for this from the migrant to the state. Historically, however, it was realized that many migrants need informal and formal networks of support to settle well, and these networks are often provided by diasporic communities. Thus, multiculturalism also contained a logic of *recognition* – formalizing and funding the role of ethnic community organizations and encouraging the maintenance of the mother tongue and homeland customs (to an extent). Such a logic often assumes the coherence of the 'ethnic community' being recognized – a problem we address in Chapter 2. At the same time, it was also understood that large-scale migration required changes within the wider society, not just among migrants. The development of anti-racism strategies, cultural awareness programmes and practices that mark the importance of ethnic diversity within mainstream society entail a logic of *civility* that expects all citizens to learn how to work and live together cooperatively in shared social space. This is often stressed as the ethos of multiculturalism, but it can dissolve into moralizing mantras calling for cultural harmony and an unreflexive valorization of difference.

Each of these logics can contain competing visions of social justice, national community, ethnic difference and moral imperatives, as well as contrasting views of the consequences of migration and the purpose of governmental policy. As Triandafyllidou et al. (2012, p. 3) argue in the European context, the way states pursue the inclusion of ethnically diverse populations varies widely. Current debates around social cohesion and interculturalism continue to work around these logics. But they are *competing* logics in the sense that they emphasize different policy goals, different 'problems' and objects of action, and different mechanisms for addressing these problems that may be in tension: social justice as the recognition of difference or the redistribution of social resources, inclusion into the national family or via the embracing of a cosmopolitan vision beyond nation and so on. These logics can be seen across all national formations of multiculturalism.

In the Australian context, while it represented a significant shift from the White Australia Policy, multiculturalism soon became a system of governance which, while addressing pressing social justice issues, locked community organizations into systems of funding and political representation based on simplistic notions of ethnic community (Jakubowicz et al., 1984). By the 1990s, the focus on programmes promoting participation and equity was increasingly framed by a well-intentioned identity politics which often promoted a reductive sense of diversity and identity (Hage, 2003; Ho, 2013; Schwarz, 2007). This was complicated by emerging policies of neoliberalism (Kymlicka, 2013) which eroded projects of social justice but retained the political appropriation of ethnic politics. Multiculturalism was always a 'compromise formation', articulating divergent interests and meanings (Rizvi, 2014, p. 8), but it was also a 'compromise' because it aimed to address different kinds of problems. Schools are social institutions where, as we'll argue later in the chapter, these compromises have to be worked out practically.

Yet multiculturalism is seen to encompass an overarching ethos which often obscures these interests and meanings. The 2017 Australian Government statement *Multicultural Australia* extends the self-congratulatory tone of the 2011 policy, seeing Australia as 'the most successful multicultural society in the world', built on shared values of respect, social cohesion, equality and freedom, emphasizing the commitment to national security and the economic role of migration. As the prime minister at the time announced, 'The glue that holds us together is mutual respect' (Australian Government, 2017, pp. 3, 9). It is easy to dismiss these bland claims, but the important issue is how such a statement entangles the rival orientations in political discourse around ethnic diversity: the free market, social welfare, national identity and homeland attachments. The value of focusing on these competing logics is to sidestep the endless debates over whether multiculturalism has failed, and whether it has produced a 'successful' society or is racism by another name (Lentin &

Titley, 2011) – these are important issues, but we are more focused here on what gets done in the name of multiculturalism and how understandings of multiculturalism shape what happens in schools, especially given that none of these 'logics' has a clear or explicit *educational* approach.

Surveying Teachers on Multiculturalism

Once we appreciate that multiculturalism is a complex contradictory formation, it is no wonder that, as a social ideal, it has been met by both public endorsement and confusion. Multicultural education provides an illustration of how these logics manifest in practice. As suggested in the Introduction, multicultural education covers a range of strategies which aim to prepare all students for participation in an ethnically diverse society *and* to meet the particular needs of LBOTE students. We are arguing not just that these programmes are diverse, but that they follow different logics and have different objectives: some are about equipping students with the resources they need to function in Australia, some are about maintaining the linguistic and cultural resources of diasporic communities, some are about training all citizens to be respectful of ethnic differences, some are about the specific needs of minority groups and so on. While this ensemble of programmes is seen to be held together by an overarching vision, in practice it raises a number of questions:

- How do schools implement programmes which seem to follow competing logics – social equity, cultural maintenance, community liaison, anti-racism, cultural awareness?
- Given the scarce resources and time that schools have, how do they prioritize?
- Are meanings and the goals of multiculturalism shared by teachers, students and parents?
- Do assumptions built into multiculturalism match the lives of students in contemporary societies?
- Are teachers and schools well prepared to address these demands?

To answer these questions, we need to examine the public and professional understandings of multiculturalism and the rationales and practices of multicultural education as they are realized in school communities. As indicated, in this chapter we draw on data from two of the three stages of the RMRME project outlined in the Introduction – the survey of NSW government school teachers and focus groups with teachers, parents and students in the fourteen project schools – to see what school communities think they are doing when they 'do' multiculturalism.

While the RMRME survey[1] elicited responses to a wide range of topics – on the backgrounds of teachers, their professional experience, their teaching practices in the area and their needs around multicultural education – it also asked questions around their understandings of and attitudes towards multiculturalism and multicultural education. The survey was crucial because teachers are professionals who work in institutions where multiculturalism has been adopted as a policy that informs many programmes and activities as well as offering an overall ethos to interethnic interaction. While studies across the world show that teachers and trainee teachers are generally very positive towards multiculturalism and more so than the wider population (Forrest et al., 2016; Hachfeld et al., 2011; James, 2004), some ambivalence persists among teachers (McInerney, 2003). Existing research on teachers' attitudes, however, tends to focus on pre-service training and is based on relatively narrow attitudinal surveys. Few studies actually enquire into what teachers and trainees understand by multiculturalism, but when they do, they demonstrate variable understandings of multiculturalism, ethnic diversity and multicultural education (Burridge & Chodkiewicz, 2010; Neuharth-Pritchett et al., 2001).

In our survey, teachers were most likely to define multiculturalism as the 'celebration of all cultures within one society' (31 per cent) and 'a society made up of many cultures' (25 per cent), with smaller numbers opting for 'a mixing of national backgrounds, languages and religions' (15 per cent), 'policies which manage diversity through goals of social equity and cultural maintenance' (15 per cent) and 'a nation where people from all cultures are free to follow their own beliefs' (13 per cent) (Watkins et al., 2013, p. 54).[2] They show that there is no agreed definition of multiculturalism among teachers, just as there is no agreed view in the public at large, despite it being a central plank of social policy for over four decades. Yet the data shows several things. First, an emphasis on an orientation to diversity which fosters logics of recognition and civility through the moral imperative to 'celebrate' diversity (which presumes dispositional skills to 'appreciate' difference) is quite different to an emphasis on a simply descriptive account of diversity (the presence of 'many cultures'). Second, both of these are valued over a focus on multiculturalism as policy, as the management of diversity. Third, those emphasizing mixing were about the same as those emphasizing cultural maintenance. These responses indicate that teachers have no special insight into multiculturalism as a set of endorsed practices, suggesting that there is no shared, professionally orientated view of multiculturalism.

These divergences also manifest in other responses in the survey: while the vast majority of teachers demonstrated support for multiculturalism, agreeing that schools had a responsibility to cater for the needs of students from diverse backgrounds (89 per cent) and to address racism and discrimination (94 per cent), almost half of the respondents had neither read the NSW Multicultural Education Policy (46 per cent) nor were sure whether the policy had been implemented in their school (43 per cent) (Watkins et al., 2013, pp. 37–8)[3]. These findings suggest we needed to look more closely at how multiculturalism is perceived within school communities.

Teachers' Understandings of Multiculturalism

The second stage of the study entailed 42 focus groups involving a total of 222 teachers, parents and students in 14 schools that were nominated by the DoE to undertake the professional learning and action research projects (see Table 1). All participants in these discussions were organized by the schools themselves. The students interviewed in primary schools typically came from Years 5 and 6 (aged ten to twelve) and those in high school typically came from Years 10 and 11 (aged fifteen to seventeen). The teachers interviewed were generally not those involved in the action research teams. The views recounted here are not intended to be representative of the schools (in Table 1) nor of teachers, parents and students as a whole. Nevertheless, they provide a useful record of diverse perspectives to be found across NSW schools.

Some differences might be expected between how teachers – whose task it is to implement educational programmes and policies – articulate their 'mission' in relation to multiculturalism and how students and parents – as largely the 'recipients' of multicultural education – understand the rationales of these programmes and the policies. As professionals with years of training, a commitment to policy and the development of practical competencies, we might expect teachers to develop a 'professional vision' (Goodwin, 1994) which offers, in a coherent and sophisticated way, an understanding of ethnic diversity in all its complexity and the challenges this poses to them as educators, and with a policy as well as practical orientation. The idea of a professional vision identifies the ways teachers' training and expertise foster the encoding of educational issues around diversity, working through categories of identity which frame not just how students, their families and communities are seen but also how educational and behavioural 'problems' are constructed and addressed (Noble & Watkins, 2014a, p. 165). While teachers' perspectives will also reflect the specificities of the school and classroom context, we would expect training and expertise to be significant factors in shaping teachers' engagement with multicultural education (Horenczyk & Tatar, 2002; Thomas & Kearney, 2008). The idea of a 'professional vision', then, relates directly to what we call the 'professional cultures' of teaching (see Chapter 3), which are defined by both the perceptual frameworks through which teaching is undertaken and the orientations to practice and theory embedded in differing modes of professionalism (Goodson & Hargraves, 1996).

The variety of views found in the survey responses, however, was reflected in the focus groups with teachers. One teacher from ethnically diverse Smithton Public School (PS) responded that multiculturalism was simply 'many cultures'. The discussion at Thurston PS, where half the student body has a LBOTE (and a significant Aboriginal student population of 8 per cent), captures the divergent senses of multiculturalism:

> TEACHER 1: Lots of cultures all in one place.
> TEACHER 2: Lots of different cultures exist harmoniously, you know, within the one area, working together and – almost you would say you don't differentiate, so multicultural that you don't notice them, you don't differentiate any more.
> TEACHER 3: Well to me I suppose multicultural is just, you know, a variety of different cultures existing harmoniously and having different things to offer, different traits and experiences to enrich the other cultures.
> TEACHER 1: The more nationalities there are the greater we see the multicultural aspect of things I suppose. I mean my parents' parents wouldn't have grown up thinking that Australia was a multicultural society but my son definitely will and he'll know it too, you know, so, he is well aware of it. I think they just accept it.

The 'fact' of diversity and the moral imperative to live in harmony are conjoined, without acknowledging the tension between accepting differences while not differentiating. This Harringvale High School (HS) teacher juxtaposed 'coexistence' and community maintenance rationales, but without seeing how these could fit together:

> The multicultural idea is that cultures, yes, they share, they blend, they coexist but in some way they maintain some kind of identifiable integrity, like you can still see aspects of different cultures in the multicultural society and that's tolerated so that it's OK for religious beliefs and all sorts of things, you know music, dress, the way you work whatever, they are all the things that make a culture, language. It's OK for all of those things to exist in a multicultural society.

Many, such as these two Getty Rd PS teachers, move from the juxtaposition of mixing and maintenance to the 'problem' of others:

> TEACHER 1: I'm from Auburn. They want to put a ten-kilometre circle around . . . and nobody but Muslims can live inside that ten-kilometre circle. So they are not even making it good for everybody living there, they are causing intolerance amongst the older people in the area, and they can't understand what's going on and why.
> TEACHER 2: Just adding to that . . . multiculturalism is . . . also that you can have your own culture, that you can identify totally with your own culture, that your understanding of others' intolerance but you can still live the life that you

want within your culture . . . the Islamic community as a whole is . . . in terms of their schooling and what they are prepared to have taught in their schools in the majority of cases is still limited. So they are not wanting that input of what we deem to be the Australian school culture or the Australian way of life.

The question about the meaning of multiculturalism shifts, here, to a commentary on the changes some have experienced in Australia. The exchange starts with the valuing of difference but segues into the lack of acceptance among older 'Australians' (where difference is outside 'Australian-ness') and the dangers of 'enclaves'. It sees multiculturalism as the right to maintain your culture but shifts into the problem of intolerance among ethnic communities who are deemed to be unprepared to adopt the 'Australian way of life', including the valuing of difference. A common criticism is that Muslim communities are not being 'multicultural' enough, supposedly refusing to be tolerant (and not just causing intolerance in others) and not accepting 'the Australian way of life'. The teachers don't seem to be aware of the contradictions they are voicing, and one of them makes the spurious claim that Muslims are attempting to claim a particular part of Sydney for themselves – a view promulgated by right-wing groups. As one anti-Muslim leader of the Rise Up Australia Party expressed it in regards to the suburb of Auburn, 'Muslims [are] taking over whole suburbs and turning them into no-go zones' (Fife-Yeomans, 2013). Auburn certainly has a large Muslim population – 43 per cent of the suburb's total population – but it is constituted by people from several national backgrounds (the largest being Turkish), sects and language backgrounds. Moreover, the largest single ancestry in Auburn is actually Chinese (ABS, 2016).

We're not suggesting that these teachers share the views of right-wing groups, but they do reproduce a questionable claim without careful reflection and, as Rizvi (2014, p. 57) argues, students pick up a lot of ideas about race, and racism, from schools, even where there is a commitment to a multicultural ethos. The point here is to suggest that, when teachers talk at length about multiculturalism, we get more complicated narratives about diversity that reflect local contexts, as well as professional training, ambivalences alongside endorsements and a mash-up of the diverse logics that constitute the rationales for multicultural education.

Students' Understandings of Multiculturalism

Understandings of multiculturalism don't just inform teacher practices but pervade school committees, policies, signage, parental expectations and student perceptions (Meetoo, 2020). It is useful to consider students because they are in the midst of an institutional process where they are 'learning' multiculturalism. Not only are they subject to activities in the name of multicultural education, but they are in the process of acquiring a competency in ways of talking about and 'doing' multiculturalism. In her study of diversity training, Voyer (2011) characterizes this as being 'disciplined to diversity', the learning of a language of multiculturalism. Multiculturalism, she argues, has become a cultural (and moral) framework that infuses all domains of life and so reshapes not just the competencies we need to navigate our institutional and social lives but also our sense of self. This process is both more diffuse and sustained in schooling, if unevenly, and is manifest in events such as multicultural days, codes of behaviour and curriculum content. Each year, for example, NSW primary school students in Years 3–6 participate in the Multicultural Perspectives Public Speaking Competition, where they deliver speeches on topics such as 'same but different' and 'racism – it stops with me' (NSW DoE, 2020e).

'Learning multiculturalism' is, however, an uneven process, depending on the school and its community. Two Year 11 boys at rural Barnett HS, in an area with little ethnic diversity, were surprisingly unclear when asked to define multiculturalism:

> STUDENT 1: Um, I wouldn't know.
> INTERVIEWER: OK, is it something that is ever discussed at school in any subject?
> STUDENT 2: Yeah, Year 10.
> INTERVIEWER: What do you do around that – what do they talk about?
> STUDENT 2: Um, I forget. Um, we do it in history or geography.

This is surprising given the time and resources that are invested in multiculturalism across the schooling system. This suggests that for some students the impact of these practices is muted or forgotten, particularly in communities with limited diversity. More typically, students at semi-rural Pentonville HS, with a low LBOTE population, offered the basic definition that multiculturalism meant 'different people living together'. While a version of this was found at most schools, some students, especially those from schools with high LBOTE populations, were more comfortable with the language of multiculturalism and its different emphases. At Getty Rd, a student responded that 'I think it means, not just lots of different cultures together but it means acceptance of them'. At Eaton Park HS,

> I think multicultural is the mixing and the integrating of different cultures in something like say a community or a group, so yeah, like in this community there are various people who make up that group who come from different various cultural backgrounds and races and they mix and integrate with each other. And they share these cultural things that they have.

At Harringvale HS: 'also a bit of embracing their culture as well. So if you look at our society you have like Indian restaurants, Chinese restaurants, Italian restaurants, so embracing that culture as well is an important aspect'.

These responses convey an array of ideas, as we saw with teachers, some of which are in tension. From the initial description of the 'fact' of diversity, students emphasize more 'prescriptive' elements: mixing, moral or dispositional skills (accepting, appreciating), coming together in community, sharing cultural traditions and so on. Sometimes this is framed in terms of a local community and sometimes across the nation. Sometimes culture is understood as personal differences and sometimes it refers to groups of people; sometimes it is a vague sense of 'background', while for others it is linked to ethnicity, language or faith. These divergent elements are not 'mistakes' but demonstrate partial internalization of the disposition towards a multicultural ethos and perhaps the nature of their local context; these students are processing the diverse messages they receive in schools, their communities and the wider society about multiculturalism and ethnic diversity. Several students referred to the activities they do in school where these messages are reproduced most explicitly: through multicultural days or the Multicultural Perspectives Speaking competition. One from Smithton, with a relatively high LBOTE population, commented that 'We always do writing on it, like "is it good for Australia to be a diverse multicultural country?"'. Unlike the boys from Barnett, where there is little diversity, this student is indicating the multicultural message is constant. While generally these students had imbibed a celebratory message of diversity, few thought about multiculturalism as policy unless prompted. Some, however, had a nascent understanding of the necessity of the management of difference. At Hingston Valley HS:

> having a policy sort of makes it a little more official, makes people think that you know this country is about multiculturalism, like in some places where the government is not supporting it the people feel that there is no need to support it either, so it sort of promotes a policy which sort of promotes the peace a little more. It sort of shows that they are out for multiculturalism and that it's a serious issue and it needs to be addressed.

At Eaton Park HS: 'when those bad qualities come in, whether or not a multicultural community is successful is how they deal with those bad qualities and how they accept the person for who they are.' As students discussed these issues, they worked through particular ideas, like this Harringvale student:

> I see it as having sort of two sides . . . in a multicultural society you have lots of different cultures that learn from each other but also like when individuals . . . are allowed to retain their own culture . . . it's like

different facets on a diamond kind of thing, like they are all unique and they are all different but they come together to form a whole.

More difficult issues arose when students pursued the theme that multiculturalism meant the mixing of differences, because some argued that faith-based schools or specific suburbs were not diverse. The Pentonville group, in a semi-rural area, debated Muslim schools in this exchange:

STUDENT 1: I don't know why they have to have just a [Muslim] school, just for them, I don't understand why they couldn't go to their local school.
STUDENT 2: Let's just say the Anglo-Australians trying to build a school specific for White people, imagine the comments and the newspaper articles that would get posted, you know, that's fine for the Lebanese or Muslim, like churches and religious groups trying to build schools specifically for them.
INTERVIEWER: What about if it's a Christian school?
STUDENT 2: But can't anyone go to that anyway?
STUDENT 1: With private schools I don't think that's, if you have a Lebanese child that was you know, came from a Christian background they would still be more than welcome there, it's not, it's religious belief not, yeah. I think that's another topic.
STUDENT 3: I honestly don't see the problem. If they would like to have a school that their children can go to, to practise their religion, they should have the right to do it.
STUDENT 1: Yeah, but that's the thing, it's not a religious school, I thought it was a school based on race.
STUDENT 2: And if they build a school like that, as long as they just didn't like isolate themselves from the rest of the community, like if that happens people wouldn't be happy about it, oh they're just like not interacting with anyone else, they are just in that group.

Despite the complications around seeing Christian schools as non-religious and open to all, and Islam as a category of race, it is clear these students are grappling with the tension between the 'rights' logic of multicultural recognition and the goal of 'cultural harmony'. The discussion reflects the semi-rural context they come from, where there is little diversity – but it is also close to one of the areas in Sydney where there had been a media panic about the building of a mosque. The discussion moved to a Sydney suburb transformed by Asian migration which they visited as part of a school excursion designed to bring students into contact with ethnic diversity. While one student described it as 'cool' because of its restaurants, when asked if this place was multicultural, students disagreed:

STUDENT 4: We did an excursion there, yeah, in geography to just see the multicultural school, so yeah, I would say it was.
STUDENT 2: It's not, it wasn't particularly multicultural, it was primarily Vietnamese students.
STUDENT 4: When we went there, there are all different signs in different languages.

There is a tension between identifying particular schools as 'multicultural' (which their own school was not, by implication) because of the presence of Others, and the criticism of these Others for not participating in Australia's diversity. These responses suggest that young people were grappling in their own way with the competing logics of multiculturalism, and that a disposition towards the 'multicultural ethos' of automatically respecting difference had not been internalized evenly, despite students' immersion in programmes designed to foster this ethos. Young adults, recently in school, don't always exhibit the kinds of intercultural capacities many educators expect (Blair, 2015; Mann, 2015).

At the heart of these discussions is not simply disagreement about the benefits of multiculturalism but attempts to think through the messages of educational discourse in terms of the worlds they know. Such attempts reflect the internal tensions arising from the competing logics of multiculturalism. Contemplating whether a suburb which represents ethnic difference may not be very diverse involves confronting the imperative to 'live together' with anxieties around the myth of 'ethnic ghettoes' that underlies the desire for social integration (Megalogenis, 2002). As Anita Harris (2013) argues, young people articulate contradictory views as part of the process of negotiating ethnic diversity through competing relations of affiliation and conflict. Yet, as close as these student discussions get to engaging with the challenges posed by ethnic diversity, at no time do they engage reflexively with the *intellectual* task of making sense of the complex world around them, why these logics are in tension and the social contexts which produce them. As we will go on to explore, the absence of a shared 'ethos' of multiculturalism is less of a concern than the development of the intellectual tools to make sense of their experience of globalization and diversity.

Parents' Understandings of Multiculturalism

While there is substantial research on attitudes to multiculturalism generally, there is surprisingly little focus on the views of parents of school-age children as a specific cohort. This is surprising given the persistent emphasis on the family as the primary site for the development of attitudes towards ethnicity (Priest et al., 2014) and the congruence (or not) of parental and school discourse in students' educational experience (Bodovski, 2010). It is as parents that many adults have to deal with the institutionalized nature of multiculturalism and its role in the fostering of particular values and beliefs among children. Parents do not share a common institutional experience as students do, and they may have different experiences of education, in Australia or elsewhere, so their relations to discourses around multiculturalism are variable, based on experiences in the homeland and in Australia, social milieu, media or work and community relations. The common experience of their children's schooling, however, means that there is a salience to examining parents' attitudes in the context of their school community (Byrne & De Tona, 2014).

Responses from the parent focus groups work through the same array of meanings as students, but often with less nuance, and often reflecting the context of their school. Typical statements from parents about multiculturalism include these: 'the bringing together of many different nationalities of people', from a parent at Barnett HS; 'lots of cultures living in one society . . . and being able to all get along', from Beechton PS; 'different backgrounds congregating together' from Wellington Heights PS, and; 'living in a society with people from different, or relatives from different races', from Harringvale HS. The descriptive understanding of multiculturalism dominates, though the scale varies from being seen in terms of individuals, cultures, nationalities, races or 'backgrounds'. Nevertheless, parents tended to focus on 'mixing' and 'acceptance'. One from ethnically diverse Wellington Heights believed that there was not only mixing but adaptation: 'kids from different cultures come together, they can adjust'. An exchange between parents from Addington HS, where there is little diversity, demonstrates several ideas:

PARENT 1: Oh, basically just people from different backgrounds all coming together and I mean we all have to live in the same world, regardless of what background we are from, whether we are from, you know, Europe or Britain or anywhere . . . we just all have to understand each other and move forward as one sort of nation really so that we can all just get on with things. But it is good to understand each other's backgrounds so that, you know . . . there might be a war overseas, that doesn't mean that everybody from that nationality here is a bad person.

PARENT 2: I think the same, learning about it is important, to learn that people do come from different cultures and have different beliefs but at the end of the day we all live together and it's a case of respecting, although there are differences. Everybody deserves the right to be treated the same and to live equally.

In some ways the parents put stronger emphasis on the need for a moral ethos of acceptance and civility towards difference, but without an exploration of this. The focus on social justice tended to be weaker among parents, and there weren't the insights into the governmental management of diversity that some students noted. Despite the initial emphasis on 'acceptance', there tended to be a rapid move to the 'problems' of multiculturalism, typical of the ambiguities at the heart of 'happy talk', where people juxtapose the 'nice' and 'problem' features of diversity (Bell & Hartmann, 2007). Echoing the students' discussion, a parent from semi-rural Pentonville commented that 'the term in the traditional sense means that different cultures living separately in their own culture'. He didn't see many cultures mixing but thought, like the students, that 'they' 'stick together'. As with the students, multiculturalism quickly becomes a problem of Others. As another in this group said, it 'depends on the culture doesn't it? Yeah, different cultures just don't mix do they?' A parent from Binto Valley PS, also with a low LBOTE population but in a higher SES area, also saw problems: 'where does religion and culture sit? . . . For me that's interesting because that's when you get into extreme, you know, where does extremism sit with integration, you know, and how do you integrate extremists? It is very, very difficult. I think that's a problem.'

One parent at Getty Rd, where there was a high LBOTE population, grappled with the 'mixing' issue in this way:

> With multiculturalism is that the different cultures and the blending of them and also the differences of them? There are pockets of differences and there is great blends of – and it's just like chicken soup. But yeah it is being able to pick out all of those different things and recognize them for what they are and – it's not all good or bad or right or wrong, but its recognizing, respecting and learning to understand it.

One rare exchange was among Eaton Park parents, with a large proportion of students from Asian backgrounds in a high SES area:

> PARENT 1: Well, actually multiculturalism includes all Australians, it is not about other cultures, it's a 'we', not a 'them', you know, and to what extent our, not non-Asians, but our so-called Australian community is part of that program . . . I don't know what it means anymore . . . it is probably something as broad as that it's just people within the community of different cultural backgrounds together. Now you can't define it I think across the board . . . multiculturalism . . . yeah, I'm confused by the word.
> PARENT 2: The word has been bandied around so much now that I think people sort of have a bit of trouble. They sort of think they know what it means but because it has been bandied around so much in so many different contexts.
> PARENT 1: It is fascinating, I mean I just find the concept fascinating that people live together. . . . Sydney is very tolerant, lets things happen but it doesn't cross borders . . . you know,

> there is not a lot of crossing of borders across cultures. You tolerate this, you tolerate that, you know, you don't interfere with it, but there is not a lot of communication across those cultural boundaries, I don't know.

While parents generally don't elaborate their views as much as teachers and students, they nevertheless tended to similarly juxtapose a desire for cultural harmony, embodying what we have referred to as a moralizing logic of civility and an anxiety around the consequences of ethnic diversity without the kind of nascent 'thinking through' found in students' discussions. A few parents, such as this man from Graham's Point HS, with a sizeable LBOTE population, recognized that their children's lives entailed a different relation to ethnic diversity and deferred to it: 'multiculturalism defines what our children are now talking about. All children, they are very multicultural. We should look up to our children to learn what multiculturalism is all about.' Despite some differences, all three cohorts emphasize three key understandings: multiculturalism as the descriptive 'fact' of diversity, the moral imperative to celebrate that diversity and the expectation of 'harmony', although anxiety is never far away. Given this seeming convergence of multiple views, it is worthwhile examining how each group sees multicultural education.

Teachers' Perspectives on Multicultural Education

Documenting the complex set of understandings entailed in multicultural discourse is crucial if there is to be some agreement about the purpose and practices of multicultural education. But the absence of a clear distinction between teachers', parents' and students' views, and the evidence of limited understandings of multiculturalism across the three groups, might suggest that not only is there not a shared public idea of multiculturalism, but there is also no developed, critical approach to this complex set of understandings within the professional vision of teachers.

The survey of NSW teachers revealed interesting findings. When asked to nominate the key goals of multicultural education, teachers prioritized social justice issues: educational equity (89 per cent), social access (90 per cent), English language proficiency (90 per cent) and combating racism (90 per cent). However, cultural maintenance (73 per cent), intercultural understanding (88 per cent), sharing social values (77 per cent) and commitment to Australian identity (67 per cent) were also highly rated. In other words, teachers expect multiculturalism to deliver on all the logics of multiculturalism (Watkins et al., 2013, pp. 33–4). When asked how they would foster greater inclusion, their responses showed a relatively even spread across major areas – improving academic outcomes, intercultural relations, anti-racism, increasing parental involvement. 'Holding events to celebrate diversity' was high but ranked eighth in the options we provided. It is instructive to compare these results with those of a smaller pilot study, where we asked teachers in eleven schools to complete a hard-copy survey where, rather than give options, teachers had to come up with the strategies. In that survey, teachers were most likely to nominate the conventional multicultural days: listed more than twice as often as the next option. That is, when teachers are given options that draw on categories that relate to institutionalized rationales, the spread is even. When they are asked to articulate these themselves, the range is narrower. The multicultural day is the automatic response. While a popular event, the multicultural day does not offer strategies for promoting equity per se, except as symbolic recognition, and it has been widely criticized for promoting ethnic stereotypes (Ngo, 2010; Shankar, 2008). We take this up in Chapter 4, arguing such days constitute 'lazy multiculturalism' because they don't engage in the educational tasks of interrogating the consequences of these practices (Watkins & Noble, 2019). But the point here is that for many teachers their 'professional vision' is limited in terms of their capacity to articulate the educational options, reflecting gaps in their training.

In focus groups, some teachers were again often unclear about the goals of multicultural education. Some simply listed words like these Beechton teachers – 'inclusion mainly, harmony, togetherness', 'living together peacefully, happily, tolerance, harmony' – emphasizing the imperative of a multicultural ethos. While one teacher from Wollami Lakes PS expressed uncertainty, she managed to combine the moral disposition with a focus on knowledge of other cultures:

> I don't really know. I think the most important part is sharing different cultures and making the children aware of maybe the beliefs of different children that we might have at the school and even ones that aren't here, they still need to know about different cultures, especially if they move to somewhere else. So probably yeah, just giving them more an idea and so we have a big multicultural day here each year which is great.

Another, from Addington, went further and thought that schools had 'to make sure that they are . . . teaching different backgrounds' – presumably referring here to 'culturally responsive pedagogy'. A few, in contrast, felt the emphasis should be squarely on 'numeracy and literacy': 'the same' as any student, claimed one teacher from Barnett. Another at Thurston even doubted whether they could create multiculturalism in her school, implying that she saw it less as a practice than the 'natural' result of diversity: 'Multiculturalism is something that happens, it is not like we are going to make this a multicultural place. I don't know, to me it's something that just is.' Overall, the emphasis among teachers was on fostering a disposition towards the ethos of multiculturalism through special events, much like the pilot study suggested.

Students' Perspectives on Multicultural Education

This emphasis was echoed among students, though many balked at the idea of trying to articulate these as educational goals. Many students also thought immediately of the multicultural day, or similar events, in thinking about multicultural education. Most students thought, like the group at Graham's Point, that these days were 'awesome': 'they put on a show don't they with different cultures?'; 'they get you to wear like your cultural clothes'; 'then they have food . . . from around the world.' Yet many students were unclear about what clothes they should wear and often just came to school in jeans and a T-shirt. Other students, who had obviously experienced exchange programmes like this Hingston Valley student, thought multicultural day was 'where you get other schools, and you just talk about like their culture and how like, even their religion and how they've been brought up, like to help, explain it.' When pressed on why this was useful, students typically argued that this gave you 'a better understanding on how other cultures work'. As that student's peer said, 'racism happens because of a lack of understanding about other cultures.' Yet, while these students could articulate certain goals – celebration of difference and anti-racism – they still focused on the multicultural day as an event that achieved this rather than a more sustained approach across curriculum, and they focused more on the good feelings of civility that came from the event than the development of the critical capacities to analyse cultural complexity.

Parents' Perspectives on Multicultural Education

This emphasis on civility was common among parents too. One parent of Polish heritage from Beechton described what she saw as important: 'Basically educating children and parents as well to accept one another and to accept that some people could be a little bit different but also when they did get together to have that Australian way of living . . . accepting each other and living together and educating people to basically love one another.' These aims are worthy, but they are couched in broad terms of personal, moral attitudes and have limited translation into curriculum. Parents, like this one from Binto Valley, also focused on events: 'you would start with things like, I don't want to say easy things, but like multicultural days. They are great, they are fun things, easy for kids to understand.' One Getty Rd parent felt that the food focus of multicultural day was 'tokenistic' and didn't encourage 'genuine understanding'. This Eaton Park parent similarly questioned what the best approach was:

> [is it] setting up programs to focus on different cultures or do you have a classroom dynamic led by the teacher that somehow integrates

the cultural in the classroom? . . . Is that more important than running multicultural days or particular events? I think probably the process is probably more important than the big event, and that's not unimportant because that's where a lot of knowledge also occurs, but I expect that seeing the teaching and learning process somehow integrates cultural attitudes towards learning or towards particular subjects. I don't know how you would do that to be honest.

Intercultural Understanding

'Intercultural understanding' has become a key term within educational discourse because it shifts the focus away from the view that multiculturalism is for migrants and promises a deeper approach to intercultural relations. As we indicated in the Introduction, it is one of the 'general capabilities' advanced in Australia's National Curriculum, premised on 'three dispositions—expressing empathy, demonstrating respect and taking responsibility' (ACARA, 2013, p. 111). There is, however, much debate as to whether 'interculturalism' offers anything clearer, beyond multiculturalism (Meer & Modood, 2012). Nevertheless, its newfound status requires that we gauge what teachers understand by it. The RMRME survey demonstrated that, despite its endorsement as a national priority, 'intercultural understanding' has not entered deeply into professional discourse. Teachers' definitions of intercultural understanding were roughly divided between knowing other cultures (33 per cent), understanding cultural diversity (26 per cent) and interacting effectively with people of different cultures (23 per cent) (Watkins et al., 2013, p. 51). In the focus groups, many participants indicated they had not even heard the phrase. As one said, 'that would be the first time I've heard that term.' Others gave vague responses which aligned with what they had said about multiculturalism, emphasizing 'awareness', 'empathy', 'understanding', 'appreciation', 'tolerance'.

For many, intercultural understanding, like multicultural education, continued to be about Others. While one teacher at Wollami Lakes thought 'it is definitely the school's responsibility' to foster intercultural understanding, she could only list events such as Harmony Day and Refugee Week as examples of how this was addressed in schools. Nevertheless, she argued that,

> on a day-to-day basis it's just intrinsic in everything that everybody does here. . . . it happens just through general talk, through discussions, through formal teaching lessons, about where people have come from and my family and that sort of thing, the playground and it just, it's hard to identify exactly what we do but it happens every day.

But if it just 'happens', then why is it a general capability to be promoted through schooling? Challenged by identifying what schools might do, many teachers saw intercultural understanding primarily in terms of a need for more 'special days'. Clearly, 'intercultural understanding' has not translated into professional discourse. It was an even less clear idea for students and parents. Students often admitted, as this student from Addington declared, 'I don't know', while one of her peers guessed that it might mean 'raising more awareness of other cultures'. A Barnett parent defined it as 'broadening your awareness that children have of the differences', but his fellow discussant thought that it 'would be tricky to do here' because 'there aren't a lot of other people from other cultures'. For some, like multiculturalism, intercultural understanding was relevant only in ethnically diverse schools. This Binto Valley parent was hesitant about how interventionist a school can be on the basis of 'culture':

> that's very difficult because there is a lot of nuance in how you deal with people, it is not only about their culture, it is about their personality, and I think it would be very difficult for a school or government to regulate or provide a curriculum that says this is the way that you should deal with non-English-speaking people at your school.

If parents are voicing these dilemmas, how well equipped are teachers in resolving them?

Teacher Expertise in Multicultural Education

Given that the research indicated little evidence for a clear professional vision among teachers regarding multicultural education, it was important to gauge just what training and experience teachers had in the area. Research suggests that both pre-service and in-service teachers are inadequately prepared for the demands of teaching a diverse student body and for addressing wider issues around multiculturalism, but often feel their training is adequate or that simply being in a diverse school will be enough experience (Alismail, 2016; Caneva, 2017; James, 2004). Knowing your community is a key element of the resources schools accumulate to fulfil their mission as educators, but it has to be matched by the attributes of teachers as professionals, their capacity to work with their communities and to understand the issues in teaching ethnically diverse classrooms, yet teacher education programmes have tended to address diversity in a piecemeal fashion (Mills, 2008). This is especially important given the increasingly globalized nature of the world. Professional teaching standards adopted in 2011 by the Australian Institute for Teaching and School Leadership – the national body overseeing teacher education – may have gone some way towards rectifying this, given the requirement for professional knowledge in teaching students of culturally and linguistically diverse backgrounds, but there is little detail as to what this requirement translates to practically (AITSL, 2011, p. 5).

The RMRME survey found that the development of professional skills in multicultural education, both broadly conceived and in specific areas such as EAL/D, was uneven and limited. Fewer than half of the respondents had received pre-service training in multicultural education, and longer serving teachers had much less training in this area than new teachers. Just over a quarter surveyed had EAL/D training, and this was more likely among primary school teachers (Watkins et al., 2013, pp. 17–18). In terms of in-service training, a wide array of professional learning experiences was found, with anti-racism strategies and culturally inclusive curriculum being the most reported (almost 60 per cent of teachers), but over 20 per cent of teachers had not undertaken any professional learning in multicultural education at all.

While some teachers in the focus groups had some EAL/D, Teaching English Language Learners or Anti-Racism Contact Officer (ARCO) training, there was a similar unevenness of experiences of multicultural education both within their training and professional development. Typically, one Getty Rd teacher admitted, 'in terms of formal training . . . there was nothing really much when I was at university.' Another, from Addington, vaguely recalled a 'unit . . . to do with the people coming from other countries to school, so that's all I did . . . you had to . . . know what their needs, what their habits, or culture . . . lots of things like that'. There was also evidence of the unevenness of professional development. While one or two teachers had returned to study, more representative was an early career teacher at Graham's Point who admitted, 'since university I probably haven't had any extra training'. A Barnett teacher who had accumulated training over many years when she worked in the state of Victoria said there was 'nothing' at her present school. Another at the same school commented, 'Years ago there was, but not so much in the last ten years.' Smithton teachers talked about the 'orientation' on new arrivals each term, but 'it's more been about giving you background rather than giving you any strategies'.

To flag a theme we take up in Chapter 3, familiarity with multicultural education was seen to be about the practical experience teachers had accumulated in schools with large LBOTE populations, where multicultural education was seen as a pragmatic need. One teacher at Barnett, with few LBOTE students, said they 'had a lot of in-service training' at their previous school in south-western Sydney because there were 'a lot of nationalities represented'. For those in schools with low LBOTE populations, it wasn't seen as relevant. As this teacher at Pentonville argued, 'we don't have a massive multicultural aspect in this school apart from the Aboriginals.' When multiculturalism is 'done', a Thurston teacher explained, it is more about practical 'multicultural activities' with the students than professional development per se. Older teachers, such as this teacher from Getty Rd, described how they had lots of hands-on experience 'in terms of multicultural activities. . . . we always had the Vietnamese community and the Chinese community coming and doing things with the students, cooking, dancing, all sorts of things. We had community language teachers there as well.'

Several teachers had undertaken ARCO training provided by the NSW DoE as a requirement of the Anti-Racism Policy, but this too was cast as practical expertise. At Wollami Lakes there were at least three teachers with ARCO training. For others, such as this teacher at Thurston, anti-racism training was presented 'as part of our discipline policy', rather than a broader orientation to multicultural curriculum. The former 'corrects' a problem as it emerges, as a behavioural problem, the latter sees racism as a topic to be addressed as an educational issue. Most valued what one Harringvale teacher described as 'on the job' training when and where it was needed: they learnt 'more than I ever would have learnt by going to some in-service courses. . . . it was part of what I did every day, eight periods every day. So that's where I did my training for ESL and NESB.' For others, such as this teacher from Wollami Lakes, this was a haphazard approach:

> I don't think we can say any of us have had a great deal of training while we've been teaching in the area of multiculturalism. . . . I suppose we've had bits and pieces because of the different population that we have here . . . but . . . as a staff we really haven't had anything significant.

Some recognized the limitations of the training they had received, as did this Hingston Valley teacher:

> I did a video conference on ESL [EAL/D] multicultural education and it was quite interesting. . . . but it was a very sort of surface level discussion about multiculturalism, ESL, LBOTE students and that was pretty much it. You just came out feeling that you needed to know more because there was stuff that I didn't understand and wanted to know more about.

Many teachers felt they had a need for further training, but in specific areas such as EAL/D and culturally inclusive curriculum, echoing the findings of the survey (Watkins et al., 2013, pp. 25–6). For some it was about cultural awareness, and often for pragmatic reasons. One Addington teacher talked about the need for a 'heads up about . . . cultural do's and don'ts . . . ceremonial things that I don't fully understand, what celebrations . . . sacred ceremonies that we shouldn't go near, or there are certain people you should use if we want to get that lesson across'. One Binto Valley teacher similarly felt what was needed was a 'starter pack', 'when we have a kid from another culture arrive, just something that we can use just to start teaching these kids rather than thinking, what will I do?' For a Beechton teacher, it amounted to having 'an appreciation of all different cultures'. For another at Beechton, professional learning just wasn't a pressing need: 'at this stage of my career I just sort of go with the general consensus and currently at our school . . . we don't have a great population of multiculturalism.'

The experience and expertise of teachers in multicultural education were variable, and they had contrasting views of what they needed and what was best. This is no surprise, especially as many teachers see such needs in terms of whether they are in a 'multicultural school' or not. Few teachers grappled with the broader issues of teaching students to understand the cultural complexity of a globalized world, and their professional vision was predicated on a pragmatic response to the 'problems' that arise when you have students from 'different cultures'.

Conclusion

This chapter began by arguing that 'multiculturalism' was a difficult idea not easily reduced to simple definition, and that it contained diverse logics – of incorporation, recognition and civility. These logics are rationales that point to different objectives which, in practice, could be in competition in the ways people thought about multiculturalism and implemented it as policy. Schools reflect these, often contradictory, ideas in their everyday practice (Rizvi, 2014). Our examination of what teachers, students and parents understand by multiculturalism demonstrates that not only is there little agreement within and across school communities on what they mean but that teachers lacked a coherent professional vision in relation to multicultural education. We aren't suggesting that teachers are personally to blame for this lack of a coherent vision, but our data does say something about their professional capacities to critically reflect on how to address these issues. It is not so much about ascertaining whether people have the 'right' definitions of these ideas, because these are difficult questions often unresolved by scholars. Rather, we are suggesting there is a need to consider whether teachers' understandings provide the basis on which we can examine how the goals of multicultural education are realized in schools.

Baumann (1996) distinguishes between dominant, or institutionalized, and demotic discourses of multiculturalism: the former, he claims, tends to essentialize and reify 'cultures' while everyday discourse treats culture as a process. Such a clear distinction doesn't play out in our study as teachers seem to share the same contradictory ways of thinking about ethnic diversity as students and parents. In all three groups there was a tendency to think of multiculturalism as the descriptive fact of diversity in Australia. As we will explore in the next chapter, addressing how understandings of 'culture' play out in the lives of school communities, such a perspective embodies a specific 'multicultural imaginary' (Noble, 2011). This entails a perceptual schema which rests on reductive notions of cultures and ethnicities as discrete entities, organized around primordial difference, with little grasp of the cultural complexities deriving from global interconnectedness, resulting in a tendency to treat culture and ethnicity in ahistorical and depoliticized ways (May, 2009; Rizvi, 2014). Moreover, people tend to invest this understanding with a moralizing ethos of 'respecting' difference. Respect is not a bad thing, of course, but it is largely manifest through tokenistic, celebratory one-off events rather than a sustained feature of educational practice. Without a critical engagement with the social processes which produce difference, identity and inequality, 'respect' becomes an unthinking, moralistic injunction. The combination of reductive notions of difference and a moralizing ethos produces what we characterize as an *unreflexive civility*, where the overwhelming emphasis is on attributes of tolerance and appreciation while the reflexive, analytical skills for making sense of cultural complexity and combating essentialisms – critical understandings that should be central to the focus of schools (May, 2009) – are given little attention. Teachers, as we shall see, are not always well equipped to deal with these complexities both in terms of the uneven-ness of their pre- and in-service training and in terms of the development of a professional vision which would help them think through the complex challenges of diversity.

CHAPTER 2

Questions of Identity and Culture

'Culture' has become central to political and popular discourse over the last few decades, such that we 'see culture everywhere' (Breidenbach & Nyíri, 2009). Yet this 'culture talk' (Mamdani, 2005), which tends to see cultures in traditional and essentialized ways, has emerged politically and socially at a time when globalization has created a world marked by cultural complexity unsettling traditional ideas of identity and relations. It is this tension which makes 'culture' an increasingly important idea to interrogate. The previous chapter demonstrated that the confusion around the meaning of multiculturalism is not just semantic but relates to the diverse logics of multiculturalism. This chapter extends this argument by looking at the question of culture, which lies at the heart of multicultural discourse. We start by considering the ways teachers, parents and students actually identify themselves in terms of 'cultural background', and how this sits in tension with participants' understandings of the idea of culture and the valorization of 'cultural diversity'. For reasons we will elaborate, the problems embedded in the idea of culture mean that we prefer the term 'ethnic', rather than cultural, diversity. We examine how 'culture' is perceived primarily in terms of (exotic) difference and is used to explain a whole range of practices in school communities. These understandings structure the professional vision that teachers acquire and employ. These issues are important not just because of the need to have a clearer and more nuanced profile of ethnic diversity in schools but, as 'national populations grow more diverse . . . the need for educationalists to better understand and work with difference productively becomes increasingly critical' (Allard & Santoro, 2006, p. 115). But, we argue, this can only be productive for schools if we engage critically with these issues.

Identities Are Not Cultures!

It is often claimed that schools are places which represent the broader nature of an ethnically diverse society – at least in terms of their students and their families. They are diverse, of course, but not uniformly so. Of the fourteen RMRME schools, for example, one had a LBOTE population of 3 per cent while another had a LBOTE population of 95 per cent. The nature of that diversity is often seen in straightforward ways, with student populations organized into lists of students' language backgrounds or countries of origin. Yet diversity is much more complex than that and is becoming increasingly diversified (Vertovec, 2006). Intermarriage, transnational mobility and intergenerational change complicate the widening cultural, linguistic and religious complexity of Australia's migrants and their children (Ang et al., 2002, 2006). It is also often claimed that, while schools are places of great diversity, the teaching profession does not reflect that diversity. So, it seems useful to gain some insight into these cultural complexities 'on the ground' by asking teachers, students and parents about how they identify in terms of the question of 'culture'. We use this data to demonstrate that assumptions about the match between culture and identity, in fact, show that we need a more nuanced understanding of the relationships between culture, ethnicity, identity, 'background' and ancestry to fully appreciate the complexity present in school communities.

The 'Cultural' Identities of Teachers

Teachers are generally seen as part of the Anglo-Australian, monolingual mainstream (McKenzie et al., 2011; Santoro, 2013b) and the curriculum is, as a consequence, seen to be problematically ethnocentric (Hickling-Hudson, 2004). There may be some historical truth to this, but it is often not explored closely or with nuance. In fact, the increasingly mobile nature of teaching has contributed to a much more dynamic and diverse workforce (Reid et al., 2014). Many assume a coherence to teachers as a category that evades the complexities of the relationship between teaching, identity and ethnicity (Raible & Irizarry, 2007). These complexities are borne out by the RMRME research, which showed that NSW teachers were disproportionately Australian-born (79 per cent) in contrast to the wider population (73 per cent), but that there was also a significant degree of complexity in the ways teachers identified themselves and their backgrounds, often drawing on multiple national, linguistic, regional and religious descriptors (Watkins et al., 2013, pp. 13–14). There was a noticeable echo of this pattern in the teacher focus groups.

Semi-rural Beechton PS fits the view of teachers as overwhelmingly Anglo, all identifying as 'Australian'. In contrast, most of the fourteen schools reflected degrees of ethnic diversity, even when there was an Anglo-Australian dominance, as at Hingston Valley HS:

> I'm Australian from an Italian background.
> I tell kids I'm a Skippy [the bush kangaroo]. I refer to myself as Anglo-Celtic background.
> I refer to myself as an Australian with Lebanese background.
> I'm an Australian with an Estonian background.
> Just an Australian.
> An Australian with a Ukrainian background.
> I'm Australian with an Indian background. We speak Tamil at home.

These accounts reference 'layers' of identification, which point more towards the idea of cultural complexity than the conventional idea of 'cultural diversity', as juxtapositions of nationally defined 'cultures'. This was also found elsewhere. At Eaton Park HS, for example, a young teacher explained, 'I'm Australian but my mum is Vietnamese and my dad's Chinese, but we speak Vietnamese at home and, like, my brother, I speak English with him.' At other schools, as with this teacher from Getty Rd PS, explanations became more detailed:

> Basically, I identify as being Australian but my mother's family is a couple of generations Australian, but her mum came from an Irish background and her dad from an English and Scottish background. My father . . . identifies as being Ukrainian, but his mother came from a German-Polish background and they lived in the Ukraine, so it's quite, I guess I'm a hybrid . . . I could speak four languages before I came to school but when I went to school, I was always the child that was called out to the ESL tests and things.

There is nothing 'basic' here at all. Many teachers felt compelled to go beyond categories to describe the temporal dimensions of this complexity, as with this Binto Valley PS teacher: 'I am born in Fiji, lived in the Pacific until I was 17, lived in New Zealand for six years and then came here, so I just don't know. I still feel Fijian, but yet I don't know.'

Detailing histories means that past (and possibly future) changes to identity can be reflected upon, as this Getty Rd teacher did:

> I was born in Italy and I think for a long time I considered myself very Aussie, but . . . the last few years I've gone back to the Italian background a little bit and thinking a lot more about the Italian and thinking maybe going back to visit and listening to Italian music and getting a little bit more that way. I mean, I am still Aussie but the Italian is coming through

a lot more . . . I always sort of neglected it, and I think it also had a lot to do with being almost ashamed of being Italian back . . . when I was at school . . . it's come back now that I'm feeling a little bit more patriotic to the old country.

Like the Binto Valley teacher above, this Wellington Heights PS teacher demonstrated that a detailed account doesn't guarantee certainty of a sense of identity:

> Um, well my father's father was from Norway and my mother's family are from England, Scotland and very much entrenched in that . . . southern English way of being, so I had very sort of strong ties to that because of my maternal side and my grandmother and my great aunt speak very correctly, the Queen Victoria's English . . . so I have had that kind of European connection and I don't know if I see myself as – I don't even really understand what being Australian is to tell you the truth because it is something that I don't really feel like . . . the thing about being Australian is that you don't feel really completely tied to any one place. Because I've grown up in areas that are very culturally diverse and I was fortunate. . . . I was probably one of the only Anglo type children so I had a really good exposure to different cultures and took that as being, that's what the norm is sort of thing. So yeah, I don't know.

So, while many teachers see themselves as 'just' Australian, others point to various forms of identification that articulate national categories and histories of migration. Identity is not static but has temporal and spatial contexts. It is often linked to family ancestries, but it has a nebulous relation to the ways of life of past generations. These issues are even more pronounced in students' and parents' accounts.

The 'Cultural' Identities of Students

A revealing picture is given of the community at Barnett, a rural high school, where students in the focus groups answered this way:

> Australian.
> Australian.
> Australian.
> 100% Aussie.
> Australian.
> Australian.
> Australian.

But at Thurston PS, in the outer suburbs of Sydney, students responded differently:

> I'm Tongan. [but they were born in Australia]
> I am Samoan. [born in Australia]
> I'm Egyptian. [born in Australia]
> I have Mauritian and half Russian. [born in Australia]
> I'm from Bangladesh but I wasn't born there, I was born in New Zealand.
> I am Bangladeshi too. [born in Australia]

At Getty Rd, students responded differently again:

> I'm Vietnamese and Australian. [born in Australia]
> I'm Anglo Saxon and Australian.
> I'm Chinese. [born in China]
> I'm Syrian and Australian and New Zealand. [born in Syria]
> I'm Chinese, Cantonese and I converted to Australian citizen when I was three years old. [born in China]
> I'm Lebanese and I'm Australian. [born in Australia]

These students saw themselves more in terms of hyphenated identities. As with the teachers, some students reflected on their hybridity and how this induces uncertainty: 'I don't really know. I think I'm mixed. I've got quite a lot, well my mum is Chinese and Indian and my dad is Scottish, Sri Lankan, Portuguese and Indian. But I was born in Australia' (Binto Valley PS). Like this student, many students drew on multiple categories of identity and ancestry, often of different orders, and going beyond a simple focus on citizenship or nationality. One Binto Valley student, for example, declared, 'I am Persian and American', while a Pentonville HS student described themselves as 'Aboriginal and Croatian'.

The contrast here is not simply that some schools are very 'Anglo' and others are ethnically diverse, and some students are monocultural and others are hybrid. There is an important contrast in the nature of the categories used in these accounts. At Thurston, most students used their ancestral or 'homeland' origin (often their parents' country of birth) as singular markers of identity, whether they were born there or not, or had become Australian citizens or not. At Getty Rd, students mostly adopted a hybrid identity, adding 'Australian' to their ancestral category, also irrespective of whether they were born in Australia or not. Why these choices were made is not clear, but the fact that there are options in the ways students define themselves is important, and these choices are significant if a school is to understand its community. In some of these descriptions, the hybridity combines what we would typically refer to as an ethnicity (based on the homeland or on language and religion) and what might be for many a category of citizenship (Australian) rather than a cultural identifier, while others use what we might assume are hybrid ethnicities (Mauritian and Russian), but we can't know for sure on the basis of the word alone.

As a consequence, some students also feel the need to give further information beyond the simple homeland or ancestry category, as this Graham's Point HS student offered:

> I'm Australian but Chinese. I was born here and then I went back to China when I was three years old because my parents decided that it would be a good idea to actually learn Chinese so we don't lose our language. And then I came back here when I was in Year 6, and then I speak basically Cantonese at home but it seems to sort of like have a mix a bit with English because I've sort of forgot about some words and things like that.

Many students feel this need to tell us where they were born, where their parents were born, when they became citizens, their language background and competence, their faith, transnational movements and so on. The challenges of self-definition are stark in some responses. Not only do the identities become more hybrid, but the responses have to be more narrative, detailing something of the histories of marriage, migration and settlement. Moreover, they become more reflective as a consequence: sources of identity are often construed in terms of change (losing language) and 'amounts' ('a lot'), or reflect degrees of attachment. For some, this produces some uncertainty around their sense of identity.

The 'Cultural' Identities of Parents

There was a similar pattern of responses from the parents. There were some whose definitions entail singular categories, while others articulate degrees of complexity, combining 'ethnic' (nation, language or 'race') and citizenship categories:

> Australian. [Addington HS]
> I am Palestinian. [Graham's Point HS]
> Chinese. [Hingston Valley HS]
> I define myself as Singaporean but we have obtained the Aussie citizenship. [Eaton Park HS]
> Fifth generation Australian, German heritage. [Barnett HS]
> Greek Australian. [Smithton PS]
> Well it is hard to say, I am just sort of Aboriginal but kind of there's a lot of White blood in me, mostly White blood, but I register more for Aborigine, I don't know why but . . . I identify better as Aboriginal than as a White Australian. [Wollami Lakes PS]

Again, as identity is increasingly complex, it has to be 'explained' and contextualized and often entails a degree of ambivalence and 'confusion':

> It is quite mixed, I am born to a Japanese mother and a Taiwanese father. I was born in Japan, raised primarily in Canada and I moved to Australia 17 years ago. [Binto Valley PS]

> Born and raised in France, French is the first main language, moved to Australia around 13 years ago now and I must say I am confused. . . . I've got the dual nationality, French and Australian, which adds to the confusion. [Binto Valley PS]

This degree of complexity among parents also has consequences for their children, so some parents start discussing their children's identities in talking about themselves, because identity has to be explained in familial terms given their histories of settlement:

> I am Indian background but I was born in Fiji, born and bred in Fiji so I suppose we are called Fiji Indian, but totally Indian heritage wise . . . I came [to Australia] in 1987, so a while ago and when I was in Year 9, yeah, and my daughter though is a beautiful mixed background because my husband is Anglo Indian. . . . So she is quite a bit of Portuguese, English and Indian blood in her, so yeah. Bit of mixed cultures there. [Harringvale HS]

> If I was to classify myself, I would say I am mixed. I am half African from Zimbabwe and I am half Australian. But in saying that I am of European background. My dad is Italian and Irish. . . . I say to people I am some African and Australian and my daughter – she is actually African, Australian and African/American. So yeah there is a mix there. But that is what I say and I am proud of both too. And I was bilingual at one point. I lost it when I came here as a kid . . . I was born in Zimbabwe. My dad was born and bred in Australia. [Wollami Lakes PS]

In discussions of multiculturalism, we often conflate culture and identity, but as we can see from these comments, there is much more going on that needs some explanation.

Unpacking Identity

These accounts indicate a need for a more nuanced understanding of the complex make-up of school communities and the need for caution in the ways people, and schools, often use identity categories. Several issues emerge from this snapshot of the identity claims students, parents and teachers made in the course of our discussions. Identities don't rely just on simple categories of nationality or ancestry but use increasingly complex forms of mixing (Noble et al., 1999) which are tied to other social categories (Appiah, 2018). Moreover, identities are rarely static or given, especially for young people and those of migrant backgrounds. We need to speak of multiple identity-forming experiences which are responsive to diverse environments, relations and contexts (Moran, 2020). These combinations have to be located in narratives of changing forms of identification over time rather than singularizing notions of having 'an' identity. They operate in relation to family, mobility and histories which point backwards and forwards and entail uneven attachments to citizenship, language, faith, sub-national and supra-national regions. Such combinations are often talked about as layers or mixing, but they also involve levels of attachment – one can be a passionate Scottish nationalist, or vaguely point to great grandparents from Scotland. Sometimes these narratives entail uncertainties as well as strong, affective claims. Identities are rarely simple.

Many of these forms of identification reflect a globalizing world of superdiversity, where differences are not simply additions of two or three elements but a world of hyperdiversity, in which the dynamic interplay and synthesis of these elements produce new, fluid, hybrid and multiple ways of thinking about identities, relations, communities and belonging (Noble, 2011). A truism of contemporary educational discourse is the importance of 'knowing the student', which also entails knowing the wider communities in which they live; but it must also take into account these complex forms of identification and the contexts in which they are produced. The phenomenon of cultural hybridization, resulting from the intensifying diversification of hyperdiversity, is yet to be formulated as a meaningful focus of multicultural theory, school policy or classroom practice.

A key point to stress here is that people's identities are not their cultures, if by 'culture' we are pointing to a way of life. The Scottish nationalist may live a life very different to that of their grandparents. Identification is a layered and dynamic process through which people draw on ancestries (often framed as national 'homelands' or cultural 'backgrounds', including languages and faiths, among other things) and reassembled diasporic networks which include appropriated aspects of the country of settlement (often framed as 'ethnicity'). As one Addington student said in terms of 'being an Aboriginal', 'I don't do any of the traditions, like I just know my background.' The problem is that 'backgrounds' are sometimes treated as though they are 'foregrounds', as the ways in which people live their lives in the current moment, rather than, as they may often be, residual forms of identification that point to heritage, not contemporary, 'ways of living'. This is not to dismiss the importance of ancestry to identity but to emphasize that 'cultural background' simply can't explain the ways students', parents' and teachers' forms of identification are the results of complex distillations of diverse elements born of family histories and locations in a transnationalized world.

Not only are identities neither singular nor natural, they are not simply choices. The ways we identify depend very much on the ways others identify us, a dialogic process in which some people and institutions have an influential ability to validate identity claims (Bottomley, 1991). School is a key institution that is intimately involved in 'recognizing' students' identities or, rather, *misrecognizing* those complex distillations as simple categories of 'culture' or 'cultural background'. Schools, therefore, may inadvertently produce reduced identities, in the ways students are sorted into groups and have their needs assessed, in the ways they are exhorted to perform their identities at multicultural days or in the ways their behaviour is 'explained' by teachers. Students' senses of self are very much shaped by the 'schooled identities' fostered in educational institutions (Noble & Watkins, 2014a).

Who Is 'Multicultural'?

Before we turn to the problem of 'culture' at the centre of processes of identification, we want to extend this link between schools and identity through a discussion of the 'who' of multiculturalism. As we suggested in Chapter 1, despite declarations that multiculturalism is for all Australians, in practice it is often seen to be 'about' and 'for' migrants and their children. Students who talked about the 'multicultural school' – in contrast to their own – and the references to 'them' and how 'they' stick together, suggest that multiculturalism is not simply the description of a culturally diverse society nor a way of managing it but refer to distinct groups of people. This was particularly pertinent in the responses of a group of students at Beechton when asked why they thought they were in the focus group:

> I'm in Year 6 and my teacher thought that I should participate because I am multicultural.
> I'm in Year 6 and the reason I'm participating in this is because I'm the school captain and I'm very multicultural.
> I'm in Year 5. My mum thought it would be good for me to do this because I am multicultural.
> My mum and dad thought that this would be a good thing to speak about my multiculturalism.

What does it mean for these children – all of whom were Australian-born with diverse ancestries – to believe they are 'multicultural'? This is partly to do with the 'schooling' of identities in an educational context: certain students come to see themselves as the 'multicultural kids'. Correspondingly, the separation of students into the multicultural and non-multicultural is seen when these students were asked what multiculturalism is:

> Like lots of, um, a person from a different culture coming into another culture and having to learn about their culture and what they do.
> Well I define multicultural as like different backgrounds and your parents could be from two different nationalities and see in Australia we are very multicultural because a lot of people come here.
> I think multicultural is a variety of cultures that, so like my parents they've got – they are multicultural because they've got Australian and Maltese and Greek and everything.
> There is like a group of multicultural people coming together, getting to know each other and all that.

It is perhaps understandable that students don't think of multiculturalism as a set of policies that manage the diversity that arises from migration, but they move from seeing 'multicultural' as a description of diversity across a society to focusing on people of 'different' backgrounds. This is echoed in responses at other schools: one Eaton Park boy, for example, refers to himself as being 'from a half-multicultural background'. 'Multicultural' here refers not to the mix but to people who are different from what we can only call at this stage the Anglo 'mainstream'. This emphasis is also found within the parent groups. A parent who identified as Indian at rural Wollami Lakes talked about how 'more other multicultural people are coming into the society'. But some teachers also use 'multicultural' this way. One at Pentonville, for example, referred to a TV show that has 'a range of multicultural people in it'; another at Wellington Heights explained that when she was growing up, 'we didn't have any multicultural people at my school.'

Do these variations in the use of a word matter? They do if we acknowledge that one of the central tensions has been whether multiculturalism is about people of cultural and linguistic backgrounds other than English or is 'for all Australians', which has been central to the discourse of multiculturalism for many decades. 'Multicultural' here, however, is used to refer to people of migrant ancestry who are visibly or culturally different from the Anglo 'mainstream': the fact that the mainstream may or may not be a culture in its own right is never addressed. 'Multicultural people' are those who have been termed 'ethnics' in the past in Australia. So a 'multicultural Australia' refers, on the one hand, to Australia as a whole but, on the other, singles out specific groups who are deemed to be the ones that are actually 'multicultural'.

A similar reconfiguration has happened with the term 'Culturally and Linguistically Diverse' (CALD), which was introduced two decades ago to replace the problematic term 'non-English-speaking background' (NESB). 'Culturally and linguistically diverse' makes most sense when it is used to refer to the diversity across a population, as in 'Australia is a culturally and linguistically diverse society'. Yet it has become common to use the term narrowly to refer to specific, ethnically defined communities, or as 'culturally and linguistic diverse people' (NSW DoE, 2020a). First, this represents a confusion of the idea of diversity (variety within a population) with 'difference' or, more specifically, those who are seen to be 'different' – but it can't be both. Second, it focuses on particular 'non-mainstream' differences: Lebanese-Australians are seen to be a 'CALD community' (irrespective of their internal diversity), because they are identified as different to the Anglo 'mainstream'. Yet those of British ancestry – whether of recent or long-standing heritage – are just as much part of the cultural and linguistic diversity of Australia but aren't seen as a 'CALD community'. Third, in its most nonsensical form, we see references to 'CALD people'. A person can be different but not diverse: diversity refers to a range of differences within a population. Semantic inconsistencies aside, this usage reproduces a classic form of Othering – the mainstream is 'normal', Others are 'different' – which, just like the problematic 'NESB', reproduces the metaphor of an Anglo core and an ethnic periphery, central to conventional multiculturalism (Stratton, 1998, p. 10). A crucial aspect of the focus groups with students, teachers and parents discussed in Chapter 1 was seeing multiculturalism in terms of the cultural differences of others, of people who are different from the 'mainstream'. Our aim here is not to belittle such views but to highlight one of the difficulties around words and the ways they categorize people and shape practices.

This tension, in fact, reflects the contrasting logics of programmes: those designed to address the disadvantages resulting from migration and having a LBOTE and those designed to address all Australians in the quest for social cohesion. But as Hage (1998, p. 140) suggests, it produces a critical fault line in Australia's view of itself: Are 'we' diverse or is diversity about Others? Castles et al. (1990, p. 145) point out the importance of this tension when they argue that multiculturalism is a reformulation of national identity through the celebration of ethnic differences 'which are then subsumed into an imagined community of national cohesion'. One axis of the competing logics we have identified rests on this tension: seeing multiculturalism in terms of the recognition of proliferating differences and yet as constitutive of a new form of togetherness, a 'unity in diversity'.

The issue of the philosophical contradictions of multiculturalism is less important here than the ways the multicultural imaginary structures the ways of seeing others in a school community, and especially the 'professional vision' operating within teaching. This 'vision', which entails the codification of educational problems and solutions, rests on schemas of perception that frame the way we see people. Such schemas underlie the practices of classification and judgement through which we make sense of the world. They are largely unconscious and become 'eternal norms', naturalizing the contingencies of the social world and shaping pedagogic actions such that they reproduce the categories they hide (Bourdieu, 1996a, p. 156; 1996b, p. 73). Bourdieu focuses on the ways that these schemas operate in educational institutions in class terms, whereby the academic criteria for evaluating students hides their social construction (1996b, pp. 10–11, 167); but we argue they operate in ethnicized ways within a multicultural imaginary. Teachers' 'professional vision', we suggest, entails schemas of difference which inform the running of the ethnically diverse school. These may be progressive in intention but can be problematic in execution, as we will explore in Chapters 4–7. Central to these schemas is the idea of culture, and how perceptions of culture are crucial not just to the idea of identity but to making sense of practices of multicultural education in schools.

The Meanings of Culture

The tensions articulated here rest on the complex place of 'culture' in multiculturalism. 'Culture' is one of the most complicated words in the English language (Williams, 1976), evolving over centuries to come to refer to things as divergent as the growing of organisms, the arts, individual taste, a 'whole way of life', discrete communities defined by nation, language or faith, consumer lifestyles and an organization's ethos. An account of this varied usage is not needed here, as it is well documented by many (Wren, 2012), but it is important to see how it is articulated in participants' comments and to reflect on the consequences for multicultural education. This wider range of meanings of culture was generally not found in the focus groups; there was a narrower focus on discrete communities which share values and beliefs, which we would understand as ethnicity, often defined in terms of national origin. Since Williams's work, the idea of culture has become increasingly ethnicized and the traditional idea of culture as 'the arts' has been displaced (Berking, 2003). The emergence of multiculturalism has been a key element in the increasing centrality of the conflation of culture and ethnicity in public and private vocabularies, in business and government, across all sectors and professions (Breidenbach & Nyíri, 2009), but perceived in particular, reduced ways.

The responses from students at Barnett are a useful starting point. For them, culture is:

> What they believe in, kind of.
> How we live.
> Religion.
> Well, yeah, religion, how they grow up.

At Pentonville, one student said culture was 'where you are from, like the things that they do', a second described it as 'a mix between race and religion', and a third said it was 'their background'. A fourth at Pentonville contrasted 'Western culture' and 'Asian or Chinese culture': 'how they do stuff differently . . . like in China they will use chopsticks instead of a knife and fork.' Many teachers, students and parents found it easier to typify what culture included, rather than define it, like the Wellington Heights teacher who said culture 'encompasses things [like] dance, music, food, religion'. Many also simply glossed culture as someone's 'background' or even as a kind of possession. One Eaton Park student said, 'I've been born here, but I still have my background so I keep it with me.' As we found in Chapter 1, there was little difference between the views of teachers, as professional educators, and those of students and parents. Common ideas voiced in the teacher focus groups were variations on the themes of 'traditions', as one Eaton Park teacher admitted, and 'what you do in your country' according to a teacher from Thurston.

There are several issues here. The first is that while these ideas overlap – beliefs and values, way of life, religion, traditions, country, background, how we are brought up – they are not the same thing. In talking about a term that has become central to the ways we think about the world, few parents, students or teachers had a clear and consistent way of grappling with it as an idea, and there appeared to be no shared, coherent understanding of culture across the groups. Some people, like these Pentonville students, admitted uncertainty: 'it's all different but I don't know how to explain it'; 'Um, I don't really know, I know what it is but like I don't really think of a technical definition.' These disparities are partly explained by the fact that culture is used to refer to different 'levels' of existence (Castles et al., 1990, pp. 123–6). The anthropological understanding of culture as a 'whole way of life' points to broad forms of social organization. At this level there have been two major cultures in Australia: traditional Aboriginal culture and Western, industrial society resulting from European invasion. Many Aboriginal Australians continue to live in relation to the land that reflects this deep notion of culture. There have often been two cultures in the lives of many migrants, they point out – such as those migrants who had lived in peasant villages in their homeland – but migrants cannot bring this 'whole way of life' when they migrate. What they bring is certain customs, language, religion, food and so on, diverse practices but without the deep structural organization which gave rise to those practices. This level, however, is quite different.

The second issue is the shift in scale in defining culture, quite different to the two levels above: from a focus on ethnic groups, religion, language, nation to large geopolitical entities like 'the West' and 'Asia' all featured in responses but always point to a cohesive entity. 'Nation' is the typical way people talk about cultures, but it is problematic. In Australia we talk about the 'Lebanese' as though this is a recognizable category, but Lebanon, like all countries, is divided by 'way of life' (urban consumerism versus peasant economies), faith (Maronite and Muslim), and class, language and so on. Being Lebanese in Lebanon is a category of citizenship. It is when migrants come to Australia that 'Lebanese' becomes reinvented as a singularizing category of ethnic community. The other scales are no less contentious: speaking Spanish or believing in Islam doesn't make for a homogenous culture, whether understood as a way of life, an ethnicity or a system of shared beliefs.

Nation-based categorizations of culture were occasionally challenged. While some talked about 'Australian culture' as though it was understood, one Pentonville parent, a critic of multiculturalism, pointed out what he saw as a logical flaw in the multicultural idea of culture: if Australia also 'has' a 'culture', then 'you can't have many cultures in one culture'. Other participants, such as this Hingston Valley student, foregrounded the problem of hybridity in categorizations of culture:

> For me, this is where I was born, this is where I grew up, this is my home, so I'm Australian. My background is Lebanese, my parents come from Lebanon, that's my culture, this is how I grew up, but I'm Australian. My background is Lebanese and I associate with that and I'm proud to say it. . . . You know for me, I can't say that like Lebanese culture-Australian culture, to be honest, that is confusing . . . I am Australian or Australian culture or Lebanese culture. For me, because I have grown up with a different background, in Australia, it sort of just meshes.

This Graham's Point student criticized other categorizations of 'culture': 'I don't even know why the word culture is used. I think the word exists to classify different styles really, because for example, the first time I invite people around to my house they immediately [went] 'wow, this is an Asian house.'

One of the consequences of equating culture with country is that it encourages a view of culture as a kind of 'container' which sees cultures as fixed and ongoing groups (Breidenbach & Nyíri, 2009, p. 25). This reified take on culture (whether it be based on nation or ethnicity) has been widely critiqued (Modood, 2007) in favour of a more processual view of culture as dynamic, fluid and contested (Gupta & Ferguson, 1997). The 'confusion' among interviewees is not an intellectual failing: the tension between an 'anthropological' focus on culture as a whole way of life and a recognition of the shifting and heterogeneous nature of culture-as-process has been central to debates around diversity (UNESCO, 2009). Migration is only part of a wider transnationalization of culture which destabilizes any simple definition of culture, whether as a way of life, a nation or an ethnic community, because cultural life is increasingly shaped by complex and interactive flows of people, goods and meanings. We can see these unresolved dilemmas in this exchange between teachers at Smithton as they discuss whether there is a thing called 'Greek culture':

> TEACHER 1: It encompasses everything about their lives.
> TEACHER 2: Because you know what, our Greek culture here is not even the same as the way the Greeks do it. My parents brought it out here, they put it in a bottle, they put the lid on it and it stayed the same. In Greece it changed, yet my parents still live in that culture. . . . They preserved

what they brought . . . [but] What is Greek culture? Is it the way in Greece, or is the one that my parents brought here?

The first (Anglo) teacher then responded by declaring the parents 'more authentic' than the culture in Greece, while a third responded that culture is, then, 'what you make it'. This discussion partly reflects the 'two levels' of culture discussed above, but it also highlights the tension between a traditional and dynamic view of culture in a globalized world. The 'traditional' might be seen as more 'authentic', but it leads to a dangerous 'primordialism' in ethnic politics (Appadurai, 1996). Several interviewees voiced a more dynamic view, including this migrant parent at Graham's Point but didn't know where to go with it: 'Culture is what you make of what you see around you and how you react to it.'

The tensions between traditional and dynamic views of culture, and between culture as a 'whole way of life' and as the practices that people recreate after migration, are obscured by the useful but problematic term 'cultural background' which has become standard terminology but can refer to both near and far 'backgrounds'. The ways people use culture to identify themselves, and are identified by others, refer more to ancestry than the 'ways of life' they currently follow. This is not simply a problem of semantics, for if identities are not 'cultures' but the result of complex distillations of diverse elements, how able are schools to address complex entanglements of culture, identity, ethnicity, migration, globalization as educational issues within multicultural programmes?

For these, and other, reasons, we therefore make a distinction between 'culture' and 'ethnicity' to reinforce the separation, in the lives of migrants, between homeland and diasporic community. We use 'culture' to refer to recognizable 'ways of life' or forms of social organization with patterned relationships and systems of meaning, as we might with remote Aboriginal communities. 'Cultural complexity' therefore points to the ways those patterns and systems are thrown together and changed because of the intensifying processes of globalization. We use 'ethnicity' to refer to those forms of community organization and identity that form through the processes of migration and settlement, long after 'culture' and heritage have settled into the 'background'. For us, ethnicity foregrounds the processes of mobilization in a global context whereby a diasporic community becomes identified as a discrete entity, resulting from historical and political processes, while 'culture' tends to dehistoricize those processes, treating cultures as primordial, traditional essences (Rizvi, 2014). So we prefer to talk about the diversity resulting from migration in Australia as ethnic diversity. However, we also use 'culture' to refer to identifiable forms of social organization at the level of an institution or profession, as in the culture of the school or a professional culture. But these are compromise solutions to difficult problems. The key issue for us is to use 'culture' analytically, to interrogate what is at stake when people use the term: What is it used to do, and what might it hide? Not grappling with these issues has dramatic consequences once we consider how divergent uses of 'culture' shape school practices?

Culture as Difference

The first key issue in examining meanings of culture is the way people understand culture as difference, as we began to discuss in the last section. Culture is typically seen in terms of the division between 'us' and 'them', and especially in terms of a contrast between the exotic difference of migrant communities and the Anglo 'mainstream' (Watkins, 2014). This amounts to the 'ethnicization' of the idea of culture (Noble & Watkins, 2014a, p. 166). It is seen in the use of 'they' in many quotes above, but it was voiced explicitly by this student from Beechton: 'Culture means from a different culture, like their background is a different culture than our background.' The interviewer followed this comment by asking whether someone born in Australia had a culture. One girl gave a thoughtful, but telling, answer:

> Well depends, as you said, you were born in Australia and if you have a culture like, say your parents were born in a different country and then they had a culture and then their parents had a culture so then you would have a culture because their parents have culture and so do your grandparents. So you would have culture because they are from a different country or they were born in a different country. . . . I also think that culture is like a different religion or something, not really a religion, like Catholic or anything but like a different country so you could be born in Australia, as I said before, you could be born in Australia but your parents could be from a different country and that's culture, so it's like you are born in Australia but you've got some part of a different country inside of you.

This student grapples with the complexities of culture. She captures a sense of culture as something transmitted over time, involving many things such as religion and nation, and as leaving residues or layers in the children of migrants. Yet her starting point is the idea that culture is structured around difference premised on the idea that difference is exotic, something from 'outside' 'Australia'.

The problem is not simply that an emphasis on difference excludes Anglos from the multicultural imaginary, but that in reducing cultural complexity to simplistic relations of sameness and difference and exoticizing migrant difference, schools set up perceptual schemas of difference which shape teachers' 'professional vision', including the understandings of students, the challenges they face, their classroom practices and the role of educational practitioners (Noble & Watkins, 2014a). The focus on (essentialized) difference displaces the relation between deep and phenomenal aspects of culture, the importance of history and dimensions of class and power, and the complex and dynamic flows of the globalized world (May, 1999). This is significant when we consider how teachers, students and parents viewed the relationships between 'culture' and educational and social dimensions in their school communities: learning outcomes, student behaviour and so on. This is how multiculturalism is 'enacted' in school communities, inside and outside the classroom (Meetoo, 2020). If the aim of multiculturalism and multicultural education is to direct attention to the need to address a range of issues in the pursuit of equity, to what extent has multicultural discourse helped or hindered our understandings of the challenges facing students and parents? As we've indicated, the focus on cultural difference is a central consequence of the multicultural paradigm, but this has often produced schemas of perception which frame understandings of learning outcomes, student behaviour, parental involvement and so on.

Culture as Explanation

'Culture', as a central category in political, popular and professional discourses, allowed us to move away from a problematic language of race, but it has also served to obfuscate complicated issues around ethnicity by operating as a reductive explanation of a range of social phenomena (Breidenbach & Nyíri, 2009), or what Yudice (2003) calls 'cultural expediency'. Participants were, for example, asked whether students from particular cultural backgrounds perform differently academically. This teacher at Binto Valley, echoing many, said that 'Asian students have that work ethic, right from the start, no matter which Asian country they come from, they all seem to have it . . . that's not the case with a lot of the other races'. 'Culture', not class or migration, is used to explain these differences. Most teachers had no qualms not only generalizing about academic performance in terms of ethnic categories but in hierarchizing them. A Graham's Point maths teacher explained,

> there are certain cultures that absolutely thrive on having maths as their primary like goal. . . . Maths and science is very similar because they want to be doctors or engineers. . . . The first cultures would be, well . . . particularly Indian, Sri Lankan, so sub-continental, Middle Eastern can be but maybe not as much. . . . But definitely not Anglo-Australian.

A Wellington Heights teacher echoed this view: '[the] Indian population [has] a massive academic push in those areas and therefore when I go into their classroom they are the achieving students. The Anglo students . . . they are more the strugglers, like the lower end.'

Sometimes it could be said bluntly, in a way that reflected an older language of race. A Wellington Heights teacher, for example, explained the lack of success of Arabic-speaking students: 'that's also because the culture is different again, where the cousins marry cousins, so therefore the children's intelligence levels will be different. That's just their genetics, a scientific fact.' A Getty Rd teacher was anxious about being so explicit: 'It sounds awfully racist but not necessarily, the Asians and the Indians value education, the Middle Easterns couldn't care less. The Aussies they care more about sport.' Other teachers were more circumspect and preferred to emphasize issues like class, how long students had been in Australia, language competence and family values. Yet many agreed about the performance of Asian students. One teacher from Eaton Park talked about the idea of the 'Asian fail', 'if an Aussie beat an Asian at maths', or if they got 'below 90' – a phenomenon we look at in Chapter 5. The public perception of the successful Asian student echoed throughout the discussions (Watkins & Noble, 2013). Some teachers saw this drive as 'inbuilt into their culture', as a Beechton teacher said in relation to Indian students and family expectations, and this was often linked to the rise in tutoring colleges. A few teachers saw Aboriginal disadvantage in terms of low SES, but others, such as a Pentonville teacher, saw the problem in terms of the lack of a 'work ethic'. Such outcomes were often explained in terms of 'culture' rather than marginalization stemming from colonization.

Most teachers adopted some form of cultural explanation of success. A few raised the idea of culturally specific learning styles, an idea that became popular in Australia in the 1990s and has remained part of educational discourse despite criticism (Noble & Poynting, 1998). The RMRME survey indicated that 70 per cent of teachers viewed 'accommodating diverse cultural learning styles' as an effective strategy for fostering cultural inclusion (Watkins et al., 2013, pp. 33–5). A Binto Valley teacher raised the issue:

> the learning styles of the Islander kids and the learning style of Asian kids, they are entirely different and you have to have an understanding of that. It gives you a preparedness I guess when you get it that a child comes from a different culture, that at least you have some insight into the way that they should be learning.

While some teachers shrank from such a view, there was a strong and persistent linking of the relationship between culture and educational outcomes.

Such 'explanations' were extended to topics such as student behaviour and parental involvement. Several teachers referred to students of Muslim or Arabic-speaking backgrounds as being 'problems'. One young female teacher at Wellington Heights recounted an experience with a Muslim boy who 'was taught at home to disrespect women'. This view fits into a long tradition of Orientalist Othering (Said, 1978), but the point here is how these categories operate in discussing student behaviours. Another common view was that there were noticeable differences in parental involvement. 'Australian' parents were seen to be more likely to participate while, one Addington parent argues, 'a lot of cultures . . . stick more to their own families . . . some cultures . . . are more willing to participate and want to help out'. Yet it is 'cultures' getting involved here, not parents. In other words, 'cultures' become things which have agency, explaining individuals' actions. At Smithton, one parent felt that Greeks tend to 'keep very much . . . together'.

The point is not whether these views of culturally explained patterns of behaviour have some basis in people's experiences, but the ways these categories are drawn on to explain aspects of individual and group behaviour. Not only are they drawn on, but they harden and become taken-for-granted ways of seeing Others which constitute a multicultural imaginary. Significantly, such explanations seemed to be much more common and stronger among teachers than parents and students, suggesting that perceptions of difference were extremely salient in teachers' professional vision, shaping their practices and school programmes generally. As suggested in the Introduction, the endorsement of culturally responsive pedagogies, which has become a central tenet among some advocates of multicultural education, shares some of the problematic connections between culture and behaviour. We argue that many of the claims here rest on categories that are not meaningful, let alone useful in explaining behaviour. Given that nations are diverse societies in themselves, cleft by class, gender, faith and urban/rural divisions, and reconfigured through processes of cultural complexities of globalization, there is little cultural coherence to being Greek or Lebanese as a form of explanation. Moreover, as we have argued, being the child or grandchild of a migrant is no guarantee of continuity of 'way of life'. This is compounded by the questionable use of geopolitical categories, such as Asia and Africa, to explain behaviour. Yet such ethnic stereotypes harden into 'truths' that inform hot educational issues such as selective schools, coaching colleges, youth radicalization and so on. People, including teachers, use these categories as though they are homogenous and fixed, ignoring complexities of social causation. 'Culture' becomes increasingly essentialized and primordial, even sometimes construed in racial terms.

Culture Talk and Racism

As we have seen, the language of race often found its way into participants' accounts, but without necessarily involving explicit racist appeals. So it is interesting to look at participants' views about racism and the ways 'culture talk' may entail habits of thinking about culture, ethnicity and race which underlie assumptions about the differences between groups even when we don't think we are being racist. While the emergence of the language of culture was historically important in that it de-emphasized old fashioned racialized discourses, some would argue that 'culture talk' has simply become a way of obscuring real issues around racism (Mamdani, 2005).

Most teachers, students and parents felt, by and large, that while there were ongoing issues of racism within Australian society and their own school communities, their school did a fair job of preventing and dealing with such incidents. This corresponds with the view in the state-wide survey of teachers that racism was more of a problem outside schools than within them (Watkins, et al., 2013, pp. 44–5). By and large, people tended to see their school as harmonious. One Wellington Heights student declared, they 'get on pretty well because there is no racism in our school', which a teacher echoed: 'I've never seen racism at the school.' A Barnett student commented that 'there are definitely racist people, but I wouldn't call Australia as a whole racist'. A Smithton parent made this distinction: 'the kids know there is their school world and then there is their world when they see it on TV at home. There is more racism on TV.' At Addington two teachers agreed that the few incidents that occurred each year were 'superficial', 'like calling someone fat'; they didn't have serious problems like 'race gangs or race wars'.

The reasons why were diverse. One Pentonville parent asserted that 'there are no racism issues, and I think it's only because, or one main reason is we've only got a very small percentage of non-Anglo Saxon children here, therefore the problem just doesn't arise'. In contrast, some believed that areas that were more of what a Hingston Valley parent called a 'melting pot' were less prone to racism. A Harringvale student claimed: 'there are parts of Australia like in Sydney I don't think that racism is as common as it could be in other parts . . . because it's a matter of what you are exposed to.' Moreover, sometimes racism was downplayed or excused. A Smithton student described many incidents as 'accidental racism', rather than an intention to hurt. Some students at Hingston Valley dismissed racist remarks as 'just joking', an occasional refrain across the schools and groups. One Smithton student of Greek ancestry argued that 'nobody pays attention to racism and stuff because it's getting old . . . now we've gotten over'. One Graham's Point parent dismissed some forms as rudeness: 'I don't think it is racism. It is lack of education or lack of awareness.' There was a tendency to not only downplay cases of racism but also to see it in individual terms, and as a moral flaw in uneducated or 'racist people'. Some saw it as more or less incidental. An Addington parent agreed: 'They . . . use racism as a fist fight, it just happens to be maybe two kids from a different race fighting and other people around turn it into a race fight – just because they may call them names, they are in the heat of the moment.'

Yet many could easily point to racist incidents, and these were more often voiced by students than teachers or parents. At Wollami Lakes, students listed clear examples of name-calling: 'people call Aboriginals, "niggers" and they call Indians, "Punjabs" . . . some people tease the Indians about their turbans'; 'sometimes they call them "curry munchers" and stuff'. One parent at Hingston Valley saw particular targets:

> the African kids because they are so different in their colour of skin that they stand out a lot . . . so many of those kids have been through so much trauma that we just can't comprehend and I get really upset when I see blatant racism against them because . . . they have been through so much trauma and all some people see are these big muscular boys you know, and feel intimidated.

Students at Barnett recounted an experience when a student started saying offensive things about land rights, Aboriginal welfare and drugs because the topic they were studying involved Indigenous issues: 'me and [another] were the only Indigenous people in the classroom, so we were just like yelling and screaming at them and I know that's probably not the best way but the teacher wasn't doing anything at all.' The inaction of the teacher is a concern, but the other issue here is that curriculum designed to produce better understanding of such issues actually became a springboard for the airing of racist views.

A Wellington Heights student noted anti-Muslim feeling more generally in Australia:

> A lot of people pick on Muslim people in our country. Because they are always, all the people who have like committed crimes and wars. . . . Australians themselves think that people in this country who are Muslim also will act like that but . . . I'm not saying that Australians are racist but it is just people's opinions, after seeing what's on TV and they believed it . . . they say that Australia is a racist country but I don't think so, it is more of a multicultural country than a racist country.

So, does multiculturalism necessarily inhibit racism? Multicultural education has, as one of its logics, the imperative that we respect and tolerate those who are different to us, yet it also encourages a way of talking about others that encourages us to see people in terms of difference that is often primordial, overriding both points of connection and other explanations of conflict, despite, or perhaps because of, its good intentions. In contrast to the student who contrasted racism and multiculturalism, one Harringvale student felt that multiculturalism encouraged racism:

> Multiculturalism leads to people congregating to what they are familiar with, so, for example, if you are Lebanese like from another country

coming down to Australia you will be more inclined to live in areas such as Bankstown which the majority is Lebanese, but the thing is, I live in Bankstown . . . and I've experienced the racism in there . . . It's because they are so proud, like any person can be proud, but when you group them together and . . . they are all the same race it's so easy to become proud of your culture and to criticize others.

We're not arguing that this student is right, but it does point to a more complex relation between a multicultural ethos and issues of inequality. Indeed, some scholars have argued that 'culture talk' (Mamdani, 2005) often reduces complex social, economic and political issues – educational outcomes, drug addiction, welfare, terrorism and land rights – to questions of culture. Some scholars talk about this as a process of ethnicization or culturalization, the ways social phenomena are understood through a single lens which serves to mask broader structural relations of power by finding explanations for them in the 'culture' of a particular, often marginalized or demonized, group (Murji & Solomos, 2005). The danger is that the 'professional vision' we have documented, by focusing on questions of ethnic difference, might allow the language of 'culture' to reproduce forms of racism while hiding deeper issues of racialized inequality. At the same time, the injunction to be upbeat about difference, to celebrate diversity avoids an uncomfortable but critical language of race and racism (Lentin & Titley, 2011). The hope is that a more reflexive interrogation of the question of 'culture' will foster deeper and more productive discussions about the relations between race, ethnicity and inequality in Australia.

Aboriginal Peoples and Multicultural Education

Some of the comments above raise the vexed issue of the relation between multicultural education and Aboriginal education. It is significant that this question arose several times, especially in rural schools or outer-western Sydney schools with significant numbers of Aboriginal students, when we were asking people about multiculturalism. While Aboriginal communities and languages have often been used to exemplify the cultural diversity of Australia, multiculturalism is often seen to be exclusively about migrant communities. Such a division is built into the organization and funding of education departments across Australia, as well as school practices. As the Australian Institute of Multicultural Affairs (1986) explained three decades ago, while endorsing a greater alignment of the two areas,

The response from the Aboriginal communities has been mixed, with a strong feeling from some quarters that, at least at the philosophical level, multiculturalism denies their unique position as the original inhabitants of Australia. Indeed, it is felt that adoption of multiculturalism by Aborigines has the potential to trivialize their disenfranchizement from the land, and might limit their claims for social justice.

The language of 'culture' is used to comparable effect in Aboriginal education policies (see NSW DoE, 2020b) as it is in multicultural education policies, and there are comparable logics of recognition, incorporation and civility, a comparable ethos of respect, and a comparable stress on culturally appropriate strategies. At Pentonville, this exchange took place between parents when the interviewer picked up on an earlier comment and asked what the parents thought about the separation of these areas:

PARENT 1: Yeah, just from like talking to different adults in regards to that, I find because the Aboriginal is separate from the multicultural sort of, that sometimes that can bring a bit of – what's the word? – resentment, sort of thing, that so much is focused on the Aboriginal culture. Just from people that might not necessarily know the true past. . . . I think having that separateness sort of sometimes may cause a bit more problems.

PARENT 2: I don't think it should be separate because . . . teachers, the kids, they are separate people but you should be treating, telling the kids that we are all equals, and because we look different, believe something different doesn't mean they should be separate. Doesn't matter what your background is, we are all the same. To have it separate just means – why is it separate? Why are they different? That just creates something different – everyone should be in together.

When asked whether he thought there were similarities between educational strategies for Aboriginal students and those associated with multicultural education, one teacher at Pentonville answered cautiously that 'some places yes, and other places, no'. A parent at Smithton felt it was strange that his son 'knows more about Greek culture and mythology and stuff like that than he does about Indigenous culture'. As a Getty Rd teacher pointed out in discussing curriculum for intercultural understanding, 'I keep looking at the Indigenous culture as well, that we need to have that focus, although it is separate it is still intercultural . . . we should be going along that path. Looking at the choices and lifestyle customs, religions, that type of thing.' Indeed, another parent here believed 'there is a multicultural class that they have here, the Year 9 class and that's a mix of Aboriginal and non-Aboriginal students and yeah, no problem'. A Barnett teacher saw no problem in maintaining overall coherence of approach and respecting individual specificities, 'I think if you are looking at different cultural backgrounds then you would include everybody in that . . . you don't differentiate between any of them, I think they all have their own special needs and you need to look at them as individual cases.' As a parent at Pentonville concluded, 'Basically it is about inclusion . . . everybody should be regardless of what their race is, everybody should be given the opportunity to learn and be accepted and the school does also need to make sure that other cultures are aware of each other.'

These are difficult issues without easy answers. The positions of Aboriginal people and migrants in Australia are not the same, and the diversity that arises from colonial history is different from the diversity that arises from migration programmes (Kymlicka, 1995). The language of culture talk deployed both officially and demotically cannot do justice to these significant historical and political differences. We emphasize, again, that what is missing here is a critical approach to questions of culture.

Conclusion

Entanglements of culture, ethnicity, race and identity typify everyday life in school communities, predicated on the foregrounding of differences, and this has consequences for teaching practice. Many teachers, students and parents draw on cultural explanations of student learning, parent involvement in school communities and other phenomenon, which often harden into received truths. As in Chapter 1, there were various understandings at stake in people's discussions of culture, ethnicity and identity. Similarly, there was no coherent or professional expertise of teachers evident here; their 'professional vision' relied on similar reductive and essentializing understandings of culture. More importantly, the use of culture often fostered reduced ways of characterizing behaviour, structured around difference rather than deep or critical conceptualizations of culture, demonstrating the prevalence of 'cultural expediency' – that is, drawing upon culture to 'explain' complex social phenomena.

What this suggests is the need for a reinvigorated sociocultural focus in curriculum and professional training in which these factors are examined critically as well as ethically, where 'culture' is the basis of a pedagogical project of the intellectual comprehension of cultural complexity, not simply cause for empathetic 'understanding'. Such a focus would help produce a shared language for teachers, students and parents to interrogate the social, economic and political processes whereby 'culture' becomes significant, especially in the age of globalization, and where questions of identity are framed less as the automatic consequence of a 'cultural background'. This, in essence, was the goal of the RMRME project: to ask teachers to 'rethink' their approach to multicultural education and to apply these understandings in the context of their own schools.

CHAPTER 3

Grappling with Cultural Complexity

Knowledge Translation and Professional Learning

The previous chapters drew on findings from the state-wide survey of teachers and focus groups conducted with teachers, students and parents in each of the fourteen project schools. These findings proved insightful in a number of ways. Not only did they allow us to gauge the attitudes and understandings that these groups had of multiculturalism and the role of multicultural education in schools, but they also shed light on the increasing cultural complexity of school populations. This complexity is a product of various factors. As we have seen, schools are now faced with greater levels of ethnic diversity wherein more and more students and their families are not only migrants or can trace their recent lineage from a wider spread of countries, but they now tend to have far more complex migration histories and experiences of settlement. Added to this, there is a concomitant rise in linguistic and religious diversity which intersects with various factors such as class and gender, that require teachers to have a nuanced understanding of how these impact upon a student's education.

We also saw how this complexity is not spread evenly across schools. Those in urban areas tend to have greater concentrations of LBOTE students, whereas rural schools, on the whole, have larger numbers of Aboriginal students, though this is not always the case. Increasing numbers of refugees are now settled in regional and rural locations and government incentives for migrants to settle outside larger metropolitan centres have also led to greater diversity in rural and regional schools (Colvin, 2017; Watkins et al., 2019). Within Sydney there is also considerable geographic variation in ethnic and linguistic diversity with some schools having far greater numbers of LBOTE or Aboriginal students and some schools that have concentrations of students of particular ethnic and linguistic backgrounds. Different schools serve different student populations and, as a result, have different needs. In response, teachers must not only have the required knowledge and skills to work in these varied contexts but must ensure their students are well prepared for engagement in the world beyond school in an increasingly interconnected global community. While existing models of multicultural education address ongoing needs, such as EAL/D, they are simply not up to this task. They require a conceptual rethink and for teachers to be a part of this process whereby they consider the implications of this cultural complexity for their students and address ways of transforming multicultural education in the context of their own schools.

This chapter examines the steps involved in preparing teachers to do this. It provides an account of the training that was undertaken in advance of teachers conducting school-based action research around issues of multicultural education. In particular, it sheds light on the processes of knowledge translation as teachers in the research teams in the fourteen project schools grappled with conceptual understandings drawn from cultural theory and various sources of data to reconceive the way they approach multicultural education. The chapter documents the teachers' differing reactions to this training, providing insights into how they approached the action research that was conducted in their schools; in other words, their capacity and commitment to do diversity differently. First, we provide some background on the action research phase of the broader RMRME project before then considering the training that preceded it.

Background to the Action Research Phase of RMRME

The action research phase of RMRME, which was undertaken over the course of a school year, involved considerable preparation that commenced in the year prior to its implementation. It began with an information session with the principals from the fourteen project schools to outline the action research process. Each of these principals had nominated their school to be involved in the broader project after having been approached by either the NSW DoE members of the RMRME Project team or the NSW DoE multicultural education/EAL/D consultants who, on the basis of the demographics required for the overall sample of schools, selected those they considered most appropriate in consultation with the Project team. Teachers in each of these schools, along with others from across NSW, had already been given the opportunity to complete the state-wide survey. In the fourteen project schools, this survey was re-administered to ensure a full quota of responses with the results then matched with those from across the state in individual school reports that were later used with teachers in the training.

The information session with the principals was used to explain how the action research phase of RMRME would be undertaken in their schools including the approach to the training, the implementation model and the timeline for the year. The session also outlined how each school was required to appoint a research team of up to five members including at least one executive member. Rather than just teachers, one school also involved parents on their research team. Principals used various methods to recruit team members, targeting staff and/or calling for interested volunteers. These teams were responsible for devising and implementing their school's action research project over the course of the following year. Before this, each of the teams attended the professional learning sessions that were conducted at the beginning of the next year at Western Sydney University. Schools received funding from the NSW DoE to allow teachers to attend this training, follow-up sessions midway through the process and a presentation day at the end of the year at the completion of their projects. Additional funding was given to schools for further teaching relief for planning, implementation and resourcing. Ultimately, however, the allocation of this money was left to the school project teams and their principals to determine.

Teachers attending the professional learning sessions could use the training for accreditation purposes, registering the course and follow-up activities as part of their individual professional development.[1] Following this training, research teams received further support in their schools from the DoE consultants who had undertaken similar training in preparation for this support role. The consultants' training also acted as a pilot for the training of the school research teams. Lastly, a project website acted as an additional source for professional learning. This housed relevant resources, policy documents and a teacher portal providing all school research teams with access to each other's research plans and final reports, together with a discussion board to promote dialogue and the sharing of ideas between schools and participants.

Notions of Research: Applied, Engaged and Action-Orientated

The school-based action research phase of the RMRME Project is probably better described as engaged research with embedded action research components, though both these terms, 'engaged research' and 'action research', require further explanation and some qualification. Third (2016) makes a distinction between applied and engaged research. While both intend practical application, what Third identifies as a shortcoming of much applied research is that, despite its potential to produce viable solutions to real-world problems, this knowledge often has little impact on policy and practice as the process of 'knowledge exchange' is not factored into the overall research design. Third sees this as characteristic of engaged research, namely that researchers, government, industry and not-for-profit organizations work collaboratively to identify issues that require attention and devise research to appropriately intervene and effect change. Agonistic relations may result but, with research partners operating as a 'community of practice' (Wenger, 2000), these points of tension are viewed as productive and worked through, ultimately proving essential to the dialogic process of knowledge production. This was how the RMRME Project evolved. The Multicultural Programs Unit (MPU) within the NSW DoE sought to examine multicultural education practices across schools in light of contemporary research and a changing policy environment that required a response to increasing ethnic diversity in schools – and the diversification of this diversity – that added to the complex nature of school communities. Findings from an earlier project (Watkins & Noble, 2008) recommended professional learning for teachers to enhance their understandings of ethnic diversity and to move beyond notions of cultural inclusion as simply cultural sensitivity – often misconceived – towards a critical engagement with the cultural complexity within schools and the broader Australian community.

Working together with our research partners, we used these findings to inform the research design of RMRME which was initially piloted with eleven schools and then modified for what then became RMRME. The collaborative nature of this process, particularly the research design and implementation, is what characterizes RMRME as engaged research, but this engagement operated at various levels and in different modes (Figure 1). It occurred not only between the investigators from the three research partners – Western Sydney University, the NSW DoE and the NSW Institute of Teachers/BOSTES – but with the DoE consultants whose feedback from their own training led to the modification of the approach used with the school teams. They in turn worked with schools, to varying effect, devising and implementing their action research projects. There was also the engaged nature of the research the school research teams were undertaking, though at this level there was no feedback loop to the broader project to affect its overarching research design and implementation. At this point, engagement became embedded within an action research frame, and, in some schools, actions were modified through dialogue between schools and their communities. The macro-analysis that we undertook of these projects necessitated certain limits on engagement. As indicated, the training of the school teams was not simply a technique to effect change in the way they approached multicultural education. The macro-analysis also provided a means for us to ascertain the success or otherwise of the projects, yielding insights with broader implications for in-service professional learning.

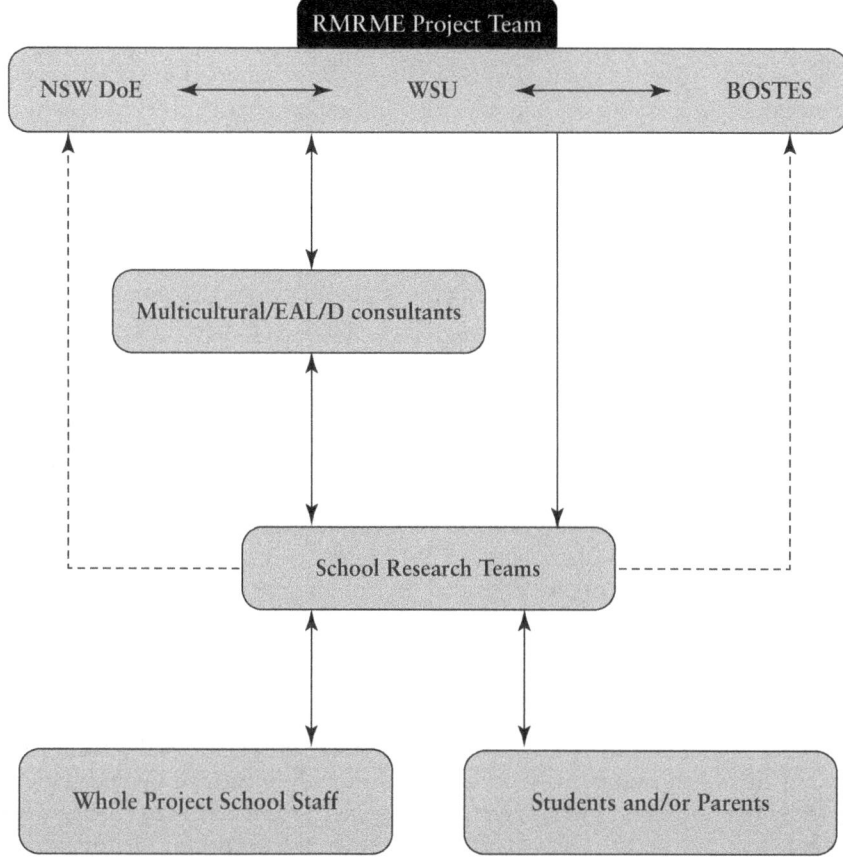

FIGURE 1 *RMRME Project Action Research: Levels and modes of engagement.*

The training also encouraged a particular approach to action research. Perspectives on action research vary enormously depending on whether emphasis is given to action or research and on the way in which research is understood (Pine, 2008, p. 43). The origins of action research can be found in the work of Kurt Lewin who, in the late 1930s, introduced participatory research methods into workplaces in the United States to improve the conditions of marginalized workers (Adelman, 1993). Together with being participatory, he drew on research methods from the social sciences to encourage a systematic approach to data collection in gauging the effectiveness of workplace practices. His ideas were later adopted in education in the United States and United Kingdom during the 1950s and 1960s where action research was refashioned as a tool for teachers to improve classroom practice (Silver & Silver, 1991) and now has broad application as a form of research-based practitioner enquiry (Kemmis et al., 2014; Macintyre, 2000; Mills, 2007). Stemming from Lewin's approach, action research tends to place little emphasis on the theoretical.

Rather, it typically involves the identification of a problem, devising an 'action' to address it, collecting data to assess its effectiveness and then reflecting upon the findings. This process is generally followed by the repetition of this cycle to monitor practice in an ongoing way. Indeed, Brown University's manual on action research in education points out that 'Rather than dealing with the theoretical, action research allows practitioners to address those concerns that are closest to them, ones over which they can exhibit some influence and make change' (Ferrance, 2000, n.p).

There is considerable debate within the field of educational action research as to the role of theory and what actually constitutes 'theory' in the first place (Carr & Kemmis, 1986; Elliot, 2005; Hadfield, 2012; Kemmis, 2008). Manfra (2019, p. 166) is of the view that 'Theory and practice are not separated in action research – theory emerges from systematic and intentional reflection on practice'. Such a perspective is not dissimilar to that of grounded theory where an inductive approach to theory, derived from the data, is favoured (Ezzy, 2002). The notion of theory underpinning the approach to action research within RMRME operated more as a dialectic between deduction and induction.[2] While theory may emerge from data, research first needs to be informed by an understanding of theoretical perspectives relevant to the field of enquiry. Without this, research design and the interpretation of data are severely constrained. This is also the case with action research if theory does not underpin the approach. As Kemmis et al. (2014, p. 2) explain, 'action research itself is a social practice, a practice-changing practice which cannot ignore the theoretical terrain that might help participants to work from a critically informed perspective on social life.' RMRME, therefore, stressed the need for teachers to engage with theoretical perspectives drawn from cultural theory around identification, hybridity and globalization to prompt them to engage critically with how multicultural education is practised in schools and how it may be reimagined.

Surveying relevant literature was incorporated into the RMRME model of action research. To some extent this was at odds with the NSW DoE's *Handbook on Action Research in Education* (NSW DEC, 2010, p. 9) which downplays the importance of surveying literature: 'In the action research cycle the literature review is not generally a formal process.' RMRME foregrounded its value and formalized this step. We also advocated a broadening of the parameters of the literature to be surveyed suggesting far more than what is usually considered under the rubric of 'professional reading' – which often has a narrow, pragmatic focus – needed to be consulted. We felt teachers would benefit from supplementing their reading with more theoretically informed scholarship allowing for the generation of new knowledge and avoiding the replication of established practice. If professional vision is part of the problem, then we cannot simply rely on teachers' reflection on their practice; we have to readjust the frame. The degree to which the teachers in the research teams took up this challenge was variable, reflective of their differing approaches to professional practice.

Knowledge Translation in Professional Contexts

Central to both this chapter and those that follow is the notion of knowledge translation, the ways in which particular understandings drawn from research are then utilized by practitioners to modify practice within their professional context. Within the RMRME Project this was a complex process involving various acts of translation as the teachers in the research teams were not simply taking a bank of knowledge and applying it but utilizing knowledge drawn from various sources: the findings from an earlier study into cultural practices and learning (Watkins & Noble, 2008); the RMRME pilot; the RMRME state-wide survey and the individual school reports that drew on this survey data; theoretical understandings gleaned from cultural theory and aspects of research methodology, and using these to frame their own action research project to address an issue around multicultural education in their school. The teams were also encouraged to draw on any school or NSW DoE-derived data to assist in the design of their projects[3] together with surveying relevant literature that they had access to through the project website and university library. Further acts of knowledge translation were evident as schools began to draw on the data resulting from the action research they undertook, using this to modify the interventions they were implementing. These are examined in the chapters that follow. Here the focus is on the training the teams received and the ways in which they made sense of what was presented.

Knowledge translation is one way of describing this process, yet various terminology is employed in discussing how knowledge derived from research is applied in terms of policy and/or practice such as 'knowledge transfer', 'research utilization', 'knowledge exchange', each signalling a variation in the actual process of knowledge creation and/or application (Graham et al., 2006, p. 15). Knowledge exchange, for example, denotes a more collaborative process of knowledge creation which was indicative of the relations between us as university researchers, the NSW DoE and BOSTES in the initial design of RMRME. This was also characteristic of relations between the NSW DoE consultants and the teams, as well as those between some teams and their participants. Another term with currency in the field of education is 'knowledge mobilization', reflective of 'the multiple ways in which stronger connections can be made between research policy and practice' (Levin, 2011, p. 15). Different terms seem more applicable depending on the stage of the RMRME Project and the participants involved, but, with the training the teams undertook, we were specifically interested in their engagement with the knowledge and research tools required to rethink multicultural education. At this stage another term associated with knowledge translation seems most relevant, that of 'enactment'. Braun et al. (2011) use enactment to refer to the processes of interpretation and translation involved in schools' uptake of policy. Here our concern is not simply policy enactment but the application of knowledge gleaned from professional learning within these varying school contexts (Kennedy, 2016; Meetoo, 2020); knowledge of a conceptual register that enables a reframing of teachers' understandings and their ability to reimagine practice.

The training of the teams was conducted at the beginning of the school year, over two days, a week apart, allowing participants time to digest material, engage in further discussion with their team back at their school and to complete additional reading for the second day. We were mindful of the limited effectiveness of short-term professional learning (Manfra, 2019), and while we would have preferred training of a longer duration – given the material to be covered and the depth of understanding we were aiming for – logistically and financially this was not possible. Bringing together teams of up to five teachers and executives from fourteen schools from across NSW was a mammoth task in itself. We hoped that having the break between the training days at the beginning of the year, a mid-year refresher and ongoing support through the project website and consultancy team would make up for the relatively short duration of the face-to-face training. The programme for the initial two days included an overview of the research process; sessions on exploring multiculturalism, culture, identity and multicultural education; presentations on the RMRME state-wide survey and; the distribution and discussion of the individual school reports. Presentations were also given on the RMRME approach to action research; a range of relevant data collection techniques; a successful programme delivered by a member of one of the school research teams involved in the RMRME pilot project; relevant resources including those available through the project website and teacher portal; how to access the Western Sydney University library for wider reading and project implementation; the timeline and in-school support. Content was delivered in various formats including lectures by us and our partner investigators, small group tutorials and other group-based activities around, for example, formulating research questions.

An important part of the training was the readings which had been distributed in advance with the questions used to frame discussion in the tutorials. These were composed of members of different schools to promote cross-school interaction. There were three tutorials of this type led by either a RMRME Project team member or one of the DoE consultants, focusing on a reading related to the following themes:

1. Exploring Multiculturalism, Culture and Identity
2. What Is Multicultural Education?
3. Conducting Research in Schools: Workload and the Professional Culture of Teachers

The readings used were:

- UNESCO (2009). *UNESCO World Report Executive Summary. Investing in Cultural Diversity and Intercultural Dialogue* (pp. 1–10). Paris: UNESCO;

- Inglis, C. (2009). Multicultural Education in Australia: Two Generations of Evolution. In J. Banks (Ed.), *The Routledge International Companion to Multicultural Education* (pp. 109–20). London: Routledge;
- Timperley, H. & Robinson, V. (2000). Workload and the Professional Culture of Teachers. *Educational Management and Administration*, 28(1), 47–62.

These were specifically chosen to address the key themes and to promote discussion around issues that emerged. The two days constituted an intense period of training. Following this, research teams met with their consultant who supported them through the process of drafting their research plans. These plans were then submitted to the RMRME Project team for feedback, prior to being revised and made available through the teacher portal on the project website. Teachers then began the task of implementing the action research they had devised. As explained, our feedback was 'light on'. While we pointed to any possible issues around each project's rationale, research question/s and research design, we were keen to see how teams would approach the process with little intervention on our part drawing on what they had gleaned from the training and with the support of the consultancy team.

Responses to the Training: Insights into the Professional Cultures of Teaching

Many found the training intellectually stimulating but challenging. As Daphne from Barnett HS explained, it 'took me back basically to my college days. I hadn't really been exposed to anything like that at that level for a long time.' This was a view echoed by Lena from Thurston PS: 'I think that's probably why it has been overwhelming for us because we have – it's a long time since I've been at uni.' The team at Getty Rd PS were pleased with the level of theoretical engagement in the training with Sofia, commenting, 'Sorcha and I were talking about, as teachers, you are often in your classroom and you don't get to go back and do things and talk to adults about intellectual things. You know, use your brain.' Harry at Smithton PS simply said, 'my brain hasn't been clicked on for a long while because here you are doing the nitty gritty.' Others, however, were less comfortable with the theoretical dimension of the training. The principal of Eaton Park felt 'it was a little too theoretical. I think it could have been a little more hands-on and perhaps the theory base could have been reduced.' Richard, from Wollami Lakes PS, was of a similar view: 'I found the first [day] difficult to sit through because it was so academic. The second one was good because it gave us a sense of, all right now we know what we have to do; we are not just talking intellectual stuff.'

For us, however, the 'intellectual stuff' was crucial for reconceiving the way multicultural education is approached in schools. One lecture during the training, for example, examined different perspectives on culture as fixed or fluid and the implications of this for understanding ethnic and cultural identity and the essentializing which certain practices of multiculturalism have tended to encourage. These issues were further explored in the extract from the UNESCO report and through findings from the earlier study around cultural practices and learning and the pilot RMRME project. Marta at Addington HS, however, saw little need for this: 'you could have condensed that day, introduction, here it is, off with your teams, here's your paperwork you've got to fill in, how are you going to do it, just let people work together.' In other words, Marta saw the training as a time when her team, released from face-to-face teaching, could plan their project with little need for further input. This was an approach the Graham's Point HS principal was critical of yet felt, 'a lot of teachers these days will say, "tell me what to do and I'll do it", rather than you know doing their own research and showing their own initiative and becoming interested in a particular area'.

Many of the teachers in other teams did not share Marta's view. Gillian at Wellington Heights valued the intellectual input and time for reflecting on different conceptions of culture and ethnicity:

> having a really in-depth look at that really made me start to think there was a little bit more to the way I was thinking and it kind of turned my thinking around to point in the direction of equity and I think that all the things that we did . . . I think the first day in particular was really like, wow, I need to have another think about this.

The training had a similar impact on Sybilla at Thurston, who began to make use of these concepts in an everyday sense: 'What's that word again? Essentialized. I've been using that on my husband quite a bit . . . you don't realize how much you do it until I guess that first week made me think OK you do do it.' As Julie, from Harringvale HS, summed it up, 'If we didn't have the professional learning, then our definition of multicultural education and any action to address it would be very limited.'

This range of comments from the principals and teachers is suggestive of two very different professional cultures, one with a narrow pragmatic focus in which professional learning serves a purely practical function, the other having a broader intellectual orientation that recognizes the benefits of theory for rethinking practice. Hoyle (1975) makes a similar distinction in his account of restricted and extended professionality that operate on a continuum. The restricted professional is reliant on their own experience to inform practice, whereas the extended professional sees the value of theory to guide teaching. As a result, teachers have differing professional visions that ultimately shape how they approach their work. While teachers need to be mindful of the immediate concerns of day-to-day classroom teaching, the extent to which this is divorced from any intellectual engagement is the point of differentiation here. The process of knowledge translation – a team's capacity to enact understandings from the training sessions – was reliant upon the professional capacities of the teachers involved and the degree to which their professional visions were formed by what appeared to be these divergent cultures of teaching. Using the term 'culture' here to refer to these differing professional orientations is quite deliberate but needs explanation. As discussed in Chapter 2, 'culture' is not only a complex term, it tends to be overused signalling commonality and providing a convenient explanation for behaviour, often problematically so. We use it here to denote a certain coherence in the attitudes and practices of teachers and how these correspond to different senses of professionalism. But, in recognizing this coherence, we also acknowledge considerable variation resulting from differing contextual factors and structural constraints within and outside schools (Ball et al., 2011) that affect teachers' lives and work which a homogenizing category such as 'culture' can often mask.

A similar range of perspectives that coalesce in terms of these differing professional cultures was evident when the teams were questioned about the readings. Richard from Wollami Lakes was initially concerned: 'when I went up and got my email . . . and I saw the readings and the questions and all that sort of stuff I just went, oh no! But I'm hoping something positive is going to come out of it.' Toby from Barnett HS felt that 'the first [reading] from the UNESCO was a chore, I felt like I was in Sociology 101 again, the second one had elements that I could follow but certainly the last paper was the best'. Such comments seem to indicate that professional reading, particularly of a more theoretical nature, is not the norm. While the extract from the UNESCO report dealt with some complex issues around globalization, cultural maintenance and hybridity, which were introduced in a lecture and then unpacked in the tutorials, it was chosen for its accessible report style. The principal from Eaton Park, however, seemed to confirm the view that such literature was not widely read by teachers: 'Oh they are useful readings, yeah, and probably you don't do a lot of academic reading when you are at school.' Alice, an experienced head teacher who led the Harringvale HS team, found the UNESCO report challenging but important: 'Well I think that it just makes the complexity of the whole idea of multiculturalism, I mean that's really what for me it underpinned, that there are no easy answers.' In reflecting on reading within the profession more broadly, she explained that

> some people would be really interested in it. I mean it depends, some people are more intellectually engaged in the theory behind educational practice and ideas so they will read . . . other people just want to get in and do the practical. If it had no relevance to what I am actually doing in the classroom immediate and I can see that I can apply it straight away, then they are a little resistant.

Clearly, this characterized Marta from Addington's approach:

> I reckon all that reading, I don't know what the point of that reading was actually . . . this is all academic writing, like we are all at grass roots, we are at things that happen every single day that we have to micro-manage . . . I know that the universities are driving the whole multicultural thing but . . . teachers need to be in the classroom teaching.

In areas such as multicultural education – though of course this is the case more broadly – certain knowledge may not appear readily applicable, packaged for immediate implementation. Rather, it is more in the realm of professional expertise to be drawn on in designing curricula, approaches to pedagogy and policy development. It is knowledge constitutive of a professional, informing practice but, importantly, at a reflexive distance from it. Dewey (1927) made a similar distinction in his discussion of initial teacher education during the early twentieth century in the difference between apprenticeship and laboratory models of teacher induction. While the latter may sound clinical in a contemporary context, Dewey favoured this model because it affords the time for trainee teachers to acquire the necessary theoretical expertise outside the classroom that they can then draw on when they commence teaching. He was critical of what he saw as 'the lack of intellectual independence' among teachers (Dewey, 1927, p. 16) and the way in which 'scholastic knowledge is sometimes regarded as if it were something quite irrelevant to method' (Dewey, 1927, p. 21). More recent scholars such as Posch (2019, pp. 498–500) also stress the importance of 'reflection-on-practice', but, unlike Dewey, Posch seems less inclined to foreground the value of 'scholastic knowledge'. He refers to Elliot's critique of the 'theory applying model of learning to teach', and the difficulties beginning teachers have in applying the abstract theories they have encountered at university to teaching. This may be the case, but no matter the stage of a teacher's career, reflection-on-practice may well need theoretical intervention of a type envisaged by Dewey to sharpen or reassess their professional vision and the way they see and address issues. In the case of multicultural education, some grasp of recent scholarship around the impact of globalization on the nature of ethnic diversity and schooling seems a necessary component of a teacher's toolkit, especially if they are to challenge the problematic 'imaginary' embedded in multicultural education which entails reductive perceptual schemas around ethnicity as community.

Marta's view, in fact, appeared a more extreme view that was not consistent with many teachers in the other teams. It was a stance of which others, such as Julie at Harringvale, were highly critical:

> at a school with a really experienced staff, if you give them an academic reading [they'll say] 'that's the same thing with a new name', like 'I've seen it before, we did it ten years ago', blah, blah, blah and so I think

you know that trying something new scares the bejesus out of teachers, because I just want to pull out my 1970s sheet that I've always used on Vikings and not have to do any more preparation.

Having said that, Julie felt there was a change in the profession:

When I first started teaching it would never have been, you know, someone would have said here's an academic reading, how about you consider this. I mean I've only been teaching 12 years so I don't see it as that long a time but I reckon for the first maybe ten years of my career it was me who sought that out . . . but in the last few years that accountability of being data driven, having the academic readings, I think that's something that is more of a buzz now than it has been in the past.

While teachers find some aspects of data-driven accountability excessive, and there is justifiable critique of the neoliberal managerialism it can promote (Connell, 2009; Keddie, 2013; Lingard & Sellar, 2013), a renewed focus on professionalism, in part attributed to the adoption of professional standards in NSW in 2004 and Australian standards in 2011, appears to be having an impact. In NSW, all teachers are now required to complete 100 hours of professional development every five years to remain registered.[4] Far from being resistant to these changes, many older teachers were enthusiastic. In contrast to some of her colleagues at Wollami Lakes, Jocelyn pointed out that 'even though I am at the end of my career I am still growing and, I'm sorry guys but, I do enjoy the academia and that. I came away from the first day feeling like I needed more.'

Raoul, an experienced head teacher and team leader from Pentonville HS, had a similar view: 'To me, I feel, as professionals, we don't get enough of that. The way I get academic input would be like if I was doing, if I went and did another degree, not even logged in-services, not a lot of academic input to it.' Raoul particularly liked the UNESCO reading: 'the quandary it put in your mind about what culture is and so we all have our own view of it and it just sort of expanded my mind a bit.' When reflecting on the readings, another teacher at Wellington Heights remarked that 'I'm not 100 per cent locked in now with what I think multicultural education is, like I'm really confused about it. Before I pigeonholed it and felt OK I've got a handle on it but now I'm just like, oh my god it's all . . .' and then laughed. When asked if she was 'good confused or bad confused', the response was, 'It's good confused because it makes us always reflective'.

Clearly, the teachers in each of the teams had differing views about the value of the course readings and professional reading more broadly. To us in the RMRME Project team, this was important as, in reassessing multicultural education, a broad spectrum of views and perspectives on professional learning was essential to gauge how teachers would go about trying to effect change in their schools. Did teachers' levels of engagement with the course readings impact upon the design and carriage of their project? What factors impeded the process of knowledge translation that broader systemic change might mitigate? Such questions were pertinent in evaluating the action research projects examined in the following chapters.

Delving into Data

In addition to lectures, tutorials and a range of other activities, the RMRME training also presented the findings of the state-wide survey of NSW DoE teachers and distributed the reports of the school-specific surveys which compared each school's data with that gleaned from teachers across the state. These findings included information on the ethnic composition of the teacher workforce in NSW government schools and in each of the RMRME project schools, their knowledge and use of relevant policies and attitudes and understandings of multiculturalism and multicultural education. The presentation and discussion of this data was designed to serve a number of purposes. First, the findings of the state-wide survey had implications for how schools might approach their own projects. For instance, data on teachers' various forms of cultural identification – such as their use of hyphenated identities and descriptors that varied in terms of nationality, ethnic grouping, religion, geographic region and race, as discussed in Chapter 2 – demonstrated how a similar complexity may underpin students' identities rather than the singular categories of, for example, 'Chinese', 'Lebanese' and 'Pacific Islander', that were generally used, even for students who were Australian-born or had complex migration histories. Such descriptors easily masked this complexity, leading to reductive notions of ethnic identification typical of what we have called the multicultural imaginary. These findings demonstrated the potential complexity of school populations and Australian society as a whole.

Second, the findings regarding the knowledge and use of the NSW DoE Multicultural Education Policy by teachers in schools across the state and by those in each of the project schools would alert each research team to the levels of teacher awareness of the policy in their schools and how this compared to others across NSW. These and other findings from the school survey reports could operate as valuable baseline data from which issues around multicultural education in the project schools might be given sharper focus. For example, if a school recorded low rates of awareness of the NSW DoE Multicultural Education Policy, they may want to address this in their action research project by adopting various implementation measures and then evaluating their effectiveness. Third, the discussion of the survey during the training provided a useful model of survey design, one of the data collection techniques that was discussed in the training.

By and large teams found the school-specific survey data interesting, but some recognized the potential for this to inform their own projects more than others. Toby from Barnett HS explained that 'after scrutinizing it a couple of times it was quite interesting to see that on some things we were pretty much in line with state areas, others we weren't and I mean obviously from the data admittedly pointed to our weaknesses and what we need to do to develop'. After the training, Toby presented the findings from the report to his whole staff, as did many other team leaders in their schools. Given Toby was from a rural school, he explained how many teachers were surprised by the ethnic diversity of the staff, something which had never been acknowledged. He also saw the survey as useful in identifying issues that could be addressed in the school's action research:

> I tried to make sure that we were looking at more where there were inconsistencies with the state data and certainly when it came to awareness and reading [of policies] it stuck out. People aren't aware of cultural diversity across the board, so it was obvious that was where the data shows us we have to go, even with our anti-racism policy.

Like Barnett, the research team from semi-rural Pentonville also considered their staff to be predominantly Anglo-Australian and were similarly surprised this was not the case. Vera remarked: 'We realized that there was more diversity among the teaching staff than what may have been initially perceived.' This, of course, is not just a matter of interest but demonstrates the increasing ethnic diversity within schools – even among those that may consider their staff predominantly Anglo-Australian. The intention here was not to use the data to allow staff to pinpoint ethnic differences but to disrupt their perceptual schemas of difference and illustrate the fact that culture and the ethnic mix of school communities are both more fluid and complex than might be acknowledged.

Some research teams, such as that at Wellington Heights, examined the findings of their comparative report in some detail. Isaac, who headed their team, explained, 'we really pulled apart the survey . . . and what we considered to be more important, what would have the biggest impact [in terms of our research project]'. Caitlin, also on the Wellington Heights team, agreed: 'we pinpointed the two greatest needs that were shown in the survey and we isolated them down to two, one of them being understanding of cultural background and engaging parents and the other one was the language side of multicultural education. So, we chose one, we ran with the parent engagement one.' While this data was used effectively by some schools and served the intended purpose of helping schools to target an area of concern, there were others who couldn't see its potential for their action research project. Marta, from Addington, for example, commented: 'basically it really sort of confirmed what we sort of knew.' Anita, another Addington team member, chose to focus on the data regarding the ethnic background of staff: 'It was interesting that one of our other team members, and me included, [said] "Oh where's mine, where's me? Did you list mine?"

Yeah, we found it there. So, it was really cool', although she added, 'but also you know quite a few people wanted to learn more about multiculturalism or do more'.

These comments regarding the findings from the state-wide survey and individual school reports not only reveal a range of perspectives but also differing abilities in the use of data. Clearly, some teachers were more adept than others in not only synthesizing the key points of comparison between their own school and the state-wide findings but then conceiving how this may inform their project. The collection and analysis of a wide range of data are now commonplace in schools (Cope & Kalantzis, 2016). To utilize this data to improve practice in the context of an action research project is a far more difficult task. The RMRME training sought to provide assistance to school research teams in doing this with further support offered by the DoE consultants who were assigned to work with teams in each of the project schools following the training.

Grappling with Action Research

As a precursor to the teams drafting their research plans, the training also provided guidance on how they might formulate the question/s to frame their project. RMRME encouraged a process not dissimilar from a standard social sciences approach but inflecting it with aspects of action research methodology, largely drawn from Macintyre (2000). This involved the following processes: identifying the issue; surveying relevant literature (throughout the process); formulating a research question; planning a series of actions to investigate the question and deciding upon data collection techniques; taking action; analysing the findings; evaluating each stage of the process; reporting the findings to relevant parties; and, finally, considering the next step. We stressed the importance of the literature survey not operating as a discrete activity that only occurred prior to finalizing a research question but rather that literature needed to inform the research in an ongoing manner. Within RMRME, we considered this important given the cyclic nature of action research. Becoming acquainted with relevant literature was encouraged to inform and extend or modify the research question/s depending on the stage of the action research cycle.

The degree to which the teams surveyed relevant literature in devising their research question/s varied. As mentioned, the teachers were given access to Western Sydney University library during the year they designed and implemented their projects, with some making more use of this and other resources than others. Many found it challenging to arrive at a research question or questions, as opposed to just deciding upon actions they would take as part of their project. The importance of research questions was discussed in detail with the Beechton PS team who, in deciding upon some of the possible actions they would undertake, were reminded during their post-training interview that 'it isn't just about developing a kind of activity'. Selena, the principal who headed the team, pointed out how 'the wording is going to be really important because it is actually going to have an effect on basically the test or the goal that we are going to, you know, how we are going to collect it'. Other teams were also able to make this observation of the relationship between a research question and the data required to 'answer' it and the extent to which this is reflective of the overall aim of a project. Anita, on the Addington team, explained:

> yeah, we found that hard to come up with a question first up, so we had to work backwards or actually we started from the middle and worked out what we wanted to do and then from that we developed a question and then worked down the list again to work out how we are going to collect data because we had to ensure that it was measurable.

In terms of the importance of framing a research question, she added, 'It gives you focus I think, yeah because when you look at what you are doing, all the different things that you are going to do, you need a central idea where all that stems from, so yeah you do need a question that is really important and making sure it's not too complex.'

Sybilla, on the Thurston team, also commented on the importance of spending time formulating the research question: 'it's making us question what can we do? If we do this, will it help? I suppose until you research it and question it and see, we are not going to be able, we can't answer that.' In summing up the focus the training put on methodology and guidelines for formulating research questions, Gary from Pentonville explained:

> all of us took that, from the two days the end message was try and come up with a nice, specific question that's not going to be so nebulous as to, you are going to find it really difficult to frame, like put the framework together for the action research and how are you going to pre- and post-test and evaluate it and that sort of stuff and we found that difficult I think.

Melody, on the Smithton team, found the process equally challenging: 'it is a bit daunting though, like you are actually doing a project, you are actually creating it from scratch!' Many teams rose to this challenge and embraced the approach to action research that RMRME encouraged.

While the teams were given the opportunity to reflect on the research process after having implemented their project, they were also asked to offer a view on completion of the training as they were finalizing their research design. As with Melody at Smithton, Julie from Harringvale also found the process challenging:

very overwhelming, we kept choosing gi-normous areas to discover and we just kept thinking how, how will we get through this in the timeframe and then we stopped, let's be more specific . . . then we took out that sample you gave us about the school and there were the questions: 'How are we going to get the data? What data do we want to collect?' So, we started thinking of it step-by-step rather than what do we want.

To Julie, this was an effective and rewarding process: 'so, now we have some things to do but we are really in the process of, well now we have our question, we have this common goal and we are starting to get excited about the practical application of it.'

Adrian from Eaton Park not only reflected on the process from the perspective of a member of a school research team, but he also thought about how the RMRME Project team would conduct the macro-analysis, recognizing a difference in the research orientation and skill base of the different researchers involved in the project:

I guess [you did it this way] to acquaint us with that research mindset that you know you have a problem, you refine it down, you investigate, you research and then you try and change practice so I guess to get us into that frame of thinking and I suppose for you guys [the RMRME investigators] then it's interesting to watch how if you throw a bunch of practitioners that challenge, how they handle it even though we have academic training, we are not in a tertiary academic environment so we are looking at things through a different lens from what the academics would be looking at.

Ivan, also on the Eaton Park team, seemed pleased the school was able to construct their own research project rather than merely being the subjects of research – though of course both were the case! He explained that 'by allowing people the opportunity to make their own choices of where they want to research, areas that they've identified, that they want to know more about, I think therefore it does relate to the school and makes it more real in the situation'.

While the intention of RMRME was to build teacher capacity and to encourage change around multicultural education in schools, this was dependent on the effectiveness of the research model and on teachers' willingness and ability to implement it. As Adrian explained, teachers and academics have a very different skill base in terms of research, and one aspect of our macro-analysis was to ascertain the degree to which the training prepared teachers to take control of the process and to conduct action research using the methodology we adopted. A number of teachers commented on the benefits of the approach but also on a broader need for the integration of action research within a teacher's professional practice. Mitchell from Graham's Point HS felt that it focuses us because I mean we probably all have the same experience in lots of different schools. You try one thing, it may not work, it may work, who knows? Who tested it? At least this is very, you know, systematic and we should get some data which shows whether what we've done works or not. I mean we should be doing this with a lot of other projects in schools because otherwise we are just stabbing in the dark, assuming what we are doing is correct but it may be having absolutely no impact on kids at all.

Deirdre, Mitchell's colleague, agreed:

> we go to all these meetings and everyone is doing the same thing and no one ever stops and says 'Does that work?' And if that was in corporate life, if I did something in my old life and my boss said 'Well what was the outcome?' and I just went 'Oh yeah it kind of worked, I think so, oh we don't really know, we never really got to it' . . . well?

To Melissa, the principal at Pentonville, collecting data through action research was also beneficial as it provided the evidence to shore up staff support if change was required:

> you've got to be able to show them the need for it. So, if they can see a need and can see that through data, whether that's numbers or whether that's through you know talking to people and focus groups and getting their main stakeholders that are giving you that information, so you can then show that there is good reason that we should be looking at this as a focus area and then you've got people on board.

Together with the utility of evidence, Harriet on the Getty Rd team saw the systematicity of action research as significant in effecting change:

> we get to find out more about our school and especially if we do it in a systematic way and you can measure it and, as an action research project, bring about change, so it forces us to critically look at our school, find something that we maybe think needs improvement and go through a systematic process and make a positive change in our school which is a really great thing.

Conclusion

This chapter has considered the first step in the process of knowledge translation, namely the different teams' responses to the training in terms of promoting new ideas around culture, ethnicity and identity pertinent to practices of multicultural education, together with understandings around action research and various data collection techniques that would enable them to systematically examine how these ideas can be harnessed in rethinking multicultural education. Our overarching message to teachers as they embarked on their projects was that 'the model we have of multiculturalism is too simple to capture the complexities of today's schools and the language we use to talk about ethnic diversity is not adequate for exploring these complexities'. We were asking them to reflect upon the perceptual schemas embedded in multicultural education and to transform the professional vision they employed on a day-to-day basis. We presented a different way of seeing and thinking about these issues, and we asked them to examine their own practices and to use that to reshape how they approached multicultural education offering them methodological tools to enable this. In effect, we were hoping to initiate a shift from a pragmatic professionalism to a more reflexive mode of professional behaviour that was predicated on engaging in informed, critical and intellectual work. While many found the prospect of doing this daunting, it prompted them to reconceive the way they approached multicultural education. Each of these schools, however, was very different. Their differing demographics and locations had resulted in different emphases on multicultural education prior to their involvement in RMRME, and the teachers who comprised each team also had varying levels of expertise. These factors contributed to the design of fourteen distinct projects as teams sought to address their different issues of concern around multicultural education. Some with low numbers of LBOTE students took various measures to lift the profile of multicultural education among their staff, students and broader communities; some designed and implemented programmes of inclusive curricula. Others with high LBOTE populations developed programmes addressing issues of academic literacy, parent engagement or intercultural understanding, and still others devised projects directed towards improving the educational outcomes of particular groups of students.

The macro-analysis of these projects that we undertook and which is the focus of the following chapters was designed to gauge the extent to which the knowledge and skills acquired in the training would then inform the approach to multicultural education they adopted. As such, the implementation of each project functioned as another step in the process of knowledge translation. We were keen to see the ways in which conceptual understandings around culture, ethnicity and identity as more fluid constructs – entailing notions of cultural essentialism, hybridity and complexity – would translate once the teachers returned to their schools and were largely reliant upon their own professional capacities, and their functioning as a team, to guide their practice. While each school was supported by a DoE consultant and could utilize the resources of the university library and project website, our intervention was minimal. Once school research teams had received feedback on their initial research plan, the degree to which teams surveyed relevant literatures, their utilization of data collection techniques, and their adherence to the action research model became matters for each team. In the following chapters we examine these projects, grouping them in terms of the ways they approached their projects and the outcomes they achieved. As we indicate in the Introduction, our intent is to provide 'ethnographies' of both the fields of multicultural education and the professional cultures of teaching. Each chapter, therefore, provides an account of the composition of the research teams and the projects they undertook. Our focus, however, is the extent to which teams met the broader project aims of not only effecting change in their school but rethinking multicultural education. In other words, were they able to 'do diversity differently'?

CHAPTER 4

Lazy Multiculturalism
Civility, Celebration and the Limitations of Cultural Recognition

Recognizing, respecting and celebrating ethnic differences have been central to the ethos of multiculturalism since its inception. Yet, as many scholars have pointed out, not only is this not enough, it can also be problematic (Baumann, 1999; Hage, 1998). Nevertheless, forms of celebration are often the starting point – and the end point – for many school practices around multicultural education, intended to produce a 'feel good' ambience but which can result in an unreflexive and moralistic version of the logic of civility discussed in Chapter 1 and a downplaying of the other logics of multiculturalism. We portray this as 'lazy multiculturalism', not because these approaches don't involve hard work on the part of teachers, but because they are intellectually lazy in not interrogating the assumptions and consequences of these practices or the complex nature of culture and ethnicity that mark a highly globalized world (Watkins & Noble, 2019).

This chapter examines the projects that were conducted in three of the fourteen RMRME schools characterized by such forms of lazy multiculturalism. Among other things, these projects placed emphasis on reduced forms of cultural recognition and a bland celebration of ethnic diversity in events such as multicultural days, and activities of a similar ilk, often preceded by units of work taking a similar approach. The teachers in these schools invested considerable time and energy in these projects, but they exhibited a reluctance to take up the invitation to critically interrogate their assumptions and practices, which inhibited both the approaches they undertook and their use of action research in evaluating them. Given their relatively small populations of LBOTE students, none of these schools had much experience with multicultural education, and each of their research teams was challenged by the ideas presented in the RMRME training and had difficulty applying them in practice. Their projects represented little movement towards 'rethinking' practice, and they largely reproduced traditional forms of multicultural education that tend to prize the moralizing civility of simply appreciating diversity over a more complex treatment of the resources required for understanding and living with difference. Here we examine the reasons for this and what they reveal about the anti-intellectualism of the pragmatic culture of teaching that influenced their professional practice.

Addington High School: A Case of Arrested Development

Addington HS is located in Sydney's outer south-west, in a suburb of considerable socio-economic disadvantage and limited but increasing ethnic diversity. Addington's student population mirrored this profile. As Lara, the principal, explained, 'there are people from non-English speaking backgrounds, a lot of Pacific Islanders are in public housing but there is a hell of a lot of, a lot of Anglo families. Many of them third- and fourth-generation welfare, so, you know, we're looking at quite a lot of disadvantage.' Of the 22 per cent of Addington's students with a LBOTE, there was a concentration of Pacific Islanders of mainly Samoan background, together with Fijian Indians and smaller numbers of Filipinos and Arabic speakers of various backgrounds. Added to this was a 7 per cent Aboriginal population. What characterized the student population as a whole was the high level of socio-economic disadvantage. Given this, there was a strong focus on student welfare which Lara felt, once provided, would 'clear the way for good learning'. A similar pastoral approach was taken with multicultural education which was incorporated within a broader values education programme. Generally, though, it received little attention apart from a multicultural day every two years of which Lara had mixed feelings: 'I think it has had the potential to slip into a bit of ad hoc, "let's have a multicultural day, a few food stalls", and we continue to tick that box. I think we were slipping in that direction.' By and large, the school was perceived as being relatively 'harmonious'. Any issues that did emerge, such as racism, were viewed through the same pastoral lens and framed in terms of bullying. The Anglo students were seen as chiefly responsible for this behaviour and teachers were hesitant about how to respond. Anita, one of the members of Addington's team, described how

> we get a little bit scared about bullying issues, I suppose, or the Pride Australia . . . the Bra boys[1] and you know, people, you know, certain cultures being more dominant over others. You get paranoid about it,

what's on in the media and then, you know, what might happen in the school, it may not happen but what could happen.

Outside influences, particularly that of the media, were viewed as fanning any latent racism within the school. Given the heightened media focus at the time upon issues of migration, refugees and Islamic fundamentalism, and the prevalence of right-wing commentators fuelling negative sentiment in response to this (Noble, 2012), Anita's concerns were very real. Yet, with multicultural education primarily approached as a form of welfare, its utility in combating this was limited. In thinking through its role within the school prior to RMRME commencing, Peter, another member of the team, commented: 'multiculturalism can be dealt with in, say, bullying and not seen just for multiculturalism but seen as being part of bullying which we could address as a whole school.' Marta, who headed their team, viewed multicultural education in a similar way, as primarily a matter of student welfare: 'if you look at creating a safe learning environment and the idea of students' background knowledge being valued, their cultural knowledge [it] makes classrooms inclusive, I think it's built in.' Such views came to colour Addington's project. While Lara felt that, 'it's good for the whole school community to have multiculturalism right back on the agenda', a view the research team shared, it was difficult to see them adopting the alternative view from the training that emphasised critical understanding rather than their focus on simply appreciating difference within a values education framework.

Teachers as Pragmatists: Expedience over Intellectual Engagement

Together with Marta, Peter and Anita, Addington's team included another member, Eleni, though she seemed to have a minor role. As the school's deputy principal, Marta's oversight of Addington's project afforded her the opportunity to extend its reach beyond that of this relatively small team and the faculties within the school they represented: English for Peter and the support unit for students with learning difficulties, for Anita and Eleni. It seems poignant that Anita and Eleni were not located within one of the disciplinary faculties of the school but rather had special education training and taught a life skills curriculum with a strong welfare focus, typifying how the team tended to see multicultural education. Also of note is the ethnic background of the team. Marta was born in Ireland, though she had lived most of her life in Australia. Anita and Peter had Dutch and German heritage, respectively, while Eleni referred to herself as 'pure Egyptian' having migrated to Australia in the late 1990s. As a team, they had direct knowledge of the migrant experience but, rather than drawing on this in thinking through some of the ideas they had met in the training, they tended to simply personalize their experience neglecting its potential as a pedagogic resource.

The team's inability to make these links may have also been a function of their approach to the training more generally. Marta's criticisms of the readings have already been discussed in Chapter 3. She could not really understand why they were used. Given this, it was unlikely she would encourage Eleni, who didn't attend the training, to complete the readings and consider the issues they raised nor to suggest that other staff, who might be involved in the project, undertake this professional reading. From Marta's perspective, it wasn't necessary as she and her staff knew about multicultural education and any further training was a waste of time. As she explained, 'Our core business is teaching and learning. Pulling us out of classrooms to do multiculturalism, that's robbing could be up to 30, 60, up to 90 kids, more probably if we are looking at a team of four.' Quite clearly, multicultural education wasn't 'core business' for Marta. She saw it as peripheral to a practitioner's main task of teaching the curriculum as if multicultural education was something quite apart from this. With Marta expressing such a view, it is difficult to understand why Addington chose to be involved in RMRME and, what's more, why Marta opted to head the school's research team. A key driver may have been the DoE funding attached to the project that schools could use with considerable discretion in the implementation of their project.

It was important that schools such as Addington were included in RMRME to ascertain how those with limited experience with multicultural education would undertake their project, what sense they would make of the training and the reasons behind the approach they took. What they did over the course of the year was not only of value in terms of understanding practices of multicultural education in schools where it had received little attention but for what it revealed about the professional capacities of teachers and the nature of the profession more broadly. It is too easy to see Marta and her team as simply resistant, or even that their main issue was a matter of enactment, the inability of some teachers to apply understandings from professional learning in practice. Rather, Marta and her team seem guided by a particular view of the profession – the teacher as pragmatist who eschews theory, seeing teaching as a purely task-based process. Unlike the pragmatist philosopher who prizes the utility of theory, for the pragmatist teacher it has no such role. In effect, Marta and her team are emblematic of the teachers Dewey (1927, p. 21) critiques for lacking an understanding of the relationship between scholastic knowledge and method. For the Addington team, their RMRME project was simply a task to complete which all too readily led them to replicate the lazy multiculturalism that had characterized the school's approach to date. They felt they could easily link their project to what was already occurring at Addington. As Marta explained,

We are just going to work off our school values and I suppose go through and embed those values in multicultural lessons. We have our PBL, positive behaviour [for learning] in schools, so that's what we are going to use it for. And then we are going to use the funding to release teachers to develop those lessons. And once those lessons are developed, they can be taught year after year after year, so sustainability!

In some respects, this seems like an effective model, drawing on what already exists, freeing up teachers to design units of work related to this and embedding it within classroom practice but, with the exception of the funding, all this could have occurred without RMRME. There was no uptake of the ideas from the training, the teachers who were devising the unit of work received no professional learning in relation to this and, most importantly, the sociocultural understanding for rethinking multiculturalism was sidelined in favour of a pastoral approach that emphasized positive behaviour and viewed racism as simply a form of bullying. Despite this, neither Marta nor her team saw any conflict between the aims of RMRME and what they were proposing, and the DoE consultant, who was advising them, had little success in shifting this mindset.

Framing the study as action research at least provided the possibility of some reflection upon the actions they were undertaking. Lara and Marta indicated how they and the school had previous experience with such projects, and the team seemed unperturbed about the prospect of collecting data to measure the effectiveness of their actions. Anita explained how 'we decided on collecting data from a survey and we are going to do a survey, a pre-survey and a post-survey, so we can measure the differences, collect student work samples that are done as part of this project and also conduct some interviews with students as well to see how we are going from there'. In the end, Addington's project encompassed several actions. Its primary focus, however, was the design and implementation of a ten-week unit of work for Year 10 students (aged fifteen to sixteen years) on the topic of refugees which was aimed at addressing the misinformation in the media that the team felt was unduly influencing students, fostering the racialized 'bullying' they were keen to curtail. While Marta had viewed multiculturalism as distinct from teaching and learning, within this unit of work it was now front and centre, though not in a way that RMRME encouraged. While having the potential to engage critically with this topic and to equip students with the skills to scrutinize media reporting of refugees, given the pastoral focus of the school's approach to multicultural education, a softer option emphasizing empathy through a study of literature was adopted. Media reports were examined, but they tended to operate more as stimulus for creative responses such as letters and poems written by students from the perspective of refugees. Teachers, it seemed, were hoping the empathetic understanding this might produce would create a more positive attitude towards refugees and counter the prevalence of racism at the school. A more critical take on the topic was not evident, an absence illustrated by the activities undertaken to celebrate United Nations' World Refugee Day, held during Addington's project.

The team decided to use this day to mark the culmination of the unit of work and ran a series of workshops that Year 10 students attended, enlisting other staff, particularly teachers from the art faculty, to organize some of the activities. The combination of workshops, however, seemed to send confused messages about the plight of refugees and the overall intent of the day as presentations on Australia's treatment of refugees were held alongside those discussing boy soldiers in Africa and jewellery making. A similar incongruence was evident in the juxtaposition of a presentation by a Vietnamese refugee with a tile-making workshop. The last of these activities became a key feature of the Addington project extending beyond Year 10 to include all students and teachers who each designed a tile using motifs to exemplify 'their culture' which was incorporated into a whole-school mosaic. Some of the activities did provide the opportunity for students to gain a better understanding of refugees but framed, in Lara's words, as 'a celebration day', it is difficult to gauge the extent to which they grasped the tension between such celebration and acknowledging the plight of refugees, its relationship to issues of racism at the school and to broader questions concerning the changing nature of Australian multiculturalism which was the overarching aim of RMRME.

Action or Research?

In discussing the degree to which their project had led to a new approach to multicultural education and any sustained change at the school, Lara commented, 'I don't think we know until we look again. We have to look again. We have to continue to embed the program, we have to keep raised awareness and then we have to look again and measure again in a year, in two years.' These remarks suggest a certain commitment to both the continuation of the project at Addington and the use of action research in evaluating it, but whether or not action research provided the most effective means for doing this, or at least how it was applied at Addington, is another matter. The findings from the attitudinal surveys the team administered, and the samples of creative writing they collected, may have suggested a shift in students' empathetic understanding, but this does not necessarily entail any intellectual shift in terms of their understandings of the complexities of culture and ethnicity. While these ideas may have been broached in the teaching of the unit of work, Lara felt the rationale for the multicultural mosaic was unclear:

> everybody did a tile, but their capacity to link that tile to why and what we were doing, even though I thought the delivery was very good, the delivery did a lot of prep work. The term before we did the tile, staff were spoken to as a whole staff about why they were doing the tile, how it was

going to fit into the project, how it was an opportunity for them to go home over the holidays and think about what were some symbols which were significant to their culture, or to their perspectives on multicultural society and to bring that back in to create their tile.

Despite resulting in what was an enjoyable activity for students and staff, the mosaic is emblematic of early forms of multiculturalism wherein Australia is viewed as a patchwork of discrete cultures – a perspective that tends to essentialize and trivialize ethnicity and encourage the forms of racism the school's values education was working against. Of course, the tiles may have provided a springboard for the examination of an alternative perspective on ethnic diversity, allowing staff and students to reflect on the process and what the mosaic may represent about the changing nature of the school's population and Australia's ethnic diversity, but this was not the case. If the rationale for the mosaic was to raise awareness, what this entailed and what those making the tiles were being made aware of was unclear. Certainly, there was a disconnect between the rationale for the mosaic and the understandings it promoted, which a greater engagement with the ideas from the training would have made plain. When these matters were raised with the research team, Marta replied: 'oh we did a pre-survey and a post-survey and yeah, we've got the results there but [with] the pre-survey, we looked at how harmonious the students think [the school is] . . . we got 90 per cent saying it was a friendly school.' When questioned further, it became clear that the survey was only used for the unit of work. In terms of evaluating the mosaic, the following discussion ensued:

> MARTA: I don't know how you do that.
> ANITA: They were done. I mean it's physical evidence and every student has had some . . .
> MARTA: And all of them, if you look, have taken pride in them and you know . . .
> ANITA: And not [one] child has said 'nah, I'm not doing it'. Every single kid engaged in this activity.

The measure of effectiveness, therefore, was the activity itself, the completion of a tile and the satisfaction in doing so. Yet, even with the unit of work, the evaluation relied primarily on an attitudinal response to enable what seemed like a dubious quantification of school harmony. While the post-unit survey on refugees included some factual questions, it was also largely couched in attitudinal terms, for example:

> Question 6: Do you think refugees value their Australian citizenship after they get it?
>
> ☐ Yes   ☐ No   ☐ Some do/Some don't   ☐ Don't know

Question 7: My opinion about refugees coming to Australia has changed.

☐ Yes   ☐ No   ☐ Not sure   ☐ Stayed the same

Leaving aside the issue of survey construction, the team focused on promoting an attitudinal shift in students, reliant on the development of empathetic understanding that the unit of work, tile-making and other activities were designed to elicit. Yet, the ability of empathy alone to foster intercultural understanding is a matter of some dispute (Boler, 1999; DeTurk, 2001; Lather, 2009). Much work examining its role in the teaching of students of ethnic minorities indicates empathy provides little more than a superficial understanding of these students' experience. It entails a highly moralistic version of the logic of civility, involving an injunction to sympathize with victims of trauma rather than understanding the socio-historical origins of conflict and flight. As these various activities lacked a clear purpose, it is not certain what understandings students may have acquired and the data the team collected was ineffectual in determining this.

Postscript

With an emphasis on moral civility over critical enquiry, it seems that students were inadequately equipped to examine the complex issues associated with the plight of refugees and the ways in which this is represented in the media. The intention here is not to simply find flaws in Addington's research design, or the limitations of the activities they conducted, but to reflect on the process of action research and to rethink how multicultural education is practised in schools. Clearly, it demonstrates that action research, as with any research, is a complex process. Being a form of practitioner enquiry does not make it any less so. Addington's experience demonstrates the potential pitfalls when insufficient thought is given to survey design and the overall suitability of data collection techniques to produce the evidence required to judge the effectiveness of the actions performed. The problems with Addington's project, however, do not only relate to research design but stem from how the team approached the project in the first place. As was evident, Marta and her team saw little need for wider reading and relied on the knowledge they already possessed to frame their project. As a result, the team seemed to reproduce the assumptions that had informed early policies of multiculturalism, empathy for 'Others' and the recognition of ethnic difference constitutive of the forms of lazy multiculturalism that occur when practitioners lack the necessary critical understanding to reflect upon their practice. Despite this, there were some positives resulting from the work undertaken. Closer ties were formed with an external refugee agency to lend support to lifting the profile of multicultural education at the school, and Lara also recounted a conversation she overheard among a group of students following the Refugee Day: 'the argument was around what we do with boat people, that's what they were arguing about and what was the most humane solution and you know who should be taking responsibility. It was sophisticated intellectual discussion and it was really powerful, and I thought if nothing comes of the project but that, the project was worthwhile.' While this provides some evidence of the impact of Addington's project, greater emphasis on developing students' critical capacities rather than a focus on empathy and reduced forms of cultural recognition would arguably have resulted in more such discussions.

Binto Valley Public School: Let's Celebrate!

Binto Valley PS had a demographic profile in stark contrast to that of Addington's. While it had comparably low numbers of students with a language background other than English, the LBOTE population at Binto Valley was mainly European, the majority being French-speaking with recent arrivals from Japanese, Mandarin and Cantonese-speaking backgrounds. There were no Aboriginal students at the school. The key difference between the two schools, however, was the SES of the students. Binto Valley is located in the affluent eastern suburbs of Sydney in an area Samira, the principal, described as 'very exclusive'. Many of the LBOTE parents were highly paid professionals on temporary visas for two or three years before moving elsewhere, reflective of their transnational lifestyles. Those of Anglo-Australian background were of an equally high SES. As Samira quipped, 'they'll fly to Aspen to go skiing in the school holidays.' Samira was keen for Binto Valley to be involved in RMRME to lift the profile of multicultural education at the school and to increase the participation of LBOTE parents, particularly at Parents and Citizens meetings which were generally only attended by the Anglo-Australian parents and some of European backgrounds. Another reason for involvement in RMRME was that there was some concern about racism at the school especially towards the increasing number of children from Asian backgrounds who were treated by some as a less acceptable 'difference' within the school community. In relation to this, Samira felt there was a certain 'cultural snobbery' at Binto Valley: 'one type of culture is better, and our culture is all European. So, you are Italian, you are Swedish, um what else do we have, French, yes, the French group is incredibly big. So, the European multiculturalism is better than the new Chinese or Japanese multiculturalism.'

In terms of the parents, the way in which this 'snobbery' manifested itself tended to be quite furtive. Samira explained that 'the parents are incredibly politically correct so the racism is really hard to put a finger on'. She felt a similar type of racism was evident among staff in 'aside comments' which she referred to as 'covert' and 'unconscious' wherein teachers assigned particular characteristics to students and parents on the basis of their ethnicity, such as 'oh well, they're Japanese aren't they'. Given this, involving the school in RMRME presented a real challenge especially as Keith, the assistant principal and a member of the team, stated, 'I don't think the staff has a commitment to multiculturalism.' Starting from such a low base, it was Samira who was the main driver of the project. She had a personal commitment to multicultural education. Having Chinese and Sri-Lankan parentage, she had been a victim of racism growing up in Australia and in her first years at the school, and she wanted students, staff and the broader community to be far more inclusive. As a result, Samira decided to lead Binto Valley's team which also included Keith and three classroom teachers: Annelise and Marilyn, who, like Keith, were of Anglo-Australian background, and Rhys, who was born in Fiji with Anglo and Samoan ancestry but had lived most of his life in Australia.

Perspectives on Multicultural Education

Samira came to the project with a wealth of experience having worked in high LBOTE schools in the past and written curriculum materials for the NSW DoE around issues of ethnic diversity. Her perspective on multicultural education, however, tended to foreground cultural recognition through celebratory events and 'culturally sensitive' curricula. As she explained, 'We're got a lot of kids who are maybe second generation Australian too so helping them appreciate their own cultural heritage. I want multicultural education not to be tokenistic. I actually want it to be authentic . . . so I am wanting to help teachers to create an inclusive culture.' Marilyn, on the team, had a similar view. She was keen to develop 'an understanding of all cultures in my class, on the ethnic backgrounds in my class to make sure that I'm not doing something or asking them something that is inappropriate in their culture that might be OK in Australian culture. I think that's really important and also dealing with parents too, you know, treading gently.'

Despite good intentions, Samira and Marilyn seemed to be working with contained conceptions of culture. In Marilyn's case, it informs an approach to multicultural education that is about developing particular rules of engagement around cultural difference, the dos and don'ts of interacting with Others (Noble, 2009a). Such limited notions of culture have long been characteristic of multicultural education. Tellez (2007, p. 547) refers to how competencies-based education in the United States has required pre-service teachers to memorize 'a laundry-list of cultural features as a demonstration of competency for multicultural education'. Together with a troubling essentialism, such approaches may promote the kind of uneasiness evident in Marilyn's remarks of 'treading gently', not wanting to put a foot wrong in relations with LBOTE students and their parents. If understood in this way, what is deemed 'culturally appropriate' may in fact delimit the possibilities of engagement, policing the parameters of interacting with Others on the basis of an assumed ethnicity and concomitant cultural mores.

Yet Marilyn and Samira expressed these views following the training that was designed to challenge such thinking, views that other members of the team shared. Unlike the lack of interest that Marta and the team at Addington displayed, the team at Binto Valley had a far more positive response. All seemed to relish the opportunity to engage in professional reading. For Samira, this was standard practice. The content may have been new, but she viewed reading as an essential aspect of professional practice and was pleased her team, at least initially, seemed motivated to do the same, particularly as she remarked that 'professional learning wasn't a big part of the school culture before I came'. Annelise explained how she was 'really thrilled to be reading actual academic papers on something. . . . it did feel like going back to uni', and Marilyn referred to the importance of the training content: 'there are incredible changes at the moment, particularly with multiculturalism in Australia because of what's happening with migration . . . and I think everybody should be doing something like this because it certainly opens up your mind.' Despite this enthusiasm, Samira and the team had difficulty translating these ideas into practice. This was particularly the case in relation to undertaking the project as action research. While Samira indicated that she had used a similar methodology in the past, it was new to the other team members who found the prospect of designing and implementing a project 'overwhelming'. As Annelise commented, 'I thought, oh my gosh, what have I got myself into!'

The Essentialism of the Multicultural Day

The research team decided to focus on community liaison in their project with the intent of improving the participation of LBOTE parents, particularly those of Asian backgrounds. It was felt that lifting their profile would also have payoffs in countering the underlying racism which Samira and others had identified. The team first decided to have some measure of parental involvement in the school and so conducted an online survey of the parent body which they hoped to follow up with a series of focus groups. The survey yielded very few responses, and the focus groups were abandoned for a similar lack of interest with the intention of revisiting the issue of parental involvement later. Instead, energy was focused on the development and implementation of units of work for Years 3 to 6 (aged eight to twelve years) taught over two terms, in which each class chose a different country and investigated its 'culture' including language, traditional dress, music, history, customs and food. As Samira explained,

'I want to generate an understanding, an appreciation of different cultures. . . . I want them to appreciate the multiple sort of diversity that would be in every child's heritage.' This seemed an attempt to engage with ideas about cultural hybridity from the training but understood here as a patchwork of different cultures characteristic of traditional forms of multiculturalism that still heavily influenced the team. Following completion of the units of work, it was decided that the school should then hold a celebratory event. Referred to as 'Multicultural Cafés', the occasion proved to be a variant of a standard multicultural day held with the additional rationale of involving parents.

On the day itself, students in each of the Years 3 to 6 classes set up a café in their room serving food and conducting activities related to aspects of the culture of the country they had been investigating. These countries included China, France, Spain, Italy, England, the United States and Australia. The audience for these activities, and the 'customers' in the café, were Kindergarten to Year 2 (K-2) students (aged five to eight years) who moved from class (country) to class (country) using a 'passport' that had to be stamped on entry to each. Parents had been notified in advance of the day and some attended, assisting in preparing and serving food. This constituted their involvement. In the China classroom, for example, one mother of Chinese background was busy steaming dumplings and passing them to the 'Chinese' students, that is, students dressed in 'traditional Chinese' attire, to serve to those from the K-2 classes sitting at tables replete with Chinese bowls and chopsticks (and knives and forks, just in case). Other activities in the China room involved participating in Chinese dragon dancing, making lanterns and watching the Chinese-themed Disney animation *Mulan*. A similar formula regarding the organization of activities operated in each of the other rooms where food associated with each country's culture was served, and students could participate in an array of what were considered culturally specific activities.

Of particular note was the Australia room which, given the foregrounding of multiculturalism, we anticipated would present food and activities representative of various ethnic groups including others not yet considered. Instead, on entering the Australia room, the nation's diversity was ignored with a focus on stereotypical aspects of Anglo-Australian culture including a mock beach with umbrellas and towels, a thong-throwing[2] competition, pin the tail on the kangaroo, making paper koalas and adding to a wall chart of typical Australian expressions. The food on offer included traditional 'Aussie' fare: sausages cooked on a barbeque, meat pies, Vegemite[3] sandwiches and lamingtons,[4] with a boy wearing an ANZAC-style slouch hat[5] as one of the waiters. The only concession in terms of incorporating elements not obviously associated with Australia's dominant Anglo culture was an activity to make an Aboriginal hand mural and the inclusion of an Aboriginal flag alongside the Australian flags adorning the room and as fake tattoos on many students' faces.

In discussion with the research team following the event, the day was considered 'a positive start' and a 'success'; as Marilyn pointed out, 'the kids were immersed in [these] cultures.' Even though the team was disappointed by the limited involvement of parents, Annelise felt that 'the Multicultural Cafés will continue into next year and that will evolve into a greater forum to involve multicultural parents'. After the disappointment with the parent survey and focus groups, however, there was no attempt to collect any data beyond anecdotal comments to determine what parents thought of the day nor to gauge what students and teachers had learnt from the experience. In many respects the action research component of the project had all but been abandoned, and the initial rationale for the team's actions around increasing parent involvement and combating racism was given little attention. With the exception of Samira, the team felt they had completed what was required:

> So, for them they've done it, because they created a project. But it is the analysis phase and where we go to next, and understanding that this is not a one-off, it is a cyclical thing where it is building and building and embedding into a culture, and I don't think the teachers at this stage are very clear what the practices are or the products that we want and that's what we've got to get from this first cycle of learning.

This is an interesting comment from Samira given she was leading the school's research team. While it shows some understanding of the cyclical nature of action research and an intent to progress the project, she also seemed to have distanced herself from the process. As was the case with the other team members, it seemed RMRME may not have been what Samira was expecting, as it entailed far more intellectual commitment than her previous experiences of professional learning: 'If I had known what we were going to do, so I only had the experience of working on (the NSW DoE curriculum materials) which were really fun. This is incredibly mentally intense, the research aspect of it. I didn't realize that it was going down that track.'

'Despite also expressing misgivings about the 'lack of rigour' in their project, Samira tended to agree with the team that the Multicultural Cafés had been worthwhile: 'I think what was big for the school is that it has always been a very European/Anglo school and it was big to actually have a celebration of different cultures. I think that was a first big step.' Binto Valley may have had limited experience with multicultural education but, even as a first step, this approach was grounded in assumptions that did not operate as a good foundation for future initiatives. To what extent, for example, had the event shifted teachers' understandings of culture and, importantly, those of their students and the parents they had hoped to involve? As the emphasis clearly involved the logic of recognizing and affirming difference, culture was still perceived as bounded and static, and multiculturalism little more than an acknowledgement of the variation of distinct ethnic groups set apart from the Anglo mainstream – a view that activities on the day reinforced. Multicultural education provided the rationale for the celebration and – in the process – the instantiation of difference. It seems highly likely that activities such as these, as well meaning as they are, led to the equation of culture with difference. With the exception of the Australia room, the school's Multicultural Cafés were representative of the 'cosmo-multiculturalism' that Hage (1998) critiques but, at the same time, was distinct from the lifestyles of some of the so-called 'multicultural parents' whose transnational lifestyles were more commensurate with a cosmopolitanism suggestive of hybrid forms of cultural identification and an easy mix of cultures rather than belonging to 'this' or 'that' culture.

Thinking Differently

The day in fact presented many opportunities for a more nuanced examination of culture and interrogation of multiculturalism as did the many lessons conducted in advance of the day. In the China room, one of the activities for K-2 students – while eating dumplings – was to watch excerpts from the Walt Disney movie *Mulan*, with Chinese characters speaking in American accents. Rather than simply presenting this as an example of traditional 'Chinese culture' – which clearly it was not – it could have acted as a useful stimulus for children to discuss globalization, hybrid identities and more fluid conceptions of culture. Students could have been asked questions such as the following: Where was this movie made? What type of accents do the characters have? Who are the actors voicing the characters? (Eddie Murphy, an African-American actor, and Pat Morita, a Japanese-American actor, both voice characters.) Is this a Chinese or an American movie? Do you think people of other nationalities were involved in its making? What's the difference between nationality and culture? What is similar/different in culture between China, as depicted in the film, and China today? What connections do we have with China today and in the past? What aspects of culture do we share? What does travel, technology, migration do to culture? And so on. Yet such questioning did not eventuate. Instead, given students were in the China room, this was simply presented as an example of 'Chinese culture', one of the many cultures that were presented as constitutive of Australia's multicultural whole.

These cultural influences, however, did not feature in the Australia room. Rather, as discussed, here the focus was on Australia as a predominantly Anglo country with a symbolic nod to its First Nations People. Yet, as with the China room, there were many possibilities for teachers to develop students' capacities for critical thought, pedagogic interventions that would promote a more complex understanding of Australian multiculturalism.

Teachers could have asked: What's missing here? Is this an accurate reflection of Australian culture? What's the impact of the cultures represented in the other rooms on Australia? What does this tell us about culture? Are these separate cultures, or are they a part of Australian culture? In fact, many of these questions could have been asked in the process of organizing the day and perhaps have produced very different representations of cultures within each room. There was a view that perhaps some of these ideas were far too difficult for primary school-aged children, but the professional expertise that teachers possess should equip them to translate such knowledge for students, making complex ideas accessible and encouraging questioning to allow students to better understand the contemporary world. Yet, there was also a reluctance to engage in critique because multiculturalism was something to celebrate and activities should simply be fun. As Marilyn said, 'The children just had a lovely time.' In a similar vein to Ahmed's 'feminist killjoy' (Ahmed, 2010), questioning the multicultural day seemed tantamount to being a multicultural killjoy, raining on the parade of a celebration of difference. But this need not be the case. Celebration can be coupled with critical enquiry; it simply entails reflection upon what is celebrated and how.

Postscript

The research team at Binto Valley found this difficult to do. The readings they had undertaken during the training and as part of their professional learning seemed to have had little effect on broadening their perspectives on culture and any reflexive capacity in relation to their practices around multicultural education. When interviewed separately, Samira indicated that, after the initial enthusiasm, she had encountered 'massive resistance' from the team given the time and level of commitment required to undertake the readings and conduct the project. Once again, the point here is not simply to critique these teachers' practice and limited application of the conceptual resources the training afforded – in fact there are important lessons here regarding the complexities of knowledge translation and professional learning for teachers – but to think through how they could have reflected on the actions they undertook. This is an important aspect of professional practice and key to successful action research. What was needed was more than just commitment in terms of the time devoted to organizing this initiative. Though important – especially given the busy nature of teachers' day-to-day responsibilities – rethinking multicultural education requires stronger intellectual engagement with the conceptual tools which can bring new insights to understandings of culture and schooling and to making effective interventions in improving the practice of multicultural education. Without this, it is all too easy to resort to the lazy multiculturalism that the teachers here adopted.

Beechton Public School: Counting and Consuming Culture

Beechton PS, a small school in the semi-rural outskirts of Sydney, has a long history having been established in the late nineteenth century in an area of some of the early land grants to White settlers during the period of British colonialization. To this day, Beechton remains a primarily Anglo-Australian school with an Aboriginal population of just under 10 per cent and a LBOTE population of 19 per cent.[6] The LBOTE students included those who were migrants or had a parent who was a migrant from a range of different countries: Bosnia, China, Iraq, Lebanon, the Philippines, Poland, Spain and the Netherlands. There was no concentration of any one group with only one or two students from each. The category 'LBOTE', however, which is applied if students, or one of their parents, speak a language other than English, fails to capture the prevalence of Maltese and Italian speakers in some students' families and within the broader Beechton community. These people were either the grandparents or other forebears of a number of students at the school who had arrived in Australia in the post-Second World War wave of migration and settled in rural Beechton where many had established market gardens to service the expanding city of Sydney. While students' parents worked in various trades or had their own businesses, on the whole, Beechton's population was of a relatively low SES, slightly higher than Addington but far less than that of Binto Valley.

Even prior to Beechton's involvement in RMRME, the school executive, comprising Sheena the principal and Sally the deputy, both of whom had teaching roles given the school's small population, had expressed concern about what Sheena referred to as the 'narrowness of their lives living out here'. They had coined the phrase 'the Beechton Bubble' in recognition of the insularity of the area. Both felt students and their families had little engagement with, or understanding of, the ethnic diversity of the broader Australian community and were keen to change this. In previous years, the school had undertaken a 'cultural exchange' with an inner city, high LBOTE primary school, but Sheena and Sally felt this programme had not had the desired effect. In discussions with students following these visits, they simply focused on the differences between their school and those from the inner city, reinforcing a view that 'people of diverse cultural backgrounds live elsewhere'. Sheena explained how she was dismayed by 'comments from the children, particularly the Year 5-6 children's derogatory comments about other cultures that you know have come from home'. These remarks were no doubt fuelled by a bitter campaign in the local area against the siting of a Muslim cemetery in Beechton; its cheaper land prices on the outskirts of Sydney were an attractive option for the city's growing Islamic community. Given these factors, RMRME seemed to offer the school an opportunity to rethink how they approached multicultural education and to lift its profile in the school.

A Research Team with a Difference

The composition of Beechton's team was very different from those of all the other RMRME schools. Along with Sheena and Sally, Beechton's research team included six parents, all mothers of students at the school, two of whom worked in teacher support roles at Beechton and another four whom Sheena had invited to be involved because of their active roles in the school community. These parents were an interesting mix. Apart from the two who were teacher support staff, two of the other mothers were undertaking university degrees, one in law and the other in education, and a third had a degree in accountancy, meaning most of these parents had a much higher level of education than was the norm within the Beechton community and was perhaps why Sheena asked them to join the team. The ethnic mix of this group of parents was also interesting. Five referred to themselves as 'Australian', though four did so with some qualification. Sarah considered herself 'straight Australian', an acknowledgement of the dominance of Anglo-Australian ethnicity, Selena pointed out that her in-laws were of Maltese background, Talia had Aboriginal heritage and Heda was Australian-born of Lebanese background. Ellie, on the other hand, was a Polish migrant who had been in Australia for over twenty years. Sheena and Sally were also of Anglo-Australian background though Sheena had been born in New Zealand.

The rationale for including parents on the school's research team was twofold. As a small school, Sheena and Sally felt it would have been too disruptive to include another two or three teachers on the Beechton team as they would have been off class during the training and planning meetings. Also, given there was a view that whatever action Beechton undertook it would involve the whole school community, parental involvement was considered crucial. These parents had a strong personal commitment to multiculturalism and were keen to see changes not only within the school but, given the tensions over the Muslim cemetery, within the Beechton community as a whole. Heda, as probably the only Muslim parent at the school and whose wearing of the hijab made her difference highly visible, wanted to broaden community understanding and counter the racism she experienced. In hindsight, including parents on the team at the expense of classroom teachers may not have been a good idea. While the parents' involvement did prove valuable for some aspects of the Beechton project, having a couple of these parents attend the training, as not all did, meant that other teachers on staff, apart from Sheena and Sally, missed out on this important professional learning. Community involvement may have been a key aspect of Beechton's project, but it also included a school-wide curriculum component, and the training of teachers would have been valuable in this regard, particularly as Sheena acknowledged that her staff were 'unaware of multicultural policies'. The same level of enthusiasm that

Sheena, Sally and the parents on the team displayed did not appear to be matched by the teaching staff as a whole. In fact, prior to the project, Sheena was wary of her staff's level of commitment, 'I actually think . . . they are resistant to change because they don't want to feel that they've been put upon and pushed into a situation'. Such comments did not augur well for the year-long project that the school was about to embark upon. There was some attempt to engage in additional professional reading as part of the literature survey to inform the research design of the school's project, but this was only undertaken within the research team and, even there, it was not sustained. The Beechton team also had difficulty framing their project as action research. Despite having undertaken a previous action research study, like Addington and Binto Valley, they tended to put emphasis on developing a range of activities rather than letting their research question guide their approach.

Celebrating Difference and the Problem of Enactment

Cultural recognition and the celebration of diversity were the key aspects of what developed into a multifaceted project at Beechton with the aim of promoting attitudinal change towards ethnic difference within the student body and the school's broader community. To this end, the school embarked on a number of activities. From a community perspective, the school wanted to collect data on the ethnic heritage of students and their families extending back to students' grandparents as a way of revealing, as Sheena explained, that Beechton was part of 'a very large multicultural community', to burst the 'Beechton Bubble' and the perception that all those who lived in the local area were of Anglo-Australian background.

The survey that was distributed to parents yielded a wealth of information about families' ethnic and linguistic backgrounds. With 72 per cent of families completing the survey, the school was able to show that while Anglo-Australian heritage was indeed dominant, there were students whose grandparents had been born in twenty-two different countries throughout Europe, Asia and the Pacific. This exercise also revealed the strong Maltese and Italian heritage within the community which, as mentioned, was not captured in the school's LBOTE data on students. Of course, once this data was collected, the point was what to do with it. How was it to be utilized within the community and by students at the school? The initial rationale had been that this information would be relayed to the community via a multicultural day involving students, their families and community members and also used to inform teaching programmes at Beechton. There was indeed a multicultural day towards the end of the year, but, disappointingly, the data was not used by classroom teachers in their teaching programmes, even in Sheena and Sally's classes. This seemed like a missed opportunity given the richness of this data. The way it provided evidence of previous waves of migration into the Beechton area could have operated as a powerful resource to tackle some complex issues with students around globalization, migration and reasons for settlement and, importantly, for them to see that people of diverse ethnic backgrounds don't simply live elsewhere but were part of their own community. As was the case with Binto Valley, these ideas could have been approached in age-appropriate ways and drawn upon in activities during the school's multicultural day but, given most of the teachers didn't attend the training and there was little follow-up at the school in relation to this, such possibilities were not considered.

Instead, each of the different year groups in the school undertook literature-based units of work with a 'multicultural theme' ranging from topics such as colours and food in the junior years (students aged five to eight years) and refugees and migrants in the more senior years (students aged nine to twelve years). Teachers were hoping their students would exhibit attitudinal change and greater intercultural understanding as a result of undertaking this work. To determine the extent to which this had occurred, teachers conducted pre- and post-tests with their classes which involved students responding to a range of images and questions before and after these units of work to elicit a series of attitudinal responses. In the junior years the focus was on identity and belonging such as 'What does an Australian look like?' and 'Who should live in Australia?' In the more senior years, students were also asked these questions together with their opinions on migrants, refugees and the wearing of the hijab. Some teachers, however, felt uncomfortable about broaching these issues with their students, particularly those with junior classes. As Sheena explained,

> The Kindergarten and Year 1 teachers were a little bit perplexed about how they could raise the notion of prejudice and racism or that will come out and I said I think you are thinking too deeply, this is Kindergarten and Year 1. What they need to realize is that there are different, different people who have different backgrounds, because children do recognize differences with people and if they go to tease then they will tease them on those physical aspects. So they were a little bit tentative about drawing those out in the classroom, they just wanted to look at community and stuff. We wouldn't want to put viewpoints into their heads and we had to say, no it's actually celebrating, it's not the negative, but it is actually celebrating.

Rather than tackling difficult issues of racism head-on, Sheena's suggestion of celebrating difference was the approach that was taken in the junior years. While there was evidence of younger students parroting the prejudices of their parents, it seems they were deemed too young to examine these topics in class or at least their teachers' discomfort overrode the possibility of doing so. Instead, emphasis was given to simply celebrating ethnic differences. In the composite Year 1/2 class that Sally taught, for example, where texts about 'multicultural foods' were the focus, she explained how

> We actually made pappadums, yeah and we had spring rolls one day and we had, we made fried rice and what else did we do . . . Yeah, so we connected literature from different cultures and then gave them a hands-on experience. Oh, we made pizzas, one day, yeah. I think that was easier for them to associate because we got to eat at the end of the lesson.

Sally was one of the teachers who did attend the training where the limitations of such forms of multiculturalism were considered and how culture in an era of globalization is far more fluid and complex than how she presented it to her class. In the training, culture was also examined as not simply constitutive of difference but as that which is shared – things in common in an interconnected world. Although Sally was critical of the understandings the cultural exchange programme seemed to generate in students, her unit on 'multicultural foods' had a similar effect. By focusing on foods as representative of different cultures, it was 'difference' from the Anglo mainstream that was emphasized much in the same way as the Multicultural Cafés at Binto Valley.

It may seem harsh to critique these activities in this way, but the key point here is to consider the meanings they evoke and the extent to which they assist young children to better understand the culturally complex nature of the world in which they live. This celebration of difference served to both erase relations of connection and processes of fluidity, on the one hand, and avoid confronting problems of racism on the other. Sally's lesson exhibited a similar problem with enactment as with the teachers at Binto Valley. While lacking the kind of reluctance to change seen at Addington – in that both the research teams at Beechton and Binto Valley seemed far more committed to the aims of RMRME – neither was able to formulate curriculum that engaged with the intellectual challenges the training presented. It is poignant, for example, that in explaining her unit, Sally simply lists the various activities her class participated in. There is no account of the ideas she was hoping to convey, indicative of the more pragmatic professional culture that the teams in each of these three schools displayed. In each case, the intellectual dimension was excised from these teachers' practice, focusing instead on the activities themselves devoid of any overarching conceptual frame or meaningful pedagogic direction. It seems this approach was deemed suitable for children of this age. As Sheena remarked, 'I think you are thinking too deeply, this is Kindergarten and Year 1.' But such a perspective not only underestimates the capacity of children to understand more complex ideas but also a teacher's ability to devise the ways in which this can be done. Sally's unit on food simply required a different framing, one that applied the ideas from the training and drew on the school's own data on their students' and their families' ethnic heritage.

Rather than seeing these foods as consumed by Others and representative of different cultures, students could have linked them to the ethnic heritage of people within their own community, that is, not so much a focus on 'them' but 'us'. More importantly, this could prompt a discussion about culture more broadly, how students themselves have no doubt eaten pizza, fried rice or pappadums, and so how these are very much a part of the heterogeneous mix that is Australian culture. Such a discussion and its attendant activities could easily segue into an examination of the interconnected nature of the world, how culture – the way students and their families live – is a product of various influences related to waves of migration, phases of settlement and the increased cultural flows that digital technology and travel enable. Framed in this way, many other aspects of life could have been considered such as religion and people's beliefs beginning with those of First Nations People. This would also allow for some engagement with 'the negative' that many teachers were keen to avoid, namely how disagreements over aspects of how and where people live are ongoing, and we need to find ways to live peacefully especially when differences become difficult to reconcile. If approached in this way with younger children, a curriculum could then develop these ideas in later years to think in more critical ways about the reasons for conflict and discrimination, who are targeted by whom and why, and how this may be addressed. Sally's unit, however, provided little foundation upon which to explore such content. Rather, it reinforced a notion of culture as difference through its celebratory mode of multiculturalism that emphasized the discrete nature of ethnic groups rather than the heterogeneity of national and global cultures.

Policing Borders

In the senior grades, attempts were made to grapple with more complex issues as teachers opted for texts around the themes of refugees and migrants in the literature-based units they taught. The attitudinal pre-tests that the Years 3–6 teachers conducted showed a worrying racism among students informed by a combination of ignorance and fear. In Sheena's composite Year 5/6 class, students were asked a set of questions prior to reading and engaging in activities related to the text they were to examine:

1. What does an Australian look like?
2. Who should be allowed to live and stay in Australia?
3. Why do asylum seekers want to live in Australia?
4. What should we do with boat people?
5. Should Muslim women living in Australia be unveiled?
6. Should a Muslim cemetery be allowed in Beechton? Answer yes or no and why.

The first thing to note here is that the problem is cast in terms of the behaviour of asylum seekers and Muslims, not the behaviour of those who attack or criticize. So, what is most striking about these questions is the way that many of them seem to mirror the xenophobic discourse of the right-wing media that dominate such debates, how students themselves are positioned as border police determining who should and shouldn't be allowed in Australia, and how they should live once there, with a similar logic governing how students should respond to the local issue of the Muslim cemetery. Quite clearly, this wasn't Sheena's intent. She was simply hoping to garner students' attitudes prior to commencing a unit of work that would engage with these issues in more detail but, by introducing the unit this way, she seemingly reinforced the prejudices that many held and their schemas of perception for understanding the issues. While the class continued to explore these issues in the context of the literature they examined, it is difficult to determine whether there was any appreciable shift in students' attitudes and level of understanding regarding migrants, refugees or on the matter of the Muslim cemetery, as Sheena did not conduct a post-test on completion of this work. Instead, the class and the rest of the school focused their energy on preparation for the multicultural day held towards the end of the year. This was a first for Beechton with Sheena's Year 5/6 class taking a key role in its organization under the direction of the research team and other staff who coordinated the various activities that occurred on the day. These included a lunch, involving a barbeque and food provided by parents from their 'country of origin', cultural displays and live music including a traditional Filipino dance performance and an art show of work from students across all year groups showing, for example, flags of various countries and collages that 'symbolized students' identities'. The event was well attended, no doubt aided by the involvement of parents on the research team.

From the team's perspective, both this day and the project as a whole was a great success. As Heda, the parent of Lebanese Muslim background on the team, pointed out,

> I truly believe that people in the school, it has changed people's views . . . because when we first came to the school three years ago . . . my children weren't sure what to say what nationality they were. I said, you were born in Australia, you are Australian, but your background is Lebanese, and don't, and you know, well they don't want to say because, that's what it is. People have to accept you for who you are and now they could say it and be relaxed about it. So, it does make a change.

Postscript

Clearly, the project at Beechton had contributed to far greater community involvement in the school and, to some extent, a better grasp of the ethnic diversity of its student population and local community. However, it is the way in which this diversity was perceived and the implications of this that are important. The reductive forms of cultural recognition that the project tended to foreground have little value if they serve to merely pigeonhole students and their families, curtailing a more complex understanding of identification and the factors that inform this, of which ethnicity may play a very minor role. It is pleasing that Heda and her children felt far more accepted within the school community, but how far did this acceptance extend? Did it have any bearing on students' attitudes towards the siting of the Muslim cemetery in Beechton and of migrants and refugees within and beyond their own community? To what extent did it aid their understanding of globalization and the way in which it impacts upon their world? Approaches to multicultural education that simply favour the logics of recognition and moral civility that resulted in Heda's feelings of acceptance are simply not up to this task. They operate as a kind of fall-back position when the required intellectual commitment to engage with more complex ideas in rethinking multiculturalism is avoided. In many respects this project was a mammoth undertaking for the team at Beechton. The school had relatively little experience with multicultural education and having parents on the team, despite their commitment, contributed to the type of approach they undertook, emphasizing community involvement over skilling teachers to embed the ideas from the training within their teaching. While the use of action research provided the means by which the team could have reflected upon and modified their actions, this was applied in a piecemeal fashion. It was prescient therefore that Sheena could remark at the beginning of Beechton's project that,

> I don't think schools are places that absolutely follow through to the end, or go back and reflect at the evaluated process, and I think that's extremely important to make the next decision whether it's, if it's working and you are getting results, fantastic. It's not working and the evaluated process will tell you to pull the plug and for kids you have to do something better. So, I think that's the bottom line.

Conclusion

These accounts of the projects at Addington, Binto Valley and Beechton highlight the lazy multiculturalism that has become institutionalized in many Australian schools. As indicated, we are not arguing that the teachers themselves are lazy, nor are we suggesting that all forms of multicultural education reflect this problem. Conventional practices such as multicultural days, and the teaching of units of work with a 'multicultural' theme that take a similar approach, require significant amounts of labour in preparation, coordination and delivery, but the key educational dimension

– the intellectual labour of examining the assumptions and purposes of such approaches – is often missing. Using action research may have revealed these shortcomings but, at each of these schools, emphasis was placed on action rather than research. The research teams were far too focused on simply doing things and either unwilling or unable to implement their project in a way that would allow them to determine the effectiveness of their actions, to the extent that Rhys at Binto Valley could comment at the end of the year that 'I don't really know what an action research project is. A lot of that kind of high-brow stuff was lost on me because it's years since I've been at uni.'

Of course, the problems that emerged with each of these projects were a function of a number of factors. Given their limited focus on multicultural education prior to RMRME, projects that primarily focus on cultural recognition may have been perceived as the most likely first step towards lifting the profile of multicultural education. While this may be the case, critiques of such perspectives and their potential to promote forms of cultural essentialism – issues given consideration in the training – seem to have made little impression upon these teams, despite being raised in feedback on their initial research plans. This suggests that greater levels of academic support were required in the framing and carriage of these projects. Another factor impeding these teams' ability to devise and implement their projects was time. Despite the funding for teaching release to undertake professional learning, project planning and implementation, teams were required to complete their projects on top of their many other responsibilities. While there was a substantial time commitment involved, there was an expectation that teams would engage in ongoing professional dialogue and reflection upon how their project was progressing, how it was implementing the ideas from the training and, depending on the phase of action research, whether any modifications were required. Given the pragmatic culture of teaching that influenced these teams' professional practice, these expectations were not always met, and they simply reproduced the lazy multiculturalism that all too often governs how multicultural education is approached in schools.

CHAPTER 5

Engaging with Others

Constructing Educational Problems

'Engaging communities' is a key tenet of multicultural education, with perceived benefits including improved community relations, enhanced parent participation in schools and better student educational outcomes (NSW, 2020d). But how such engagement occurs, and what it requires of teachers, is a complicated question. This chapter examines three projects which, while similar in their intention of engaging students and parents, took quite different approaches in response to the needs and demographics of their schools. The projects at Eaton Park HS and Thurston PS were directed towards addressing the needs of specific groups of LBOTE students, while Thurston also aimed to draw parents of LBOTE backgrounds more into the school, and the third, Pentonville HS, aimed to engender greater awareness of ethnic diversity among their largely Anglo-Australian student population. The chapter documents how teachers had difficulty enacting the ideas from the training in their action research. Despite the inclusionary aims of their projects, their 'professional vision' continued to rest on the limited perceptual schema of the 'multicultural imaginary', which tends to essentialize and reify ethnic difference premised on a reduced logic of recognition and on a pragmatic orientation to teacher expertise. These constrained the ways they constructed and addressed their educational problems. To varying degrees, the teachers' commitment to action research provided some means for reflecting upon the limitations of their approaches, allowing them to begin to modify school practices in line with their findings. The chapter examines these insights comparing and contrasting the teams' capacities to reorient how they engage, and engage with, Others.

Eaton Park High School: Struggling with the Disengaged Other

Eaton Park is a large boys' school in a relatively high SES suburb of north-western Sydney that, while once very Anglo, has been transformed by large numbers of arrivals from East and South Asia – producing anxieties about the 'Asianization' of the area. As one student of Anglo background had said earlier in the research, the suburb had become 'like a different country, Asians have taken over the place'. About 60 per cent of Eaton Park students came from thirty LBOTE backgrounds, with students of Chinese and Korean backgrounds the largest groups. Eaton Park prided itself on this diversity, but it was not the major focus of the school. It put more emphasis on boys' education. It was also described by one of the deputies as 'a sporting minded school [with] a very good academic record'. Nevertheless, it was clear that its ethos included the desire that boys have an appreciation of Australia's multicultural society, as stated in the school's annual report. That report described its commitment to Harmony Day which entailed a week of events planned by the prefects to celebrate diversity and reconciliation, aimed at 'encouraging harmonious interaction' and 'improving appreciation of differences'.

While some teachers commented that there was not a lot of mixing among ethnic groups, there wasn't major concern around ethnic tension in the school. There was, however, concern about some boys of Korean background who were increasingly 'disengaged'. As the principal Percy admitted, 'we've been struggling with our Korean community in particular and ... whether that's boys or whether because of their Korean background, we are not sure.' Of the Korean cohort, of around 100 students, two-thirds were born overseas. The school had ongoing concerns with some Korean students and had already reached out to the Korean community, including an information night on the Higher School Certificate (the graduating qualification in NSW), presentations by the DoE community liaison officer to staff and parents, a homework club (open to all but primarily for Korean students) and mentoring of these students by senior students of Korean background.

From Cultural to Professional Engagement

Eaton's research team consisted of two teachers – Ivan, the deputy principal and Adrian, the head teacher of social sciences – in consultation with Percy. Other teachers were involved, but none came to the professional learning days nor the presentation days. While one of these teachers was involved in part of an interview at the beginning of the project, none attended the final interview. Percy came to part of the professional learning but had no direct involvement in the practical side of the research. Schools were required to have teams of five people including a member of the executive, and they could include specialist EAL/D teachers, Anti-Racism Officers or community liaison staff. Ivan, Adrian and Percy all identified as 'White' or 'Caucasian' Australian. Of the staff who were involved in delivering the project, but did not attend the professional learning, one was of Vietnamese background and the other was Korean, and both were young female teachers. The project was driven by Ivan and Adrian; it was their professional vision which defined the 'problem' they were addressing.

Eaton Park's involvement was unusual in that they had a specific focus for their action research from the beginning, from which they didn't waver despite the professional learning. The action research plan articulated the research question as whether there was 'a discernible difference in engagement in learning between Korean and non-Korean students at our school'. Disengagement was evidenced by low attendance, limited participation in class and poor outcomes, so the team collected data from attendance records, student and staff surveys, focus groups, classroom observations, and classwork and homework samples. The research also identified the aim as 'To identify, specifically, pedagogical strategies which successfully engage LBOTE (Korean) students in their learning'. This entailed trialling whether 'cooperative learning' strategies rather than an 'individualized approach' was a better strategy for Korean students.

Perhaps because they had a specific idea of what they wanted to do, the team did not make use of the RMRME school survey report nor the professional development. Ivan said he didn't find these days useful and felt that he didn't need any further professional development in the area: 'after all the years of teaching and being involved in these sorts of things ... I've done a bit in multicultural education.' He 'had lots of dealings with the different nationalities' and described himself as experienced in 'using the cultural background of students to be more engaged in lessons'. He described some of the presentations at the professional learning as 'insulting to the intelligence' of participants – 'it was stuff I was already aware of' – and he felt the time could have been better spent if teachers shared their experiences rather than listening to academics. As Peta, the DoE consultant working with Eaton HS, said, she didn't think the 'messages' from the training were 'taken up': the 'issue was there before the project actually started. I think it was a fairly firm idea and I don't know how much that changed because of the [training].' Despite the intention of the training to challenge multicultural orthodoxies, Ivan felt the 'content hadn't shifted that much' from his early days as a teacher. Ivan was a languages teacher with a deep investment in having his expertise, not just in languages but in LBOTE 'cultures', recognized and seemed professionally disengaged from the challenges offered in the training.

'Korean Boys... Are Causing Us a Fair Bit of Grief'

The action research project focused on twenty-two Korean boys in Year 9 (aged fourteen to fifteen years) across five subjects: maths, visual arts, personal development, health and physical education, history and Japanese, but not English. The boys were surveyed on attitudes to truancy, learning styles, good teaching practices, others' views towards them and so on. Only seventeen of the twenty-two completed the survey, however. Two students, for example, were truanting. Significantly, the survey provided little data about birthplace, SES details, prior educational paths or language competence. In each subject, students were given a cooperative task and an individual task, and the classes observed. The teachers involved were asked to reflect on the strategies and their success, and several questions were posed, around whether they thought the boys needed structure, whether creativity was more important than factual detail, the usefulness of technology and so on. Follow-up interviews with the students were conducted to garner further details about the boys' experiences. The report contained much data, but not all this was used in formulating the problem and response.

Initially, the set of issues had seemed open-ended. As Percy explained,

> I would like to see what we can do better in the classroom to make sure that every kid, no matter what their cultural background, is engaged in their learning. Now whether that's because of language issues, do we need more intense ESL [EAL/D] support in the classroom there? Is it because culturally they are not engaged with what the material is, or the resources are? Is it because of communication, do they not understand what the teacher is saying and therefore you know, they are passive... if it's a broader thing about a lack of cultural understanding then how do we address that?... that's why we are trying to think this through.

The project focused quickly on a particular issue: the 'discernible difference' between Korean and non-Korean students stemming from what Percy said were significant behaviour issues:

> you have a small percentage who are just totally intransigent... we've got three-four boys at the moment, all Korean, who are having meetings with the home-school liaison officer because of their non-attendance. Parents just cannot get them to school, and there was an incident where we had three Korean boys involved in a gang who bashed up another Korean boy from another school and a problem from outside from gangs down in the local shopping area... we've got... Korean boys truanting, Korean boys going down to the local... parlours where they play games during the school day.

It is important to stress that, as the teachers admit, there was only a small number of boys involved in such activities, and these activities are common among many young men. They pointed to a wider problem of disengagement among Korean students but admitted that their prime concern was the twenty-two boys in Year 9 – less than a quarter of the Korean-background population. Significantly, they didn't contextualize this by outlining problems of engagement among other boys in the school. While Percy was keen not to 'stereotype' students, he insisted on the 'reality' that they have 'a group of Korean boys who are causing us a fair bit of grief, but that's about eight or ten boys out of a hundred'.

Initially there was elasticity in the scope of the problem, but several assumptions framed the team's perspectives, resulting in a particular defining of the problem, primarily understood in terms of 'culture'. These perceptions were qualified by the team, but they nevertheless defined the problem. Social problems are typically ambiguous situations that can be interpreted in different ways, but the ways they become defined legitimizes particular actions (Grint, 2005; S. Harris, 2013). In this case, the definition entails an institutionalized but seemingly benign pathologizing around 'Asian-ness', shared by others. Teachers in the earlier focus group, separate from the research team, echoed the concern about Korean boys truanting while also talking about how certain subjects – physics, maths and chemistry – were 'Asian' subjects. Similarly, Korean students were seen as 'hard to read' because 'Asian kids are less expressive'. Part of the context of the formation of the educational problem were local perceptions about 'Asianization' that were interwoven with wider social discourses.

The organization of the team did not encourage alternative views of 'the problem'. As Adrian said, most of the 'decision-making' was done by Ivan and him. While other teachers were involved in discussions, such as the younger women of LBOTE backgrounds, it was clear they delivered rather than designed the research. The DoE consultant, Peta, whose role was as the 'critical friend', said: 'I have not had much discussion with them . . . I don't think they felt they needed me.' Ivan's role was especially significant because his investment in his own expertise in multicultural education made him resistant to discussions involving diverse perspectives. Ivan had a specific view of the research project being 'about investigating whether culture, specifically our Korean boys in Year 9, impacted on . . . their preferred style of learning or preferred style of teaching . . . whether it was group or individual . . . so whether their cultural preference was for one or the other.' Despite being urged to read widely, the literature consulted was selective. It was primarily learning styles literature – work criticized for its reliance on reified and psychologized notions of culture and learning (Noble & Poynting, 1998). Ivan liked this literature: 'as I was reading it . . . yes that's the Korean boys . . . [it was] stating the obvious but it's nice when somebody's put it in print.' In fact, he was selective in his interpretation of this literature which shows that Korean students show preferences for a variety of instructional strategies (Park, 2002). As Peta argued, despite the reading, the project had 'a very practical focus'.

The team's views of what they were doing are significant because they frame the problem in cultural terms. Percy criticized the Chinese and Korean parents for 'incredibly high expectations of their children that can't be realized . . . they push them pretty hard'. He qualified this: 'that's not to blame them, it is because where they come from in China or Korea, or India, "marks is opportunities!"' While he was anxious not to blame them, he added that the usefulness of having a Korean teacher running the homework club is that 'she can talk their language and she's also very assertive . . . that they are Koreans and that they should be proud of that and so she can use that as a Korean herself, just to say, "listen you are letting the side down" . . . so you know it works extremely well'. This cultural pathology allows teachers to use essentialized views of Asian-ness to explain things it didn't actually explain. Korean students are typically included in the perception of 'Asian success' in schools (Kim-Renaud, 2005; Ripley, 2013). Because these Korean students at Eaton Park didn't match the stereotype of 'Asian success', they were 'Asian Fails', common parlance for the result which is not up to the benchmark of the successful Asian learner (Noble, 2017). One of the other teachers explained that 'if an Aussie beat an Asian at maths . . . [or] if [their mark] was below 90 . . . "oh, Asian fail".' The 'Asian fail', like 'Asian success', ascribes educational success and failure to cultural orientation while hiding enormous diversity and structural factors (Chang & Au, 2007/2008). At Eaton Park, the Chinese comparison was clear, as Ivan asked, 'we really don't have that problem with our Chinese population and so why the Koreans specifically?' Percy echoed this: 'a lot of the Chinese boys have got that Confucian kind of sense of, "got to score high marks", and that just is who they are, their parents push them hard, they push themselves hard'. So, a small group of Korean boys comes to stand as a failure and Korean culture is seen as the cause. Despite the training challenging forms of essentialism that underlies a lot of these assumptions, and offering insights into the complexity of identity, the teachers' vision at Eaton Park operated with a hierarchical arrangement of the culturally produced capacities of students.

Making Little Sense of Data

The power of this cultural pathology is crucial because, despite having collected a lot of data, when the teachers reported their findings, their conclusions were limited. As Adrian admitted, the results showed that the boys prefer groups sometimes, and sometimes prefer individual learning, depending on the subject and the task. If they do group work, then they want to do it with friends, but these aren't always other Koreans. Some said they spend enough time with other Korean boys anyway. Despite their evidence, Percy agreed that it confirmed the value of group work: 'we were genuinely pleased that a cooperative model was seen to be a very positive thing for these boys because that sense of individual performance all the time was partly the reason for the disengagement.' The significance, however, was unclear because there was no comparable data for other students, so the specificity of the problem as 'Korean' was untested. Percy admitted that comparative data would have helped:

> it would be good . . . to test this with the other groups, with our Chinese kids, with our Indian kids, with our Sri Lankan – our Afghani boys . . . [but] the indication seems to be that Korean boys like working in groups, they seem to feel better about themselves, they seem to be on task more, they seem to achieve better.

Percy cautioned that 'we need to get away from the notion that . . . all Korean boys are like that . . . the Korean boys responded to both strategies in their learning, either group work or individualized, dependent on the subject'. It is 'dangerous' to make generalizations about students and culture, but Eaton Park's report did:

> the Korean boys were definitely more engaged in the group activity and there should be more use of groups in future lessons to engage the boys . . . from an Asian perspective . . . boys tend to not want to lose face in front of their peers and ask questions. . . . They do not like to engage in front of a wider audience if there is a chance of failure. . . . This is not necessarily a personality trait [shyness]. They see group work as a safety mechanism.

From their report's 'evidence', there were both cultural and non-cultural reasons for engagement. Many of these are obvious – students like to see outcomes, they need support and structure, they don't like to be embarrassed – and yet it is presented as insights into Korean learners. Even the truancy problems, Percy admitted, were more about family dysfunction. There was obviously little in the teachers' professional capabilities to grapple with more complex findings. In fact, a key contradiction was only mentioned once. As Ivan pointed out, in passing, 'in Korea everything is individual. . . . there is just about zero group work and [yet] they really liked the group work'. In other words, the team had identified in their culturalist framing of the problem that Korean education was dependent on individualized modes of learning but concluded that the students' culturally preferred learning style is for group work. Further, they assumed that a traditional background in individual learning was somehow an obstacle to success in the Australian education system, but it can be fixed by collective methods which treat them as an ethnically defined group that likes to stick together. Nevertheless, Ivan believed that 'I think perhaps it does have something to do with their cultural upbringing but they are seeing this sort of approach, this sort of method of teaching as a better method for them to learn'.

Postscript

The major achievement of this project was the varied data it produced, but there were limitations with it. There was no comparative dimension (with the 'good' Korean boys or other students). Key social factors weren't considered, nor was there assessment of the quality of work. The data actually provided many nuanced insights into the views and outcomes of the students, but the data was selectively used. Peta felt that it had been very 'useful' for the school, with 'a lot' of research, but the key finding, about the value of group work, wasn't sustained by the evidence. An issue at Eaton Park was the unquestioned focus on the construction of the 'problem' as 'cultural' despite the frequent cautions against doing this. This was largely the consequence of a deep investment in a certain way of seeing the relation between teacher professionalism, cultural difference and educational outcomes. The project was dependent upon the practical experience of Ivan, who knew what he wanted to do and what he wanted to find. It was his professional vision, whose expertise was born of a pragmatic culture of teaching, which provided the intellectual leadership for the project. The professional learning was dismissed despite asking teachers to question assumptions about cultural essentialism and complexity, and to think carefully about research questions, methodology and data. Research literature was used selectively. A wider array of teachers was not brought into the team leadership – despite the ethnic backgrounds of teachers delivering the project. There was no real dialogue with Korean parents. The DoE consultant was not much involved.

The Eaton Park project reminds us of the point made in Chapter 2 that categories of cultural identity are not primordial 'givens' in a world of complexity but are perceptual schemas or ways of 'seeing' groups of people which shape the ways we act (Brubaker et al., 2004). Yet while cultural and social analysis has talked much about representations of Asian-ness in Australian media, political debate and public policy, little effort has been given to the ways these categories may be operationalized problematically in specific contexts. Schools are places where practical understandings about ethnic differences inform daily decisions about curriculum, institutional procedures and parent liaison. At Eaton Park the connection between this schema and the pragmatic culture of teaching was deep and constrained the enormous effort put into the project.

Thurston Public School: Engaging Students and Parents

Thurston is a small primary school in a low SES, south-western suburb of Sydney with about half the students coming from language backgrounds other than English, including Bengali, Maori and several Pacific Islander backgrounds. About 10 per cent of the students were of Aboriginal backgrounds. The area around Thurston has undergone significant redevelopment, with new housing estates and increasing numbers of migrants, producing what Lucy, the principal, referred to as 'coming and going' between schools. Although the school is in a low SES area, some of the Bengali parents, she explained, are 'quite well educated but aren't working in their field'. Despite this diversity, multiculturalism wasn't a major focus of the school, concerned as they were with more practical issues around student outcomes. As Lena, one of the members of the research team, argued, there was a feeling at the school that 'we don't seem to have any problems based on culture'. Lucy also felt that the students 'mix' well: 'we don't have any issues with racism . . . they feel safe in a cohesive environment.' She added that 'the Bengali kids and the Indian kids are perfectly well behaved', and if there was a problem, it tended to be 'the Aussie kids'. Some of the Anglo-Australian students, she said, 'have had minimal pre-school and minimal [life] experience because it is low socio-economic [while] the multicultural groups haven't had a lot of experience in Australia'.

There were, however, two interconnected concerns that were related to this diversity. First, that some students, particularly those of Pacific Islander backgrounds, were not strongly orientated to schoolwork and struggled to complete homework. There was a feeling that this was tied to a lack of parental involvement in homework. Second, there was a concern about the lack of parental involvement in the school generally. Parental involvement is an interesting phenomenon at a small school. On the one hand, Lucy knew 'a lot of the parents by their first name' and yet 'our parents aren't very involved'. The school had run parent events over the years, but Lucy indicated that 'we don't get a big response'. She didn't think there was a 'huge issue' around parental involvement, 'but it is that real involvement that we don't have'. Being a small school, however, posed real challenges around resources, and there was little flexibility in moving staff around to cover any special programmes. The staff consisted of experienced teachers who had been at the school a long time but who, according to Lucy, 'don't know what other schools are like', and a number of early career and casual teachers 'lacking experience'. This was an issue for a small school like Thurston where the changing demographics of the area required teachers with experience working in schools with significant diversity.

'I Don't Think We Really Knew What We Were Getting in for'

It was perhaps because multicultural education wasn't a priority at the school that the training proved to be a challenge for the team. The research team consisted of Lena, the only permanent member of staff on the team, and two classroom teachers, Sybilla and Mia, all of whom identified as 'Australian'. It was also because, as Lucy argued, being a small school meant any change could result in 'overloading staff. . . . it's also a challenge wanting to be current in educational theory . . . and not having the funding to properly implement that'. Lena said she'd had 'a terrible weekend, thinking about all those things' raised at the professional learning days. She admitted that 'I don't think we really knew what we were getting in for' adding 'that's probably why it has been overwhelming for us because . . . it's a long time since I've been at university'. She found the discussions of multiculturalism 'informative' but sessions on designing the project 'very rushed' for someone 'who had absolutely no idea how to approach that kind of investigative experimental type report'. The team obviously needed more time and support before commencing the project.

Mia and Sybilla, as young temporary appointments, had joined the team just before the professional development, so it was a dramatic learning curve for them. But the training had a less negative impact on them. Sybilla said the discussion of essentialism in particular made her 'rethink'. Mia also saw this positively, reminding her of studying at university: 'I kind of forgot a lot of it so then that sort of refreshed my knowledge of multiculturalism and culture . . . it just reminds me that you sort of need to continually learn about it so that it doesn't just get pushed into the back of your mind and revert to your old stereotypes.' But Elaine, the DoE consultant, felt that, despite the training, the team was not able 'to get a basic level of understanding'. She didn't think they were 'well prepared' and had difficulty 'understanding the wider aims of the [RMRME] project [and] the theoretical concepts'. As a result, they also had 'difficulty in devising their question'. Confronted by the demands of the professional learning, the school almost pulled out of the project but negotiated a way in which, Lucy said, their workload would be 'manageable'.

Culture, Parents and Homework

Nevertheless, the team had a sense there was a problem that had to be addressed. There was a recognition in the school that there was a poor response to homework by students from some ethnic backgrounds and that this may be due to an inability of many LBOTE parents to support their children in this way. Yet reading and behaviour programmes had been prioritized over multicultural education. As Lucy admitted about their decision to be part of the project, she didn't really know what was involved but was 'interested in the funds that we might get from it'. There was a sense that they could do what they wanted to do with their RMRME project, a common, 'no strings attached' view taken by other schools, like Eaton Park.

The team eventually phrased their research question as: 'Will the provision of targeted homework support strategies for families/parents from culturally diverse backgrounds improve student engagement and participation in homework tasks?' This was attached to the second concern regarding parental involvement. As the school's final report indicated, they were interested in examining whether there was a connection between 'cultural groups and completion rates' and whether by 'trying to get parents more involved in helping their children with the homework' they could enhance parental participation. Lucy was hoping the project might give them 'more direction in ways that we can involve the community'. Sybilla, one of the team, said that while parents come into the school, they often talk to each other during the assembly: they don't exhibit 'the right etiquette', they let their pre-school kids 'run wild', so they need to be taught 'about school culture'. Lucy didn't think there was a 'huge issue' around parental involvement, but the school hoped that more 'active parent involvement', according to Lena, would 'improve children's outcomes'.

The project focused on Years 1–6 (aged seven to twelve years) and families of Bengali and Pacific Islander backgrounds, but the data collection was wider. It involved surveys of all parents and teachers across the school, as well as focus groups with parents from targeted backgrounds, with the aim of documenting 'cultural understandings' of homework. The choice of the groups was astute given, Lucy explained, that the Bengali group 'is always looking for more homework', while 'the Islander group are more easy going'. She added that the Bengali students tended to be good performers and that the parents were supportive but have 'expectations that are too high'. Data was collected on completion rates before and after the employment of a homework grid for a term, as were homework samples. The project's aim was 'to revise the homework policy and to provide targeted homework support strategies for families/parents from culturally diverse backgrounds'.

There were two early changes to the project. First, a plan to introduce a 'parent café' to increase parental presence at the school was postponed because parent information sessions to explain this 'new style of homework' were poorly attended. One of their means of having ongoing parental involvement and cultural inclusion was foregone. Second, and more importantly, the team adopted the 'homework grid' devised by Lillico (2004) at the suggestion of teachers from another school during an RMRME session. This in itself is not a bad thing – it says much about the value of giving schools the space to learn from each other through such projects – but it meant that the use of the grid didn't come about through their own research, nor was it researched. Its effectiveness was assumed. They cited four references in their report – of which one was a DoE document – but didn't actually use them. Lillico's homework grid is primarily about redefining the idea of homework, arguing that many of the 'real life' things that young people do involve learning practices and so should be acknowledged. The grid allowed for extension work 'for those who wanted it'. Students had to fill in the grid to show what they had done across twelve components (some compulsory, such as reading and housework, some not, such as shopping and games). As such, it is partly about seeing learning as a more holistic range of life skills beyond the strict focus of school, to ease pressure on families around schoolwork and 'bring families closer together'. Teachers therefore had to be provided with examples 'of what their homework "may" look like'. The school believed that implementing the grid would provide flexibility for those with little time and provide opportunities for the inclusion of ethnic community practices.

Their survey showed that parents overwhelmingly supported the idea that 'homework is an important part of my child's education', and there didn't seem any differences in 'cultural understandings' of homework. Yet it produced what the team saw as 'contradictory information' from the Bengali and Pacific Islander parents. While the survey indicated that the school needed to provide support for parents to help children with homework, it also showed that they were already able to do this. But the main issue with the survey was that the response rate from the two target groups was low: only twelve were returned by Bengali parents and eleven from Pacific Islander parents, so the data was not extensive. Follow-up focus groups showed that Bengali families thought that teachers should include extension work, while Islander families felt they were 'time poor' due to family and community activities, and this affected their ability to help. Consequently, parents liked the idea of a homework club at the school. The focus groups were also used to establish whether 'cultural lifestyle' was affecting students' ability to complete homework. Both groups were seen to have 'regular cultural gatherings' – a number of Bengali families in the wider area meet for 'cultural learning', such as community language and religious instruction. The team believed that Islander groups differed somewhat, but there was still an emphasis on organized sport, church and music. Unfortunately, however, only three parents participated in each group.

What to Do with Data?

The team believed their project was beneficial. The teacher feedback in the report supported this. Comments included 'more variety, students having more fun with it, students who never did homework are attempting some (not all) of the homework'. The action research, it concluded, 'has offered an opportunity for teacher's [*sic*] to assess how they previously viewed homework and develop a new way of thinking that includes valuing a student's cultural identity and recognizing more out of school activities as learning moments. It has [changed] the teacher's notion that homework is only about literacy and Numeracy.' Moreover, 'both Bengali and Pacific Islander students expressed a more positive attitude towards the new homework grid in comparison to the previous homework formats.' However, the report noted that completion rates across the school dropped significantly over the period. Although rates of partial completion improved, non-submission rates increased. The team felt that this could be explained as 'a natural decline of decreased homework completion rates over the course of the year, either due to a decrease in student/parent motivation, interest, values or expectations'. This drop was also found in the target groups, though it was not as dramatic. As the team pointed out, the numbers were too small to be statistically meaningful, but this is not the issue here. Oddly, the team reported that the results 'hold validity' and that the smaller drop in completion rates and the smaller increase in non-submission 'suggests that the new homework grid was more successful . . . for Pacific Islander students than it was for Bengali students'. The report also speculates that parental motivation may 'hold more influence in homework completion' than student interest in the grid, but this is not grounded in the data. Lucy commented that 'some of the kids are actually completing the non-compulsory parts of the grid, and not the compulsory part, but they are doing something'. She also indicated that parental participation hadn't improved. Elaine, the consultant, commented that they had,

> collected a lot of data . . . but I don't think they were understanding what to do with the data afterwards and how to address it and how to approach that with the action research project and address the question that they had placed themselves. So, I think there was a lot of confusion with them. . . . they just kept going back to the same thing.

Lessons Learnt

Despite being hesitant at the beginning, the team seemed to find involvement in the wider project 'worthwhile'. As Lucy elaborated, 'without the input of the research we wouldn't have known about the homework grid which has actually enriched our homework . . . it has changed practice for us.' Once they saw the 'relevance', the team was 'hard working and very cohesive' and engaged in 'meaningful dialogue' with staff. However, though the project seemed to be initiating a process of change for them, it was incomplete and not clearly focused. Their results indicated that despite the report's positive interpretation, the grid was not as successful as the team had wished. As Lena admitted, 'I don't think [it] has made that much difference.' Surmising that the data, gathered on the basis of a short-term implementation, may not be a true indication of whether the project was a success, the school decided to continue with the grid and reassess after a year's implementation, an indication they recognized the need for ongoing evaluation. The team also realized that the lack of parental involvement in the focus groups and information sessions indicated they had a lot of work to do in increasing the presence of parents in the school.

There were also other issues that the team needed to address. There was a shift in the project's focus, which was initially about improving homework completion, involving parents in its completion and increasing parental presence in the school. With the adoption of the homework grid, however, it became more about acknowledging the extracurricular activities students and their families engaged in as 'homework', 'adding value for what they did at home', Lena argued, and thus being more 'inclusive' of ethnic differences. Perhaps misconstruing the training's criticism of essentialism, the team ended up emphasizing reductive notions of culture. There were several consequences of this shift which would have consequences for future work. The quality of homework waned during the investigation. Completion rates, assessed differently by different teachers, and on the basis of new definitions of what counts, became of more concern. While going shopping with your parents may be a 'learning moment', the team didn't address whether it should be considered a useful learning moment, or whether it contributed to the child's development as defined by school curricula. Nevertheless, they realized that those parents who wanted more homework could be accommodated under the new practice, even as they grappled with the problem of finding, as Sybilla remarked, 'a balance between the time-poor Islanders and the "wanting more" Bengalis'. Yet, as Lena pondered, they were starting to think that 'time poor' may actually be 'commitment poor', especially among the Islander parents, and that they needed to look at broader issues around parent involvement.

As a consequence, while the homework grid seemed to recognize the importance of ethnic community activities, this was largely a symbolic inclusion of parents which didn't necessarily bring them structurally into the educational process. Moreover, the task of providing support to parents who don't feel included or capable of being involved in their child's education waned. Further, this may have alienated parents who put greater value on traditional goals such as literacy and numeracy. The school's report acknowledges this as an issue with the Bengali parents: because the grid 'does not emphasize these skills . . . this could explain the greater number of "not completed" numbers of Bengali students'. The school was in danger, therefore, of discouraging Bengali parents. Linked to this, the school hadn't thought enough about its notion of 'cultural groups', a problem raised in the training. Given that any cohort defined by ethnicity will be internally differentiated by class, faith and so on, claims about the uniformity of 'cultural values' are always problematic, especially in the case of Pacific Islander communities which are comprised of people from different places, with different languages (Watkins & Noble, 2013). Indeed, in the school's use it seemed to include Māori students. Any action on the basis of assumed cultural coherence should have been undertaken with caution.

Elaine, the consultant, felt the team needed more input to develop the project. There wasn't a strong link between the action research plan and multiculturalism, she argued, and particularly not to the critical approach foregrounded in the wider project. Lena said she found it 'really difficult' to 'define multicultural education', especially after the professional learning challenged some assumptions: 'you are posing more questions than you are giving answers', which is a challenge about the relation between the nature of scholarly knowledge and pragmatic professionalism we take up in the Conclusion. Elaine commented that it took the team a long time to have a clear perspective on what their research was showing: 'they stuck to what they wanted to do. At the end they saw that they needed to look at it differently . . . it took them a long process to finally [say] "that didn't work and we really have to reassess how we look at this for next year if we are going to continue it". I think that's positive.'

Postscript

Thurston's project says something interesting about strategies of inclusion. It began with an approach that ostensibly adhered to a logic of incorporation – improving outcomes through greater emphasis on homework completion – but it did this through the logic of recognition – accepting ethnic community activities as 'homework' and seeking 'culturally specific' understandings of homework. But the tension between these is never addressed. Moreover, the team held firm to an ethnicized schema of differences which saw problems in 'cultural' terms. Through limited community consultation, the team were able to identify some issues that LBOTE parents were experiencing in relation to their child's homework and issues in the ways the school managed homework. In light of this, the school revised their homework policy allowing for greater flexibility and the acknowledgement of differing cultural practices. Enhanced community dialogue could provide the basis from which to consider other issues that may affect students' education at the school, but the staff would need greater attention to conceptual issues and to their support mechanisms. The discussions with the team suggested they were continuing to think about these issues, and in relation to further evaluation, or what Lena referred to as 'a bigger push'. In our final discussion they raised the issue that 'it's our Anglo kids we had a lot of problems with but we were steered away from having a focus on them' because they weren't seen as being 'multicultural'. Continuing with their evaluation would hopefully prompt them to fold that concern back into the mix.

There is a lesson in Thurston's project about how the challenges of time and workload are magnified in a small school and educational systems need to consider how to differently resource them when they take on programmes such as RMRME. But there was also a bigger issue about teachers' orientation to practice. The team clearly found the training 'daunting', as Lucy explained. Asked if they saw 'action research' as an extension of what they do as teachers, Mia answered: 'doing the changes in the school . . . may be part of what we . . . do, but writing it and analysing those results is additional to what we would normally do.' Moreover, finding the time to think conceptually was outside what they were able to 'normally do'. As Lena argued, 'the benchmark and the goals were set a little bit high.' But without this conceptual work, programmes in multicultural education fall back on reductive and ultimately counterproductive understandings of 'culture'. Symptomatic of the pragmatic culture of teaching found across many schools, the focus was on finding ways to endorse what they thought seemed a good idea and to celebrate the efforts of teachers in undertaking this work. As Timperley and Robinson (2000) argue, in the article we gave teachers, professional collegiality often gets in the way of a deep reflection on practice because teachers are often keen to reward peers rather than engage in constructive critique.

Pentonville High School: Bridging the Cultural Chasm?

Pentonville is a large high school on the outer, semi-rural fringes of greater Sydney, in a low SES area with little ethnic diversity. Accordingly, the school had a very low LBOTE population of 4 per cent. It did have, however, an Aboriginal population of 9 per cent and a strong focus on support programmes for them. While the school's research team noted the presence of wealthy families, they were predominantly self-made tradespeople and farmers, with few professionals or people with university education. The principal, Melissa, pointed out there were a lot of 'mortgage poor' people in the area and a significant public housing population. As a result, the school had an emphasis on vocational programmes. As Raoul, the experienced head teacher of science who led the team, said, 'education is not valued probably in our community.'

The concern for teachers here was that Pentonville was a very 'Anglo' school – what Gary, head teacher of welfare, and a member of the team, referred to as 'a bit of a monoculture' – where students had little exposure to ethnic diversity. As a consequence, many students were seen to have simplistic and problematic attitudes to 'non-Anglo' cultures. As many of these students would have to work in ethnically diverse areas of Sydney in the future, the teachers felt that they required assistance to successfully meet the challenges this would pose. For this reason, the school's team decided to focus their project on evaluating an existing unit of work on 'Communities', delivered in Year 9 geography, which included a school visit to a high LBOTE high school, to increase the cultural awareness of their students.

'Why Are We Doing This?'

The team consisted of five head teachers, led by Raoul, plus Gary, Vera from social sciences, Shreya in charge of teacher mentoring and Mack, who led secondary studies. The three male teachers identified as 'Australian', but Vera had a Maltese mother, and Shreya had been born in Fiji of Indian ancestry. The team had uneven and limited training in multicultural education in their initial degrees, and their experience of professional development in the area was dependent on whether they had, like Mack, previously worked in a diverse school. The team was initially interested in developing strategies for their Aboriginal students, but, as Melissa admitted, 'I don't know if they come under a multicultural label. . . . I've never heard . . . them being identified that way.' Gary similarly said they originally 'were keen to look at our Aboriginal students and trying to foster greater understanding of their cultural identity . . . [but] we were sort of told that we need to . . . change our focus'. He hadn't thought they had much need for multicultural education, but once he started on the project, he decided that 'we actually do have a greater need'. Yet, he admitted, teachers at the school 'have a general apathy' towards issues of multiculturalism. Vera agreed: 'they wouldn't see our school as being multicultural, it's majority Anglo and that's the way it's always been seen so it would be all "why are we doing anything to do with multiculturalism?" because it doesn't affect us.' She pointed out that there were students from Lebanese, Chinese, Maltese, Italian, Indonesian and Pacific Islander backgrounds, even if they were few. Mack felt these students were only noticed if they were problems, or were 'in my face'.

Melissa elaborated the typical teachers' view:

> I see multicultural education and funding and programs in schools that have got a high NESB population and that's where I've only ever seen those sorts of programs operating. I've never seen them in a school that is so inherently known as an Anglo school as ours is.

Melissa, however, felt things were otherwise now, pointing out that,

> it's about learning to live in a community and a society that is very multicultural . . . it is not just about the make-up of your school . . . it's got the same relevance for any other school. I mean we need to learn tolerance, respect, understanding of other cultures and of the issues that people from other cultures living in our society face.

The assumed homogeneity of the school was undermined somewhat by the report from the RMRME survey. Vera remarked, 'we realized that there was more diversity among the teaching staff than what may have been initially perceived.' This, of course, was significant not just because it showed that, like Beechton, the assumptions of a local 'bubble' could be wrong, but it also suggested that school programmes about ethnic diversity should extend to questions of staff composition.

Glen suggested there was 'entrenched' racism at the school, 'like generalizing about other cultures and even the way they speak about other cultures'. This often emerged if students or teachers had English language issues. Shreya complained that some students were not 'respecting other cultures'. She recounted the experience of a boy from Lebanon (whose parents had died) in the context of media panic about terrorism. Students seemed 'accepting' but then made 'jokes' about him 'blowing up' the school. As Glen said, 'they wouldn't even recognize that that was racist . . . that's . . . why we need to do something.' Mack agreed, adding that 'the level of antagonism towards boat people is unbelievable'. He also noted that many of the local families 'go back nine generations', so their settlement here was predicated on the 'massacre of the local Aboriginals'. He noted that there was some resentment at 'the encroachment of . . . the new urban demographics' in the area, producing a strong us/them 'mentality'. Shreya believed that 'the staff need educating too' because they were 'complacent' about racism. Mack pointed out there had been a 'really serious racist incident' at the school the previous year, but it concerned Aboriginal students, adding, 'I don't think anything will happen in the school about multicultural education until it slaps us in the face.'

Because of this, the team decided that involvement in research around multiculturalism was useful. Melissa talked about the students, like the wider community, as being 'isolated' and 'insular'. Vera, of Maltese background, realized when she moved to Pentonville that,

> it wasn't a multicultural area, so I felt there was a need here at the school to create an awareness . . . and prepare them for when they leave school to be more accepting . . . a lot of them got to TAFE and Uni but it's a shock for them to have all that cultural diversity around them.

The training helped them address this. As we saw in Chapter 3, Raoul found the training difficult but useful and regretted that, 'as professionals, we don't get enough of that'. Like the rest of the team, he enjoyed the challenge of thinking critically about 'culture'. As Vera said, 'it made me think,' but, as Gary remarked, 'it all comes back to time.' The structured event of the training, together with the readings, gave them time, albeit briefly, to think about their practice in ways that the normal school week didn't. It also gave them space to discuss what they were doing, theoretically (in terms of ideas), practically (in terms of the needs of the school) and methodologically (how they realized their action research). Gary talked about how difficult it was to devise a research question for the project, and the training helped them become aware of the limits of their 'expertise': 'we know where our weakness is.' The team agonized over the question at the heart of their change of focus – the relationship between Aboriginal education and multicultural education. Similarly, the school's RMRME report made them view their school differently. Echoing Vera's comments, Raoul was 'surprised' by the diversity in the survey. The training challenged the perceptual schema the teachers employed to understand their students and staff, their community and their educational practice. As the DoE consultant Elke said, they didn't see themselves as a 'multicultural school'. They had begun a professional process that underlined how they had 'misrecognized' their school.

A Trip to Diversity

The team was interested in examining the effect a unit of work on 'Communities', framed by the 'Changing Australian Communities' programme in Year 9 geography, and the 'cultural exchange' it included, had on students' perceptions of ethnic diversity. The aim was to achieve 'prejudice reduction' and greater 'cultural awareness' through developing 'students' knowledge and understanding of the multicultural nature of Australian society' through work in class and the cultural exchange. This was because, as the team's report explained, Pentonville students 'are isolated both geographically and culturally'. They display 'ill-informed reactions to "non-Anglo" cultures' because of 'little exposure to the variety of cultures in Sydney'. Their data was collected from three focus groups of Year 10 students (totalling fifteen) who had completed the unit the previous year, a focus group of teachers who had taught the unit, pre- and post-surveys of the current Year 9 students participating in the excursion, a wider teacher survey, an assessment task in the unit and selected student interviews.

Year 9 (aged fourteen to fifteen years) was chosen because that was the year in which students undertook the long-standing tradition of a school exchange. The choice was also 'strategically driven' because Year 9 was seen to be at a stage of development 'where attitudinal adjustment would be most successful'. Significantly, they also focused on students from the 'lower academic stream'. The rationale for this was unstated, but the inference was that less academically successful students were more prone to racism, though the report offered no evidence for that. Half of the year's cohort of 240 were given the opportunity to attend, but only 80 did. A number of students did not participate in the excursion because of widespread anxiety towards the area in which the visited school was located. As Vera pointed out, 'parents don't let them go on the trip' because of the perception that there were 'gangs'.

All students participated in two focused lessons prior to the excursion, which aimed to create a context for the excursion and expose the students to the geographical and cultural identity of the community they were visiting. The lessons and excursions were linked to an assessment task to make it a 'genuine learning opportunity'. Students' attitudes were assessed before the lessons and after the excursion. The visit itself involved worksheets where students had to provide basic information about the suburb and the school they were visiting, some of which were aimed at capturing the diverse nature of the site. Another worksheet involved a cloze exercise where students had to fill in the missing words from text on the suburb. Students were also required to 'interview' a student at that school and were provided with questions to ask which focused on the life experiences of the student: country of origin, languages and tastes. Afterwards, students had to write 'a discussion piece about the similarities and differences' between student life in Pentonville and the high LBOTE school they had visited.

Encountering 'Aliens'

Overall, the project was set up well, with clear aims and methods, addressing the school's needs and generating plenty of data to assess its success. The research and subsequent evaluation of the annual cultural exchange to a high LBOTE Sydney school, however, revealed a number of issues that needed to be addressed. While the student surveys indicated a lowering of the 'don't know' responses, something the team valued, they concluded that 'it is not clear from the responses whether the information they gained made a positive change or a negative change'. Students were often more 'strongly polarized' around issues following the visit about whether students at the exchange school were similar to those at Pentonville, for example. Confusingly, the reduction in the 'don't know' responses resulted in the findings showing both that more students agreed that Australia had benefited from migration and that more disagreed. In written responses, students actually continued to highlight 'stereotypical differences – culture, race, language and appearance', and the team concluded that 'the visit reinforced the stereotypes' students held about migrant communities. While the post-survey showed that students 'know much more' about the place they visited, it also showed an increasing equation between migrants, poverty and crime, on the one hand, and between migrants and 'unusual' food, on the other. There were fewer ambivalent responses towards the trip after they had been but a slight majority continued to believe that it was not a valuable experience.

The survey responses from staff generally indicated that they thought these 'real-life experiences' were valuable in challenging students' perceptions, but comments suggested that some students were 'overwhelmed and disliked the experience' and even 'voiced openly racist remarks'. Our observations of the field trip registered a degree of awkwardness and anxiety among both the students visiting and those visited, and little time for them to establish a relaxed exchange. The responses from the Year 10 students – those who had undertaken the visit the previous year –

were more positive. While they registered a degree of shock because they were not used to such a visibly 'multicultural' environment, they enjoyed talking to students from the other school. Yet while they thought it was a 'valuable experience', they 'felt like they were spying into the lives of the other students as though they were "aliens"'. The research showed, the team concluded, the limitations 'of having a "one-off" visit to somewhere that is different': 'the differences . . . are most strongly remembered.' This is akin to the effect of the multicultural days we explored in Chapter 4 in exoticizing difference. The team acknowledged that the programme needed to 'move away from a "sightseeing tour"' to deepen the intercultural experience that students attain from this excursion and to focus more on their 'shared experiences'. The excursion was less of an 'exchange' than a brief 'encounter' with Otherness, one that offered no lasting change in perceptions despite the original aims.

Opening Eyes

The team at Pentonville were consequently not entirely happy with the results of their project, but they realized they had learnt from it. As Elke, the consultant, said, it took a while, but the realities of what they were finding 'hit home'. In examining an existing programme that was considered to have had merit in raising students' awareness of ethnic diversity, the action research led them to question their approach. Raoul explained that 'one of the things in schools that you have a hard time doing is evaluating programs and that's probably one of the best things that's come out of it for us, to actually evaluate that'. He added,

> we did little focus groups, kids that had been on it in previous years and they were really good. Like the kids straightaway identified some things that they thought didn't have a lot of value . . . they were saying that they like, they think it would be even more effective to set up some shared experiences between the two schools, not necessarily at one of the schools, but they go out and do an activity together and they spend more time . . . because for some of them it was, not confronting, but yeah, just a bit artificial.

The students, therefore, helped the teachers to recognize the limitations of the excursion. As a trip to visit the 'exotic Other', it tended to objectify cultural difference reinforcing rather than breaking down the cultural stereotypes many students held. The results of the action research prompted the realization that a more meaningful course of action would be to involve the schools collaboratively undertaking activities. Gary also reflected that he had begun to think more deeply about racism, questioning how he had characterized it up to this point, in particular not really feeling that racist jokes towards some students were 'intentionally racist':

> it's opened my eyes and now I am more aware of the general comments that they are making because I think to be honest, I was coming from my own, probably as an Anglo-Saxon perspective ... remember we were talking about and I said I don't think the kids are, like they generalize and they are generally racist but in terms of the respect they pay to students from other cultures within the school, I would say that it's generally, it's good [but] they are not really and it's all here about those kids fitting in and accepting the comments that are made.

Through this discussion Gary came to realize that just because the students who were the object of these remarks did not respond, it did not make the jokes any less racist, and as a teacher, it was his role to intervene, rather than being complicit in a form of 'bystander racism' (Nelson et al., 2011). By lifting the profile of multicultural education at the school, the project gave Gary a greater understanding of racism in its various guises. As in some other schools, the systematic nature of the research process led the team to begin questioning and modifying their practices because of the challenge to rethink how multicultural education was approached at their schools.

As part of this process, the team continued to grapple with the complicated relationship between multicultural education and Aboriginal education. They didn't 'solve' this problem, but they had embarked on a process of recognizing it more complexly. As the principal said, when asked how the two were connected in relation to the increasing emphasis on 'intercultural understanding' as a capability in the National Curriculum, it was still an 'us and them':

> It's a hard question and I think you'd get a very different answer from the Aboriginal community themselves, they certainly want to be seen ... locally as separate, however, not because they are trying to be separate within the community but because their needs are really very special in terms of both cultural understanding for their own students and sharing that cultural understanding for the wider ... coupled with improving the learning outcomes for the students, and there is a really big focus on trying to raise the standards for them ... I don't know if I can answer that.

While the research suggested the programme did not achieve its goals, as research the project was successful. The team understood the problems they were facing more clearly, had a better sense of their own community, had reflected on the limitations of their practice and had learnt from this. The school had committed to changing its programme to deepen the intercultural experience of the curriculum and the exchange: it had committed to strengthening the partnership between the two schools providing an opportunity for students to participate in an overnight joint school camp and to conduct joint programming around multicultural education. These were just two of the thirteen 'future directions' the team wanted to introduce as a result of the research.

Postscript

The dissatisfaction expressed by the research team at Pentonville with their program reflected their professional growth. A key principle in the literature on teacher professionalism is the need to engage in continuous learning, which requires ongoing reflection upon the limits of one's knowledge, skills and practices (Goodson & Hargreaves, 1996, pp. 20–1). This requires time and space to think and talk, which are in short supply in a school. Yet it also reflects differing cultures of professionalism discussed in previous chapters. The tendency to valorize practice underlies a pragmatic professionalism, but 'reflection' needs to be more than just thinking about classroom practice in restricted terms. It should mean thinking about social contexts, to analyse and use theory, what Hoyle (1975) calls extended professionalism. The team thought seriously about the specificity of the semi-rural location of Pentonville and its largely Anglo-Australian population, and the consequences of this for students' educational and social experiences, to think about what Melissa referred to as 'educating for the wider community'. This also requires intellectual labour. First, they took the research part of action research seriously, producing rich and complementary data. Second, the team engaged with the literature provided in the professional development sessions to think about 'culture' – though they could have made greater use of the resources we offered. As Vera commented, 'I would like to read more and do that more intellectual side of it, but . . . it comes down to time. . . . The more you know you are going to be a better teacher because you're making yourself more aware.'

While they may not have 'bridged the chasm', by engaging in an evaluation of the cultural exchange, the team realized that the programme could be broadened to allow students to engage in more meaningful dialogue around diversity. Given Pentonville had few LBOTE students and little emphasis on multicultural education, these were positive developments indicating the school was moving towards rethinking their approach to multicultural education. This may also help them in the future think about the central problem they grappled with at the beginning of the research: the complicated relationship between multicultural education and Aboriginal education. But this will only be possible because they combined their reflections on practice with thinking about social context, engaging with conceptual issues and producing significant research data.

Conclusion

These case studies are examples of three approaches to action research that are constrained by different factors: Eaton Park produced rich data but were too wedded to the ways they had constructed their problem; Thurston produced uneven data, and the limitations of their conceptual framing meant that they didn't get to the heart of their problems; Pentonville, grappling with trying to make multiculturalism relevant for an 'Anglo' school, realized that their research challenged what they thought was a good practice and were reflecting on how to do things differently. All demonstrated the difficulties, as well as the possibilities, of asking teachers to undertake 'serious' research and to think through difficult issues.

Similarly, each reflected in different ways how a perceptual schema of difference structures the 'professional vision' and practice of teachers (Noble & Watkins, 2014a). As Brubaker et al. (2004, p. 38) show, categories order the world for us. The logic of recognition underlying multiculturalism has been important in giving ethnic communities political validation, but it entails ways of seeing which carry assumptions of how people behave which affects the way we behave towards them, thus shaping ideas of engagement. This is significant in places like schools because educational problems and their solutions are constructed on the basis of these schemas. While teachers' vision may be less formalized than other professions, they nevertheless operate within ways of seeing people, tasks and environments acquired from educational training, professional development and practical experiences. These may be contested and plural in nature, but they nevertheless set the parameters of professional orientation to practice (Sherin, 2001).

In an education system with a focus on multiculturalism, such schemas of difference may encode educational issues as cultural ones which can work to 'naturalize' the origins of educational outcomes and encourage teaching practices that reproduce those reified categories and ignore the cultural complexities of hyperdiverse societies. Teachers do not 'see' the educational outcomes of Anglo-Australian students in terms of 'ethnicity', yet they do so with students of non-Anglo backgrounds. Teachers' professional training does not necessarily equip teachers with the research skills to investigate the problem in more complex ways, nor the critical capacities to think through those complexities.

The 'professional vision' based on a pragmatic culture of teaching privileges a way of seeing that shifts responsibility for those outcomes onto 'culture'. Rather than engage the Other, it continues to Other them. These three schools demonstrate the need for a more nuanced sociocultural understanding in multicultural education, which needs to be embedded in pre-service training and professional development, and in models of action research in schools that extend that understanding. The Conclusion to this book takes up the issue of what exactly are the capacities teachers need to move beyond this impasse, but, in the following chapters, we continue to explore how teachers reflect practically and theoretically through action research and professional learning.

CHAPTER 6

From Inclusive Curriculum to Cultural Intelligence

A key aspect of multicultural education has been the teaching of an inclusive curriculum (Banks, 2009). What this means in practice, however, varies considerably. While it can operate as an important way of ensuring curricula has content representative of all groups in society, in many schools it simply provides another opportunity to blandly celebrate diversity engaging in the forms of lazy multiculturalism that we saw evident in previous chapters. In these cases, students typically learn about cultural festivals and national days or the customs of 'exotic' cultures. Such approaches have limited value in assisting students to make sense of the culturally complex world in which they live whereby globalization and the transnational flows of people, goods and information suggest 'cultures' are not so clearly defined and where 'the exotic' may now be far more familiar. Diversity cast as exotic difference may even run counter to inclusion. How, for example, does it promote a sense of belonging for those who are constantly considered 'different'? This chapter engages with these issues as it examines how teachers in five schools approached devising and implementing various forms of inclusive curriculum. Some had difficulty in moving beyond how this is traditionally understood, whereas others managed to traverse new ground working with their students to rethink the inclusionary nature of their curriculum and the purposes of their work, evincing the nascent development of 'cultural intelligence' (Ang, 2011).

Barnett High School: 'We Are a Monoculture'

Barnett HS is located in rural NSW. Its student population was generally of a low SES and predominantly Anglo-Australian with 8 per cent identifying as Aboriginal and only 3 per cent with a LBOTE. Toby, the acting principal, could only think of one Thai student and another of Congolese refugee background with a LBOTE, the latter having just left the school. It is for this reason that he remarked at the beginning of the school's involvement in RMRME: 'I don't know why we were selected . . . I've often thought about it. Maybe, perhaps that we are a monoculture, because we have a high Anglo population and we don't have many students of, who are ethnic background.' The previous principal had agreed to Barnett's participation in RMRME after first being approached by the NSW DoE. Toby's confusion over the school's involvement in RMRME, however, seems emblematic of a broader issue of leadership within the school which had a constantly changing senior executive that ultimately impacted the carriage of the project, the membership of the research team and the approach that was adopted. Yet Toby's inkling as to why Barnett was included was correct. All schools in NSW are required to implement the DoE's Multicultural Education Policy, but this can be undertaken in various ways depending on the nature of a school's population. We wanted to see how this was broached within low LBOTE schools, and Barnett's rural location made it particularly interesting. Toby, however, was still unsure about the relevance of multicultural education to Barnett: 'Well, until we wind up getting more and more people from an ethnic diverse background I would always say that the Koori[1] issue with education far outweighs that of multicultural at a school like ours because we deal with it on a daily basis.'

As was the case at Pentonville, comments such as these are pertinent not only for what they reveal about the status of multicultural education in low LBOTE schools but of the relationship between multicultural education and Aboriginal education. The twin foci of Aboriginal education are to improve the educational outcomes of Aboriginal students and to ensure students, as a whole, have a good grasp of the histories and cultures of Aboriginal Australians (NSW DoE, 2020b). Multicultural education, on the other hand, has a wider remit. While it calls for students to 'recognise and respect the cultural linguistic and religious backgrounds of all students' (NSW DoE, 2020d) including those of Aboriginal backgrounds, its original and continued focus on programmes directed towards students of migrant and refugee backgrounds often overshadows its intent to promote intercultural understanding more broadly. Understandably, Aboriginal Australians resist the collapse of Aboriginal education into multicultural education that would seemingly erase their status as Australia's First Peoples. What is needed is not a conflation of these differing perspectives but a productive dialogue, one in which Anglo-Australians are more firmly embedded, relinquishing their implicit authority of overseeing the management of Australia's non-Anglo others. In such a way, the NSW Multicultural Education Policy to 'recognise and respect the cultural, linguistic and religious backgrounds of all students and promote an open and tolerant attitude towards cultural diversity, different perspectives and world views' could be more fully realized (NSW DoE, 2020d).

Clearly, Barnett was not a monocultural school; it simply had greater numbers of students of Anglo-Australian backgrounds. Referring to it in this way not only excised Aboriginal students from the cultural mix of the school but failed to acknowledge the diverse cultural heritage of many members of the school community. Twelve per cent of Barnett's teachers, for example, were born outside Australia, including in Afghanistan and Algeria. Toby, himself, was a migrant, born in the United States of Irish, Polish and Croatian ancestry, yet his Whiteness allowed for his identification with the Anglo majority within the racial divide between Aboriginal and non-Aboriginal that characterized the school and the broader community. RMRME provided an opportunity to examine the complex interplay of factors that contributed to the ethnic composition of the school community. Approached in this way, multicultural education could fulfil its broader remit of intercultural understanding and bring a much-needed interrogation of race, ethnicity and culture to Barnett.

These issues were of concern not only in relation to the school but to the broader Barnett community. Toby, for example, described the overall ethos of the school as, 'redneck, bigoted in many respects, very polar when it comes to issues that deal with race. There is a lot of derogatory, inappropriate comments made on a regular basis going in both directions between the Koori and the non-Koori students. Yeah, there is still that backwater attitude . . . and it permeates through our community as well.' This was a view that Shirley, a member of the original research team, shared:

> we probably all agree that the community is quite entrenched in some of its views. . . . I think one of the issues that we as a school face is actually coming to terms with the fact racism isn't just about Indigenous, non-Indigenous relations; it is much broader than that. There is a lot of generational ignorance and intolerance in Barnett.

A Study in Team Dysfunction

Shirley was of the view that Barnett's project should focus on the professional development of staff, that broadening students' perspectives on the world and countering racism had to be premised on teachers having a better grasp of multicultural education to address these issues within the curriculum and in day-to-day interactions with students. She drew on the school RMRME survey data to support this view. As Daphne, her colleague on the original research team, explained, 'the results from the multicultural survey showed quite clearly the fact that they've had very little training and you know that clarification of what multiculturalism actually is.' Toby's comments on the RMRME survey, mentioned in

Chapter 3, indicated teachers at Barnett lacked knowledge of multicultural education: '. . . it stuck out, people aren't culturally aware. People aren't aware of cultural diversity across the board.'

Despite this apparent need for professional development around multicultural education, Toby felt this was not necessary, 'until our cultural diversity increases'. His perspective on the direction of the programme created friction with Shirley and Daphne who were keen to explore what staff already knew about multicultural education and then to pursue the professional development of teachers across the curriculum. Alan, the fourth member of the team and an executive member of staff, had a similar view to Toby's. While ultimately taking a lead role on Barnett's team, Alan, unlike the others, had not attended the training. He saw himself as primarily about 'logistical support', looking after the project finances, organizing teaching relief, etc., rather than providing any intellectual leadership, especially with regard to multicultural education, and so didn't feel his attendance was necessary. As a result, Alan missed discussion of key concepts around multiculturalism, together with the examination of the readings that informed it – all of which Shirley and Daphne considered of importance in thinking through how they would approach the project. As Daphne pointed out, 'going through the process of defining culture and intercultural awareness and things was very interesting to me and it certainly refreshed my view of looking at things.' As we also saw in Chapter 3, Toby dismissed the training. Unlike Shirley and Daphne, he found the reading 'a chore' and the treatment of conceptual issues like being in 'Sociology 101 again'. Shirley and Daphne had greater affinity for multicultural education and for engaging with issues of sociocultural enquiry. As social science teachers, there were synergies between their disciplinary content and that provided in the training. They could see the need for staff to consider these issues if only to meet the requirements of the DoE's Multicultural Education Policy. They felt RMRME offered the opportunity to do this, but Toby and Alan thought otherwise, reluctant to involve staff in broader professional development around multicultural education. Speaking without Shirley and Daphne present, Alan described what they were proposing as having 'an audit feel', that their 'aim was to make faculties accountable and was almost punitive'.

Faced with this opposition and lacking any leadership position within the school, Shirley and Daphne left the team, but neither they nor the school notified the DoE at the time. As a rural school, there were no regular face-to-face visits with their DoE consultant, Dario, but once he was aware of these issues, it was too late. Shirley and Daphne had been replaced by another teacher, Michael, a young English teacher relatively new to the school who, with minimal support from his head teacher, Milly, took on the responsibility of designing and implementing the project. Toby, too, had left the team and so there was no one remaining who had attended the initial training. Given this, the consultant's role became key in not only briefing Michael about how to undertake the project as action research but the approach to multicultural education within RMRME. Yet Dario had difficulty fulfilling this role. Despite undertaking the training himself, he still seemed wedded to a more traditional approach to multicultural education. Whether or not he found it easier to endorse the revised approach the school was undertaking amid the toxic relations between members of the team, and the resistance of other staff, was not clear. Whatever the case, Alan explained how they had been encouraged to put a focus on 'empathy', and so Barnett's project was reduced to one teacher in the English faculty producing and teaching a unit of work as inclusive curriculum foregrounding a notion of empathetic understanding.

Inclusion by Empathy

Michael had indeed been put in a difficult position. While he was able to attend a mid-year gathering where the other RMRME schools provided progress reports on their projects, had access to the resources available on the project website and had some minimal guidance from the RMRME Project team, he received conflicting messages about multicultural education and the rationale behind RMRME from the various parties involved. As he explained towards the end of the project, 'This is where the training would have been really useful at an earlier point, of just having the language and having the things to talk about.' Without this, Michael resorted to what was conventional multicultural fare of promoting empathy by appreciating difference following a logic of reduced recognition having his Year 9 class of students (aged fourteen to fifteen years) devise a cookbook mapping changes in Australia's dietary habits from damper to chow mien through to spaghetti bolognaise and Middle Eastern lamb pies. Students also undertook a self-directed study of compiling a 'Multicultural Anthology' of literary texts requiring them to locate and write reviews and personal reflections on their content with Michael facilitating their enquiry.

For a predominantly Anglo-Australian school in a rural area, this dabbling with diversity may have constituted a marked change in the delivery of their English curriculum. Within the subjects collectively termed Human Society and Its Environment (HSIE) in NSW schools, such as history and geography, Year 9 students would have been familiar with content related to Australia's cultural diversity, its Indigenous foundations, British colonialism and waves of migration. It was this that Shirley and Daphne had been keen to give stronger focus across the curriculum, if not incorporating it into teachers' own lessons, at least developing greater awareness of intercultural understanding. Instead, Alan redirected the project into the English faculty becoming the responsibility of one teacher with limited expertise in relation to either multicultural education or action research thereby minimizing its impact within the school and avoiding any fallout from a largely resistant staff. But, even in relation to the work undertaken, difficult topics such as the prevalence of racism within the school and broader community were avoided. As Milly explained,

> what's really engaging about the unit of work is that it is about, that it is centred around empathy, and not let's talk about the refugee plight in Australia and the racist attitudes of, you know, none of us have gone into it with that approach and I think that makes a big difference in a school like this. I think you know having that really subtle approach and making it a fun concept is much more effective.

Alan agreed with Milly: 'It's a nice way to lead kids along a pathway before they get confronted by something too challenging.' Anything 'too challenging', however, was simply not considered, and so the unit reflected the lazy multiculturalism we saw in Chapter 4. Moreover, as Michael's approach to inclusive curriculum offered little more than a veneer of palatable diversity, masking issues of racial intolerance, it effectively operated as a form of institutionalized racism.

The means to disrupt this approach, through the use of action research, if only within the confines of Michael's classroom, were neutered. Apart from collecting work samples from what students produced in the course of completing the unit to gauge what Michael termed students' 'emotional maturity' and empathy in relation to difference, no other data was collected and neither Michael nor Alan had a clear idea as to what action research involved. From Alan's perspective 'action research is part of good teaching. Every good teacher I've ever worked with has done it on a day-to-day basis, minute by minute'. In other words, Alan saw action research as simply a matter of personal reflection on teaching, void of any formal process and disciplined enquiry and Michael echoed these remarks: 'that's what teachers do all the time. I think every unit of work we teach is action research. Everything you do.' Without any measure of the effectiveness of the unit, and lacking the required conceptual resources around multicultural education, both in the design of his lessons and assessment of his students' work, the best Michael could offer in terms of progress was that 'there are parts of the work samples where you can look at it and get a sense of the positive attitudes being projected'. There was no sense that students were able to utilize this to then reflect more critically upon the nature of race relations at Barnett and within the local community. Michael was at least aware that, for some students, his unit had simply contributed to a trivializing of what multiculturalism entails. In the case of one student, he described how 'he's like, in multiculturalism, he was still like, "Yeah, oh it's great that you can eat lasagne and you can now have spaghetti bolognaise." And that's as far as it's got.'

Postscript

For some it may be drawing a long bow, but we see the lazy multiculturalism that framed Michael's approach to inclusive curriculum as a form of institutionalized racism. He is not the only teacher who devised a unit of work around limited forms of cultural recognition reliant upon stereotypical representations of the Other and failed to engage with a more complex treatment of the nature of Australia's ethnic diversity. What characterizes his and similar approaches as institutional racism, however, needs some explanation. We are not declaring the teachers themselves racist. In fact, in all cases, their intentions were quite the opposite. Individualizing racism often obscures its institutionalization, the ways in which certain practices become embedded within institutions generating understandings that are rarely questioned. It is not only the institution of schooling that is complicit here but that of teaching. More precisely, it is the anti-intellectualism of pragmatic cultures of teaching that shirks a deeper engagement with issues around race, ethnicity and culture, allowing for the reproduction of problematic practice and for racism to remain unchecked.

At Barnett, this was particularly insidious as institutional racism was not so much buoyed by the way in which a pragmatic professionalism had prevented the enactment of the ideas presented in the training – in fact, Michael was given little opportunity to engage with them – but that there was a clear intent by leadership within the school to avoid confronting issues of racism. As a result, Barnett, or rather one teacher within their English faculty, adopted a benign approach to multicultural education favouring empathy over critique that was ill-equipped to tackle what Shirley referred to as 'generational ignorance and intolerance'. Towards the end of the year, Jason, a new principal, was appointed to the school, but he similarly seemed disinclined to tackle these issues. From his perspective: 'You can't force a concept of multicultural understanding on people. It's got to come over a period of time and you would think in the 21st century in Australia that that would be the case but it's not, it's not out in the countryside.'

Wollami Lakes Public School: Lost Opportunities

Like Barnett, Wollami Lakes PS is a rural school though, in many ways, its student population was very different. The school had a similar Aboriginal population of 10 per cent, but, in contrast to Barnett and many rural schools, it had a much larger number of LBOTE students (27 per cent). This included a substantial number of students of Indian backgrounds, most of whom were part of a long-established community working in agriculture and who were now major employers in the region. There was also a more recent population of students of African backgrounds together with smaller numbers from Burma, Syria and Afghanistan, all refugees who settled in the area as part of the Federal Government's regional refugee resettlement programme. The school also had a smaller number of students of Japanese, Indonesian, German and French backgrounds. While the school was far more ethnically diverse than many in rural NSW, the recent arrival of those of refugee backgrounds posed considerable challenges for staff. As Dina, an EAL/D teacher and member of the school's team, remarked,

> it was difficult for our school because the African population arrived really quickly, a lot of them, and prior to that we didn't have any African students at our school so we were sort of bombarded with these refugee students, bang, bang, bang, one after the other and we really didn't get any in-servicing or professional development in the lead-up to their arrival.

Jocelyn, the school's assistant principal and leader of the team, added, 'It is also not only language though, it's the cultural, like these poor children didn't know what a sandwich was and you know how to use a straw to drink their poppers and things.' The issues that emerged were not simply a function of cultural and linguistic difference but were related to a myriad of other factors such as psychological trauma, disrupted schooling, family separation, health and financial concerns, all stemming from these students' experience as refugees and for which teachers had been poorly prepared (Watkins et al., 2019). This situation was amplified by the school's rural location in that professional learning opportunities and DoE consultancy support tend to be quite limited outside metropolitan areas, except for online support which many teachers felt did not always meet their immediate needs.

In addition to the complexities of these shifting demographics, the school community was of a relatively low SES which, Perry, the principal, found the most challenging. He indicated, however, that this was not uniform, that there was 'everything from very low SES to very high SES'. These differences, evident in the broader community, created divisions which at times impacted the school especially given their intersection with issues of race. As Perry remarked, 'The situation with some of our Indigenous families is that they work for some of the Punjabi families in regards to picking and various activities so there is a bit of resentment there and of course it's unskilled labour so the working conditions and remuneration aren't fantastic.' Racism manifested itself in various ways. Exacerbated by class differences, it created tensions between various groups within the community surfacing, at times, within the school in what Perry termed 'good, old fashioned racism', though he stressed there was 'no widespread hostility'.

Relatively new to Wollami Lakes and having worked in many rural schools, Perry commented that there was a 'much more positive atmosphere than some of the schools I'm used to'. He was a little frustrated, however, with what he saw as an over-reliance on the school's EAL/D teachers in meeting the needs of the refugee students. From his perspective, this was 'part of everyone's business', and, while he was specifically referring to these students' English language needs and how these needed to be addressed within mainstream classrooms, he felt many teachers lacked the required cultural awareness to work with both EAL/D and LBOTE students. As he explained, 'too often multicultural programs aren't about cultural aspects, they are about the logistics of language learning and integration and these sort of things.' Unlike many of the principals we spoke to, Perry grasped the broader remit of multicultural education and its relevance to all students no matter their ethnic background. He recognized the need for the distinction between Aboriginal education and multicultural education but, at the same time, saw how the latter allowed for an engagement with a broader ethic towards cultural difference. He was critical, however, of conventional approaches to multicultural education such as those we have termed 'lazy multiculturalism', seeing a need for a deeper engagement within the curriculum:

> I would like to see a move away from cultural understanding being an event, you know, so we go off to the temple and that's great. We talk to the Sikh community and we tick that box, or we have NAIDOC[2] day and we have people come up and we tick that box, to actually move past that . . . and have a level of understanding which is something we discuss frequently and openly rather than being an event.

The extent to which such a shift would be realized within Wollami Lakes' project was another matter. Given his recent appointment to the school, the need to familiarize himself with its overall operation and various other initiatives, Perry was not a member of the school's research team which, as a result, lacked the kind of intellectual leadership he offered.

Anti-Intellectualism: 'It's the Nature of the Beast!'

The team at Wollami Lakes was comprised of six teachers: Richard, Molly, Julie, Dina, Patricia and Jocelyn, who, as assistant principal with a teaching load, was the executive member of the team. This was one of the larger teams in the overall project with the changing demographics within the school no doubt sparking the interest of many as to what it might offer in response. As to their own ethnic background, Jocelyn, Richard, Molly and Julie were all of Anglo-Australian ancestry, while Dina, the EAL/D teacher, and Patricia, the community language teacher, had both been born in India but had grown up in Australia. In fact, Dina and Patricia were the only non-Anglo members of the teaching staff at Wollami Lakes, and, as with most of their colleagues, they had been at the school for many years. A community language class had operated in the school for over twenty years, and over that period of time all things 'multicultural' were seen as generally the preserve of Patricia and Dina. This had changed with the arrival of increasing numbers of students of refugee backgrounds leading to a view that staff needed a greater understanding of multicultural education. The training undertaken within RMRME, however, was not exactly what many on the team was expecting. Richard remarked, 'I wondered what I had got myself into . . . it was a bit academic for me.' As discussed in Chapter 3, Richard was one of the teachers who couldn't see the point of the 'intellectual stuff'. Dina expressed a similar view, 'I am not an academic. I'm more of a hands-on person.' Patricia, who also attended the training along with Richard, Dina, Jocelyn and Julie, explained that it had made her 'a little bit scared' as she too was 'more of a practical person'. The only member of the team offering a different perspective was Jocelyn, who apologized, saying, 'I'm sorry guys but I do enjoy the academia.' Towards the end of the project, Perry reflected on these differing abilities within the team but also within the profession more broadly:

> some members of the team have not seen that side of it as being valuable in terms of the reading and what have you . . . some probably couldn't see the need for that at all. So some people are purely about practical implications, some people like to have the knowledge base behind them. It's the nature of the beast I suspect.

'Those Concepts Are Pretty Deep'

Jocelyn and her team knew full well that staff at Wollami Lakes required greater understanding of the changing demographics of their school community, as did their students. It was the latter, however, that the team chose to focus on in their project. Before determining a course of action, they surveyed all students in Years 2–6 (aged eight to twelve years) to gauge what knowledge they had of the countries of origin of students at the school and the languages they spoke. As expected, this was quite limited. Students tended to have little grasp of what was beyond their own experience. One measure of this was to ascertain students' ability to not only name these countries – fourteen in all – but to locate them on a world map which revealed minimal understanding of the world's geography. Such findings prompted the team, in consultation with staff as a whole, to focus on developing a teaching resource that would allow students to better understand the diversity in their midst and that of the global community of which they were a part. This resource involved a compilation of the stories of seven students at the school of the following backgrounds: Aboriginal Australian, Japanese, German, Indian (2), Congolese and Ethiopian; the last two both recently arrived refugees. The stories were obtained via interviews with each child and one or both of their parents, with each team member taking responsibility for one or more story. The team also collected photographs of people, places and events of significance to each child and their family, working with them to draft and finalize the stories with the intention of publishing the accounts as both electronic and hardback books.

The stories not only proved a powerful curriculum resource, but the process of collecting them had additional benefits that Perry referred to in reflecting on the project: 'it's been a real plus particularly on the community side of things with people coming in and sharing their stories and staff just developing a much greater understanding than they would have had previously. More so probably around the refugee population given that they are newer to our area.' Dina spoke of the impact of one of these stories and the ways in which it provided a counter narrative to the negative representations of refugees in the media: 'His is a true refugee story of hardship and camps. You have a totally different point of view after just reading the story, without even thinking deeply. If you were to read it to your class and say "now what do you think?" the children would change their minds very quickly.' In using this story for teaching purposes, Dina was relying on the power of the narrative itself to prompt students to reflect on the plight of refugees. While a useful first step, she seemed less certain about what to do next, the ways the story might then be used to consider the reasons behind the demonizing of refugees, the differences between asylum seekers and refugees, their increasing numbers internationally and differing global responses. As with her colleagues, Dina seemed unsure of the full potential of the resource they had developed, focusing instead on the personal narratives and not much more than a concrete treatment of each. As Richard explained, 'They will be used for lots of things. I mean we do shared reading and comprehension groups and reading groups and all sorts of stuff.' Julie added: 'I also see just using these stories in times like we have Refugee Week and Multicultural Day. This could be the lead-up as well as specific HSIE units [like] Celebrations because this child [i.e. in one of the stories] talks about celebrations so there are lots of opportunities to use it.' Jocelyn also felt that the stories could be integrated into existing programmes of study: 'we are not going to write a separate unit because in all the units we do there is some multicultural aspect that these stories fit into.' When asked whether doing this would allow for some consideration of the treatment of culture and globalization that was examined in the training, Richard remarked:

> an issue at our school, or in any school, particularly with primary kids [is] those concepts are pretty deep. I would love to get through to these kids and to open their minds to the idea that yeah OK, you can't stick people in a box and try to get them to develop these understandings but

... that's very difficult. We are talking about basic things here. So my frustration is how do we do that? I really need to know how to do that.

Each of the stories, however, afforded the opportunity to engage with a more complex treatment of the content. The story of the refugee student of Ethiopian background, that Dina referred to, was a case in point given the complicated nature of his personal journey. While this student's parents were Ethiopian, he was born and spent his first years in a Kenyan refugee camp prior to his arrival in Australia. He had never been to the country of his parents' birth, and so rather than simply referring to him as 'Ethiopian', his story allowed for a discussion about the differences between categories such as 'nationality', 'ethnicity', 'culture' and 'identity'. Taken together, the stories the team had collected provided useful examples of the way identities should not be reduced to singularities. Both the 'Indian' students, for example, had been born in Australia to Indian parents but had never been to India. The 'Japanese' student had also been born in Australia, in his case to a Japanese mother and an Anglo-Australian father, and, before commencing school at Wollami Lakes, had spent lengthy periods of time in Japan, spoke fluent Japanese and still travelled there several times a year to visit his relatives. His transnational lifestyle provided yet another instance of the hybrid mix of cultures constitutive of these students' identities and offered an example of what Richard felt was difficult to explain to primary school students, namely that 'you can't stick people in a box'. But, of course, such ideas are possible to explore in relation to any child's experience, even those of Anglo-Australian background. They, and others, don't live their lives in a vacuum. They engage with ethnic and cultural difference through consuming various foods, media, music, etc. It is disappointing, therefore, that the team did not include a child of Anglo-Australian ancestry within their collection as they too could have provided an account of their family's origins and cultural influences. In doing so, the emphasis may have shifted from what was largely an exploration of culture as difference to an unpacking of culture as a way of life in which both differences and similarities are evident and points of connection rather than differentiation are highlighted.

What Richard and the rest of the team hadn't realized is that both they and their students live this complexity. Cultural difference need not be exoticized as it is now very much the norm – a function of the globalized world in which we live and especially so in migrant-based nations such as Australia, even outside its metropolitan centres. Students need to know how to make sense of this world and this is the role of teachers. It is no longer viable, if indeed it ever was, to view cultures and identities as bounded and static, a perspective that early models of multiculturalism have tended to encourage and now, is so difficult to shift. Even when presented with so much evidence to the contrary, the team at Wollami Lakes seemed blinkered in this regard. They didn't seem to grasp the utility of the theory they had met in the training for understanding the cultural complexity evident in the stories they had collected, exhibiting the same problem of enactment as many teachers in previous schools. In fact, towards the end of the project, reflecting on these issues, Dina remarked, 'I think the best way to teach culture is to live amongst it. You can't teach it from a textbook.'

Postscript

This recurrent problem with enactment, namely teachers' difficulties in applying understandings from the training, has led us to reflect upon the research design for RMRME. Clearly, many teachers required additional academic support to implement their projects. In the case of the team at Wollami Lakes, this was to realize the full potential of the teaching resource they had produced. As Richard remarked, 'I really need to know how to do that.' The problem here, however, is not solely the need for greater academic guidance. Such comments raise questions about the professional capacities of teachers. With the exception of Jocelyn, the members of the team had difficulties with the 'academic nature' of the professional learning they received. They saw themselves solely as practitioners but, of course, knowing what and how to teach is far more than a practical concern. It requires an intellectual orientation to the content and delivery of curriculum which an academic adviser may provide assistance with, but which should be germane to the professional expertise teachers have acquired in their initial training and ongoing professional development.

Smithton Public School: Multicultural Education under Review

Inclusive curriculum was also an element of Smithton's project. Smithton PS is located in Sydney's south, in a suburb that Ronald, the principal, described as 'middle class' though having 'a good cross section from the very affluent [who] live in waterfront homes, very well-off through to families who would be in a housing commission development down the road'. Seventy per cent of the students had a LBOTE with those of various European backgrounds predominant but with increasing numbers from China and Korea. Given the sizeable numbers of LBOTE students, it was surprising that there was little emphasis on multicultural education within the school. As Giselle, a member of their team, commented, 'I still think that a lot of teachers sort of undervalue the whole multicultural education thing.' Melody, her colleague on the team, agreed, 'some people might see it as an add-on.' For Ronald, multicultural education had a specific focus: 'The main goal is to give those children the same opportunity, the opportunities to achieve the same outcomes as their Australian counterparts . . . feeling valued in the school, their culture is appreciated, that there are activities in the school for them to celebrate their cultural background.'

Despite the well-meaning nature of Ronald's comments, he saw multicultural education as simply about the ethnic Other with programmes to specifically target 'them'. The fact that the NSW DoE Multicultural Education Policy calls for a focus on all students with the intent of promoting a particular ethic towards cultural difference, and for all students to reflect upon their own positionality and engagement with others, was not fully understood by Ronald; but of course he is not alone in this regard. Such a perspective also seems suggestive of an implicit Anglo oversight of the management of cultural diversity reflected so poignantly in Ronald's use of the pronouns: 'their', 'them', 'they' and 'those' to create a clear distinction between non-Anglos and 'their Australian counterparts'. This is despite many of 'them' having been born in Australia, though, in 'their' case, of non-Anglo background. What constitutes 'these' students' 'culture' may, in fact, not be very different from those of their Anglo-Australian peers with traces of their heritage cultures interwoven with the hybrid mix characteristic of many students' lives such that any clear demarcation is relatively artificial. Such understandings around the fluidity of culture, how increasing globalization exacerbates these processes and what the implications of this might be for multicultural education, were all considered in the RMRME training which Ronald didn't attend.

A Lack of Leadership

In fact, there was no executive member on Smithton's team which was comprised of four staff: Giselle and Melody both Kindergarten teachers; Harry, a casual EAL/D teacher and; Hilda, a Year 2 teacher, who led the team. All four were born in Australia, as was Ronald, though Giselle's parents were Greek and Melody had German ancestry. Hilda, Harry and Ronald were of Anglo-Australian background. The lack of executive leadership in the team may have had something to do with the status of multicultural education at the school, but despite this, the team showed a strong commitment to the project and a keen interest in the training. Hilda saw it as an opportunity for 'something you don't get to do as a teacher, to ever sit down and discuss at that level'. Harry similarly enjoyed the intellectual stimulation the training provided. As discussed in Chapter 3, he explained how 'my brain, it hasn't been clicked on for a long while because here you are doing the nitty gritty'. Jade, the DoE consultant working with the team, commented on their level of enthusiasm and engagement with the readings: 'the whole team read them and discussed them and highlighted them. They were really very keen', though this did not seem to prompt any further independent reading. Armed with the ideas from the training, however, the team set about devising a project employing a cycle of action research to guide the process, at least initially.

Persistence Despite Resistance

Smithton's project included a number of initiatives that were loosely termed 'culturally inclusive practices'. The first phase of their action research involved the team collecting baseline data to gauge both teachers' and students' understandings of concepts such as 'multiculturalism' and 'Australian identity', reasoning that this was necessary before pursuing any intervention. They decided to survey Years 5 and 6 students (aged ten to twelve years) in the final years of primary school because, as Harry said, 'that would judge what we've been doing up until now and to see whether we were on track with what we had learnt with our in-servicing through RMRME'. The results of this survey showed students held stereotypical views of Australian identity and aspects of culture. An example that Harry offered was, 'I'm not really Australian because I don't drink beer or go to picnics', with Jade adding, 'you know, all Greek people eat souvlaki and Australian barbecues are only sausages, that kind of thing, very sort of superficial'. Teachers also seemed to have little understanding of notions of culture as pursued in RMRME and, combined with the RMRME survey data that showed 60 per cent of staff hadn't read the Multicultural Education Policy and even greater numbers didn't know if the policy had been implemented at the school, the team decided to embark upon a comprehensive programme of professional development with staff focusing on multicultural education, anti-racism, EAL/D pedagogy and culturally inclusive curriculum.

This was an ambitious exercise given that, with the exception of Hilda, the team included relatively junior members of staff. While the team conducted some of this professional learning themselves, drawing on materials from their RMRME training, Jade also delivered sessions, all of which produced a mixed response from staff. Aware from the outset that their colleagues lacked commitment to multicultural education, the team was measured in how they approached this professional learning. As Melody explained, 'when we've been presenting we are not saying this is what you have to do but these are things to start thinking about.' She felt there were some positive outcomes in that, 'once you get them thinking, and I think having the professional development that we've given them, they've then looked at in a different light and sort of gone, "Oh, OK, well we can do that differently"'. Yet, she admitted there were others who were far less engaged, some people were like, 'Oh we already do it, it's not, you know, why do we have to be taught again. I've been teaching for 20 years and I do it every day.' Jade was damning in her assessment of the staff's response and any prospect of change at Smithton: 'There were holes in their knowledge and they acknowledged holes but they still didn't see they needed to know anything. So, even in the face of evidence, there was a strong sense of I don't want to change what I do because it's going to mean more work for me.'

Despite many of their colleagues' lack of enthusiasm, the team persisted with the project but retooled it to place fewer 'demands' upon members of staff. Their goals of inclusive practice were pursued in various other initiatives such as improving their school's data collection on EAL/D students' language and literacy provision to ensure their needs were met and updating enrolment and orientation processes for beginning LBOTE students. They also revitalized the school's Harmony and multicultural days entering a bilingual film festival about the events and, lastly, devised and implemented a unit of work as an example of culturally inclusive curriculum. In the course of undertaking these activities, the action research component of the project was given less emphasis, the actions themselves taking precedence and subsuming the team's time and energy. Early in the project, when such a large number of initiatives were proposed, Jade and the RMRME team cautioned against doing so many. As Harry mentioned towards the end of the year, 'the RMRME [people]', they were saying, 'nah, too much, too much . . . but we just, yeah, we just did it anyway' with Melody justifying this in terms of 'we all had so many things that we wanted to do'. In effect, RMRME became a vehicle for attending to a number of issues at the school. One of the most pressing, however, of staff rethinking their approach to multicultural education was forestalled by the staff's reception to the professional learning sessions. In response, Hilda indicated, 'We ended up doing nice things.' Given the Years 5 and 6 teachers were resistant to devising a unit of work to counter the stereotypical representations of culture garnered from their survey, Melody and Giselle decided to undertake this aspect of the project themselves. Without access to the more senior classes that completed the survey, they developed and taught a unit of work with their own Kindergarten classes.

'You Don't Have to Be Just That Culture!'

Working with much younger children, Melody and Giselle had to devise ways in which they could deal with complex issues from the RMRME training around the fluidity of culture, its impact on notions of identity and multiculturalism, in simpler terms. Together with Hilda and Harry, they wanted to broach the issue of cultural stereotypes so prevalent among the survey responses of the Years 5 and 6 students and what they saw as the problem of 'pigeonholing'. In fact, they had a preference for the term 'cultural inclusion' over 'multicultural education' for this very reason. As Hilda explained, 'I don't like the word "multicultural education". I like the word "culturally inclusive". Multicultural education, I think, from previous

DoE mindsets brings up a different idea. Multicultural education, to me, when it was first set up, was, as Giselle said, is pigeonholing. It pigeonholes people.'

Designing curriculum for young children to address this, however, was a complex task, and Melody and Giselle had some difficulties in translating these ideas for their Kindergarten students. They decided to focus on the topical theme of 'The Olympics' given their unit was implemented not long after the London Games. But, of course, such a topic, where national boundaries are foregrounded and jingoistic symbolism is rife, could easily just reinforce national and cultural stereotypes, and some of the activities within the unit certainly had the potential to do this. As Giselle explained,

> one activity was for the teachers to go through the class and say, 'OK hands up if you have family members from this country, family members from that country.' And that kept going on and then we'd find the flags and we'd put them down as the category in the graph and then create a class graph and talk about different cultures . . . and so then it led onto the broader discussion 'Hey, we are all one and we all need to celebrate each other's differences.'

Categories of nation and culture are used interchangeably here without Giselle making any clear distinction between the two. In counting countries as cultures, she seemed to reinforce a notion of culture as difference missing the key point that cultures are not so clearly defined and that nations themselves are inherently diverse, both of which an event like the Olympics, premised on competition between nations, makes it difficult to examine. Instead, she wanted to draw these differences together, no doubt linking the Olympic ideal of the unity of nations, discussed with students elsewhere in the unit, with the standard multicultural refrain that 'we are all one and we need to celebrate each other's differences'.

Here the moral imperative of multicultural inclusiveness overrides any intellectual interrogation of culture and nation. When questioned about this, whether she had explained the differences between the terms to her class and how culture was not fixed by nation, she described how, 'Yeah, well basically. . . it was open to interpretation and we always kept saying to everybody, you know, it is not segregating each other's culture, it's letting each other know about similar, like similarities and differences', with Melody adding, 'you know, you don't have to be just that culture, like you can have lots of, you know.' Clearly, Giselle and Melody were trying to grapple with the understandings around culture they met in the training but, given the discursive dominance of culture being so strongly associated with discrete ethnic communities, endemic to multiculturalism, these ideas were lost in translation.

Postscript

The team at Smithton faced various obstacles during their project, but chief among these was the issue of leadership. They had an ambitious range of initiatives they wanted to implement informed by the data from the RMRME survey and that from their own survey of teachers and students. These revealed the need for greater awareness of multicultural education at the school which they hoped to address, among other things, through the teaching of a more inclusive curriculum. The team and their consultant guided the staff through a programme of professional development, but this seemed to exacerbate tensions within the school as to whether or not this was needed. It was at this point that some executive leadership on the team would have been beneficial but, without this, their aim of broadening the uptake of their approach was severely hampered. Designing what they viewed as a culturally inclusive unit of work became solely the responsibility of Giselle and Melody, as Hilda and Harry busied themselves with the other organizational and festive initiatives.

Yet, it was not simply executive leadership that the team required. There was also a dearth of intellectual leadership that, if available, may have assisted the team, and Giselle and Melody in particular, as they tried to formulate a curriculum around the ideas from the training. Given that the RMRME research design precluded academic support after the initial input, the team was reliant upon the expertise of their consultant and developing their own. This was not enough. While, once again, it raises the ethics of second-order action research, namely the extent to which academics should intervene when practitioners are implementing their projects, it also draws attention to the lack of intellectual leadership within schools, such as senior staff to assist with curriculum design who, if lacking the required expertise, can either source what is required or can guide staff in obtaining it. While lacking at Smithton, it seemed far more evident in the two remaining schools to be considered here both of which realized there was a need to rethink multicultural education and the way they approached teaching an inclusive curriculum.

Graham's Point High School: Thinking outside the Square

The first of these schools was Graham's Point, a very large high school in Sydney's north-west with a LBOTE population of just over 50 per cent comprised of mainly Indian, Afghani and Filipino students together with smaller numbers of those of Chinese, Russian, African and Pacific Islander backgrounds. All in all, it was a very diverse mix, though there was a concentration of students of Indian backgrounds, who were themselves very diverse. Elsa, the principal, also described the school's SES as 'a real mixture' ranging from parents who were 'very successful professionals' to 'blue collar workers who struggled financially'. Generally, the area was considered 'aspirational' with the school's catchment including many new, mid-range housing estates – development fuelled by Sydney's expanding population, much of which is derived from skilled migration. Graham's Point also had an ethnically diverse teaching population with approximately 30 per cent born overseas. Mitchell, the deputy principal, who led Graham's Point's research team, described the school as 'very settled', and Amy, a science teacher and member of the team, had a similar view: 'you know, it is quite comfortable teaching here, there is not a lot of conflict.' Despite this, the research team felt there had been a shift in the school in recent times. In response to a question about staff commitment to multicultural education, Deirdre, an EAL/D teacher, and another member of the team, remarked:

> they would say it was multicultural, but they would never think about what that means for the school [that] is never thought about. They would say 'oh yeah, we are a multicultural school, everyone gets on really well', and they do . . . but I think in the last six months, there has been quite a bit of a shift in the playground.

Neelam, a young English teacher on the team, agreed: 'I don't think there is enough focus in the staffroom on multiculturalism, or the issues that arise and I think recently, we are seeing a bit more racial tension in the playground as well and I think a lot of staff may ignore it.' Many on the team felt this shift could be traced back to an incident that had occurred at the school the previous year in which a boy of Anglo-Australian background, in one of the junior years, had been playing around and cut the hair of a girl of Sikh background in his class unaware of the Sikh articles of faith and the ramifications of his actions. While the school acted appropriately, contacting the parents of both students and consulting with members of the local Sikh community who spoke to the boy and provided professional development to staff around these issues, Elsa explained how it had 'brought to the surface' a lot of discontent among students of Sikh background who, up to that time, had not raised any concerns.

Questioning Culture

An additional friction within the school was the casual racism of staff and students directed at students of Afghani background. Elsa commented on one such incident: 'I heard a PE teacher say, "Oh yeah, but these Afghani boys . . ." and I said, "Well, hang on, Peter is not Afghani, and such and such is not Afghani. So, then they are not Afghani, they are just a group of boys you know."' From Elsa's perspective, some staff were too quick to assign certain behaviours to particular groups of students. She commented that any issues that did emerge were far more likely a function of adolescent masculinity than ethnicity, 'just a boy thing'. Yet 'culture' became a convenient explanation and, through repetition, had performative effect, such that Afghani boys became a 'problem'. Another example of this occurred on the day of the team's initial interview, involving students exhibiting the same kind of racialized thinking that the PE teacher had displayed. Mitchell recounted an incident where a group of Year 10 girls (aged fifteen to sixteen years) had accused a group of Year 10 boys of posting derogatory remarks about them on Facebook. He explained how,

> the girls would say to me 'Oh, it's the Afghani boys again, it's the Afghani boys not respecting us. They are looking at us, they are staring at us' and they bring in racial issues there to the extent that one girl said 'Well, I told them they should all go home if they like it over there'. So I am in a conflicted position because I need to show care for a victim, because stuff may or may not have be placed on Facebook, but I am also sitting back thinking 'Hang on, there is another issue here I have to address!'

Such incidents serve to demonstrate not only the prevalence of everyday racism but the ease with which it is reproduced within schools, premised on ethnicized schemas of perception that contort students' and teachers' perspectives on the world. In discussing the reasons for this, Mitchell felt that 'it's maybe a shorthand way of saying things rather than, you know, this boy did this and this boy did that, they find it easier or more appropriate just to put people in groups in schools . . . the Islander boys, the Middle Eastern kids'. Amy was of a similar view but suggested such perspectives stemmed from a grouping tendency inherent in multiculturalism and multicultural education:

> well, I just think in terms of professional development, in the past perhaps as far as addressing multiculturalism in the classroom, it does tend to identify people by groups and you know . . . if a kid is not working or not doing homework it maybe because of their cultural background. You are told to sort of identify what is behind it, which theoretically is based on their cultural background and I was thinking well maybe then professional development around that needs to be more focused on looking at individual students rather than looking at culture.

Once again, 'culture', understood to mean ethnicity or race, does a lot of work here (Yudice, 2003) providing the rationale for educational performance when, in fact, factors such as class, family experience and a myriad of other factors could be the issue. Of course, this is not to suggest that categories of ethnicity and race be dispensed with, but they need to be reconceived to avoid this type of crippling essentialism. As Modood (2007,

p. 115) points out, 'The distinctiveness of a group is neither a fiction nor an essence.... For what is wrong with essentialism is wrong with all theoretical homogenization, abstraction and reductionism. It misses out the diversity, complexity and open-endedness of social phenomena.'

Such 'groupism', and its attendant essentialism, manifested itself in other practices at the school wherein multiculturalism was more associated with some 'groups' rather than others. Expressing concern in relation to this, Reena, the head teacher of welfare and final member of Graham's Point's team, referred to an exchange with a student following the school's Harmony Day: 'I had a girl come up to me and say, "Oh, it's St Patrick's Day on Tuesday, can I do my Irish dance at assembly?" I said, "why didn't you do it at the Harmony Day?" And she said, "Oh, no that's a multicultural thing."' From this student's perspective, multiculturalism was the preserve of particular groups of students, those distinct from the Anglo mainstream, a perspective multiculturalism has often fostered, running counter to the inclusive framing of Harmony Day. Deirdre confirmed such a view among other students of Anglo-Australian backgrounds pointing out how they had said 'it's not about us Miss, Harmony Day, that's not about us'. Reena, Deirdre and the rest of the team raised such instances in light of the discussion around notions of culture and practices of multiculturalism in the training. As Amy remarked, 'What is the definition of culture? I had never even thought about that before.' Reena added, 'And every time something happens, you'd remember the training.' The professional learning, therefore, had led these teachers to question their practice in this area by applying the concepts required to rethink how 'culture' might be understood. The team presented numerous examples in relation to this with yet another exemplifying how assumptions of homogeneity operate within groups erasing, as Modood points out, 'diversity, complexity and open-endedness'. For Reena, this was evident in another student's comments following Harmony Day: 'another boy came and complimented me in Hindi and I said, "sorry, I don't speak it" and he said "you're Indian aren't you?" and I said "yes, but I don't speak Hindi, I come from a different part of India". He said, "no Miss, all Indians can speak Hindi."'

To recap, the research team at Graham's Point was comprised of the executive members, Mitchell and Reena, and another three teachers: Deirdre, Amy and Neelam. Mitchell, Deirdre and Amy were of Anglo-Australian background and Reena and Neelam were of Indian background though these descriptors mask more complex forms of identification that each was keen to discuss, prompted in part by the discussion of ethnic identification within the training. Reena was born in India but had lived in Australia for over twenty years. She described herself as 'the multiple hyphenated definition that we spoke about so Indian-Australian, so I identify with both cultural origins and the land that I've come to very strongly. I am a hybrid and sometimes it causes me great angst that I don't really fit in anywhere but other times it gives me great joy that I can fit in everywhere.' Neelam, on the other hand, was born in Australia and responded, when asked, 'I'll always say Australian', and was constantly frustrated with students who would say 'What "nash" are you Miss?' and wouldn't accept Australian when they found out her parents were born in India, 'but that makes you Indian Miss!' Amy's parents were also migrants but, given they were Anglo-British, she was never questioned about her 'nash'. Mitchell, on the other hand, reflected on being Anglo in the context of multicultural Australia, remarking: 'I often think, what is my culture? I feel non-cultural in a sense and I just wonder whether some of our kids feel that as well.' Deirdre expressed a similar view, 'I don't think of myself as an ethnicity.' Both these comments are indicative of the ways in which 'Anglo' and 'Whiteness' operate as normative categories, devoid of ethnicity or race, placing them outside multiculturalism which is viewed as the domain of Others.

Theory behind the Practice

It was these ideas around the complexities of culture and identification, and related issues, that the team wanted to foreground in their project. The training had led to a questioning of perceptions of culture and how to approach multicultural education which Elsa remarked upon towards the end of the school's project, acknowledging a change in the staff involved: 'the theory and work at those training days, I think they were invaluable for people to think outside the square and to start to think of themselves more as an educator with theory behind the practice.' The team at Graham's Point also found benefit in approaching their project as action research. As discussed in Chapter 3, both Mitchell and Deirdre commented on the value of using data to guide their practice and pursued this principle throughout their project. They took note of how a majority of their teachers in the RMRME survey agreed that racism was a problem in schools and conducted their own staff survey and found there was a similar result if teachers were asked about racism at Graham's Point. An additional finding was a concern that some students were tending to weaponize the term 'racist', using it against teachers and other students to deflect attention away from their own behaviour, a strategy Keddie et al. (2013) identify in their study of Aboriginal students who recognized the power in wielding such accusations. The team also surveyed students around these issues and, while fewer felt that racism was a problem at the school, a good number did feel that the term 'racist' was used to 'hurt, embarrass or provoke'.

Given these findings, the team felt it was best to address these issues in their project with a focus on improving intercultural understanding, though not by implementing lessons in units of work within specific subject areas but as an interdisciplinary programme of study taught by teachers from across the curriculum. As is common in Australian high schools, additional time is often allocated at the beginning of the school day during roll call to target various issues, either devoting time to reading to improve literacy or matters related to behaviour such as learning conflict resolution techniques. There had been some staff discussion around rethinking how this time might be better used at Graham's Point, and the team decided to devote five weeks over one term to a programme they devised around promoting intercultural understanding. As the time they had to work with was quite short, fifteen to twenty minutes, three days a week over five weeks (other matters were dealt with on the other two days), they decided to develop a curriculum resource for teachers to implement to ensure the best use of this time. What eventuated was a programme targeting five topics: 'Identity', 'Breaking Down Barriers', 'Migration and Refugees', 'Understanding and Respect' and 'Reflection and Action', involving three lessons for each. The resources the team produced included teacher notes to assist with delivery and a student booklet of activities. The programme targeted Years 8 and 9 students (aged fourteen to fifteen years) with twenty teachers, including Neelam, involved in its delivery. The first topic, 'Identity', explored how various factors shape identity, with ethnicity being one of a number and how problems of essentializing may occur when any one of these is foregrounded. This led onto the second topic exploring matters such as racism, prejudice and stereotypes through short but meaningful activities involving critical examination of media representations, discussion of personal narratives and contemplating scenarios involving stereotypes and racism. Together with the content and activities of the other weeks, the team's approach to inclusive curriculum was not about examining 'cultures' as discrete phenomena through a moralizing ethic of simply respecting difference, but to have students consider the complex interplay of factors constitutive of identity and to critically reflect upon forms of exclusion associated with ethnic, racial and cultural difference.

Overall, the team was pleased with the programme though its implementation did not go exactly to plan. Many of the activities generated far more discussion with students than was anticipated, and so the programme was extended for a further three weeks. This, of course, was a pleasing development and a measure of both staff and student interest in the programme's content and approach. Reena, for example, explained how 'there were some staff who were very positive. They would offer extra insights and resources. They would email all the staff and that was very, very positive and very heartening to see that kind of reaction.' While valuing this anecdotal evidence, the team was focused on the action research methodology underpinning their project and the need for more objective data to evaluate its effectiveness. As Amy pointed out, 'the process we went through in the pre- and post- surveys, sort of trying to find indicators to show, you know, what we did has had an effect, it really helped us to see how effective the program has been and what changes we could make.'

The team, however, did not rely simply on the results of the pre- and post-teacher and student surveys, and so each team member, minus Neelam who was teaching, also undertook observations of different teachers' implementation of the programme to determine, among other things, if the training they had provided at a staff development day to teachers implementing the programme was sufficient. Amy described how 'the feedback we got from the teacher surveys suggested that they didn't feel that they needed any extra training but what we observed, I think, it highlighted to us that although all teachers know that it is their responsibility, I don't know how many are well versed in addressing it'. In addition to the team feeling more training was required, they also felt it would be better to target younger Year 7 students on their entry to high school. The team, therefore, was drawing on the different data sets to not only evaluate the programme but to reformulate it prior to re-implementing it the following year, cognizant that changing perceptions and practice was a long-term process. As Mitchell commented, 'we knew that running the project wouldn't have that impact straightaway. It is something we are going to look at again for next year and hopefully it becomes a habit of the school that every year is run in some way. Then it might have an impact on the school.'

Postscript

The team at Graham's Point realized they were playing the long game with their project. They wanted to modify the school's approach to multicultural education by implementing a programme promoting intercultural understanding taught by teachers from across the curriculum. While developing an effective teaching resource, its implementation raised some questions about teacher training. Through the data they collected, they realized that teachers needed far more preparation to implement what they had devised. The training the team had received themselves had, in Elsa's words, encouraged them 'to think outside the square'. They were now questioning categories such as culture, ethnicity and identity and were considering the implications of this for multicultural education. The teachers implementing the programme, however, received far less training. Mitchell and the team thought their teaching notes would supplement any shortfall in this regard. Realizing this was not the case, they hoped to address this as they revisited the programme for implementation in the following year, equipped with the tools of action research to gauge its success and to undertake further revision.

Hingston Valley High School: From Cultural Diversity to Cultural Complexity

The final school to be considered here is Hingston Valley, a large boys' high school in one of Sydney's inner suburbs. Hingston Valley had a LBOTE population of 83 per cent with a large concentration of students of Chinese, Korean, Indian, Sri Lankan and Arabic-speaking backgrounds, and a smaller number of those of Pacific Islander, Turkish, Aboriginal, Afghani and African backgrounds. Approximately 2 per cent of the students were refugees, primarily from Afghanistan, Sierra Leone and Somalia. It was a very diverse student population that spoke over sixty-four different languages or dialects. Tony, the principal, explained how 'there is a great intermingling within this school'. He was proud of Hingston Valley's ethnic diversity and the valuing of cultural difference that he felt characterized the school. While he mentioned that students could exhibit 'a bit of chauvinism about their own culture', he contrasted this with what he saw as the 'tribalism and antagonism' of some neighbouring schools which Hingston Valley actively worked against. Tony considered the school was 'largely working class' and, while there were students whose families struggled financially, according to its ICSEA, the school was more in the mid-SES range. Parents had high aspirations for their sons' education. Tony viewed this as a function of migrant drive explaining how 'They often come from migrant backgrounds where they are extraordinarily focused on improving the outcomes of the younger generation and that makes it really easy to teach'. The school put a strong focus on academic achievement though this was not at the expense of broader educational concerns. Ekaterina, one of the members of Hingston Valley's team and new to the school, commented: 'It's a very positive culture at the school, it is quite academic . . . they are not dumbing things down, they are always trying to enhance the boys' education with sport as well.' Tony also referred to how parents were now far more open to their sons' involvement in the performing arts such as through dance and drama giving one such example: 'last year we had an Indian dance group of three boys in Year 10 and they've danced twice in assembly to incredibly enthusiastic applause and I don't believe many years ago that would have gone down to the same degree.'

The teaching staff at Hingston Valley were similarly diverse with just over 40 per cent having migrated to Australia, with the greater number from South Asian countries. To cater for the many students requiring English language support, the school had a large EAL/D department of six staff. With such linguistic and ethnic diversity within the school, of students and staff alike, it seemed little wonder when asked about the school's commitment to multicultural education that Patrick, the head teacher of history who led the team, remarked: 'Here it is pretty much front and centre' referring to the 'two prongs of multicultural education which is ensuring outcomes and achievement across all cultures you've got at the school and developing cultural harmony'. This was a view that Pallav, another member of the team, shared: 'Basically the main goal is to improve academic performance and to live amicably and peacefully.' The school's emphasis on academic performance and ensuring its many EAL/D students acquired the requisite English language proficiency to achieve this satisfied the first of the 'two prongs of multicultural education' to which Patrick referred. In relation to the second, around cultural harmony, the school was very focused on one of the key tenets of multiculturalism, that of cultural recognition. This was achieved through the observance of various cultural and religious events such as Diwali and Eid together with Harmony Day and NAIDOC week and those engaging with diversity more broadly such as through the 'Wear It Purple Day', in recognition of LGBTQI communities, and International Women's Day. The school had a strong social justice agenda and encouraged a broad acceptance of cultural difference. There was little tolerance of racism with Keya, another member of the team, explaining how 'we are pretty harsh on those people who are, sort of, bullying in the playground, having fights based on racial terms. We sort of nip it in the bud. It is a priority so that there is no place for racism.' Given the apparent success of the school, it is interesting that they wanted to commit to a project to rethink multicultural education. It was a decision, however, that aligned with the school's approach to professional development, involving a desire to constantly review practice. Prior to commencing their project, Patrick reflected on aspects of the RMRME training: 'On the first day, I did start to think about the way in which we teach culture to kids at school and I wonder if, with culture, we probably need to start moving towards a more complex way of thinking about it.' It was such a perspective that came to frame Hingston Valley's project, moving from an emphasis on cultural diversity to that of cultural complexity in a cross-curriculum initiative designed to challenge students' conceptions of culture, ethnicity and identity.

Embracing Complexity

Many of those who opted to join Hingston Valley's team have been mentioned. Together with Patrick, there was Ekaterina, Pallav, Keya and Rahima. With the exception of Rahima, a science teacher, the team taught humanities and social science subjects. Patrick, as with Tony, the principal, was of Anglo-Australian background though both preferred to say 'Anglo-Celtic' to acknowledge their Irish ancestry. As Patrick pointed out, 'I call myself Anglo-Celtic Australian. I do like the Celtic to be included. I think it is inaccurate to totally exclude that. I feel very Celtic in many ways.' The coupling of 'Celtic' with 'Anglo' is in itself recognition of the complexity inherent in the category 'Anglo' that generally ignores any differentiation. It operates as a term inclusive of all those that Ang (2001, p. 98) suggests might be part of 'old Australia' in an assimilatory move that erases difference and simply foregrounds Whiteness. Other members of the team were either migrants or children of migrants. Rahima, born in Iraq, referred to herself as 'Iraqi-Australian'; Pallav, born in India, identified as 'Indian-Australian'; Keya said she was 'a Fijian-born Indian'; and Ekaterina, born in Australia to Greek parents, referred to herself as 'Greek-Australian'.

Most of the team, therefore, had direct experience of the impact of migration and the difficulties that resettlement poses. Tony explained how the staff as a whole were 'from diverse cultural backgrounds themselves. All of those teachers bring with them a history of challenge and a history of overcoming odds in their own careers and that makes them far more sympathetic and sensitive to the needs of the learners in their classrooms.'

This may be the case, but such empathetic understanding is insufficient in assisting students to better understand the cultural complexity of the contemporary world. It is reliant on far more than a teacher's ability to simply share such experience; they must be able to interrogate it intellectually concomitant with their role as a professional. While, Tony pointed out, the team found the training 'intellectually demanding', they embraced the challenge of applying the ideas they had discussed. Ekaterina commented on how it was 'challenging us to think about what we understand by culture and so I think I needed to hear that before I went away and worked on a project. I was glad I was there for that.' In addition to drawing on these ideas in the school's project, Patrick recounted how he found an immediate application for them in his own teaching: 'I deal with immigration history in Year 10 every year and I reckon I've taught it a little bit better in the last couple of months than I've taught it previously because I've really encouraged the kids to be a little bit more complex in their thinking.' As well as broadening their conceptions of culture, Patrick referred to other benefits of the training:

> a big part of it is to do with the fact we're got five people in the school who have been trained in a formal method of piloting programs and evaluating it as in using data to evaluate, which means the school can basically run a pilot program and anyone of this team could be the chair of the program and coordinate the evaluation of it and have much better skills than we probably had before.

Armed with this greater understanding, and the tools of action research, the team set about developing their project.

The 'Wow' Factor in Evaluating Practice

Patrick summed up the school's project in the following way:

> Our project was designed to test the idea that by giving explicit good teaching of a more sophisticated understanding of culture, multiculturalism, cultural interactions and the fluid nature of culture, could we pass on some of these concepts to students and then in pre- and post-surveys and focus groups actually measure an improvement in general understanding in the sophistication of these ideas.

The team put a focus on the explicit teaching of this knowledge rather than just relying, as they state in their report, on 'informal cultural exposures in the development of values and cultural understanding'. This is in contrast to the comments of Dina, at Wollami Lakes, who was of the view that 'the best way to teach culture is to live amongst it'. To the team at Hingston Valley, this was no guarantee for understanding culture. They were not so much teaching culture as teaching about it and referred to the importance of their students developing 'a metalanguage to aid them in their descriptions of the multicultural society in which they engaged'. This would allow students to decode the taken-for-granted nature of culture, examine it as a set of practices and understand its potential to both fix and flow into various forms. At Hingston Valley, this metalanguage was comprised of terms such as 'culture', 'ethnicity', 'identity', 'intercultural understanding', 'stereotypes' and 'multiculturalism', and while we could add more, the words the team chose acted as an effective toolkit for interrogating culture with their students. As Rahima said, 'It was one of our findings that they knew what they wanted to express but now they have the tools to actually express that. They have the language to express what they are actually thinking.' The team used these terms in examining the following topics: 'Globalization and its Effects on World Cultures'; 'The Complex Exchange of Cultural Practices and Values in a Multicultural Society'; 'The Experiences of Migrants to Australia post-World War Two'; 'The Investment in Cultural Diversity'; 'The Value of Intercultural Dialogue'; 'The Changing and Fluid Nature of Cultures and UNESCO's Role in Preserving Cultural Diversity'. Lessons related to these topics were taught across English, history and geography to Year 10 students (aged fifteen to sixteen years) over a ten-week term. Forty-two of these students, who undertook all of these subjects, formed the target group completing pre- and post-surveys of their knowledge of the content and participating in focus groups around their broader discussion. The team was aiming for saturation of this exploration of culture even using some similar resources across the different subjects. They found the extract from the UNESCO report, *Investing in Cultural Diversity and Intercultural Dialogue*, that had been used in the training, useful in their work with students.

The team discussed their cross-curriculum approach as a programme of 'content integration', one of the five dimensions of Banks' model of multicultural education but, the content the team chose to integrate, was very different to that proposed by Banks. From his perspective, content integration 'deals with the extent to which teachers use examples and content from a variety of cultures in their teaching' (Banks, 2009, p. 15). As we have seen with Barnett and other schools, some forms of cultural recognition can be quite reductive, portraying cultural forms as static and discrete phenomena that can all too easily reproduce cultural stereotypes. Banks (2009) has noted these tendencies if content integration is approached in this way. These issues, however, are not always foregrounded in accounts of his model which has wide currency (Banks, 2019), and so problematic applications persist as teachers devise and implement versions of what they see as 'inclusive curriculum' or 'culturally responsive pedagogy' in their schools. The team at Hingston Valley took a different approach. The content they were integrating across the curriculum was not specific to any national or ethnic 'culture'; it was content designed to unpack conceptions of culture, to equip their students with the necessary intellectual resources to understand its complexities in the contemporary world; what they chose to call a form of 'cultural literacy' and which we have termed 'cultural intelligence'. Ekaterina spoke, for instance, of the emphasis they placed on the fluidity of culture:

> I think one of the things that we tried to stress in our lessons was the fact that people from different cultures don't stay fixed just because they come from one area and that that is something that's forever changing. We tried to articulate that through the teaching of the units and I think that the boys really grasped that very well.

The team used action research techniques to gauge the extent to which this was the case. Patrick explained how

> one of the good things of our program was the excellent work of the focus groups and Rahima did actual tracking of individual students pre and post. So, it wasn't just, you know, percentages of students, we were looking at individuals and sort of pre and post, but the survey we were able to do that too so we were able to put the kids' comments up pre and post and then compared, like the development on an actual individual level.

The team found examining data in this way enlightening, showing evidence of the impact of their practice. Patrick continued to explain their findings:

> we had a bit of a wow factor at first when we put up the boys' comments. The students were actually quite insightful in many cases. There seemed to be an improvement in sophistication over time, but I just remember looking for the results and going 'Geez', these boys have a pretty good idea of this sort of stuff. . . so rather than just a simplistic answer pre-test, they'd sort of be trying to explain complex concepts, sometimes in a roundabout way, but you could see there was more complex thinking underlying the comment than their initial response.

One example Patrick offered was from a boy of Lebanese background who, in describing his own cultural background, 'went from Lebanese to "I'm Australian of Lebanese background. My religious tradition is Islamic but most of my cultural practices are typical of many people living in

Australia."' Such a shift in this one student's form of cultural identification is pertinent in terms of Tony's earlier comment about the propensity for cultural chauvinism among the boys. By examining culture in this way, and questioning categories such as nation, ethnicity and identity, this boy had moved from a focus on his own cultural difference to also understanding his cultural affinity with others, an important step in countering the excesses of identity politics.

Postscript

The team at Hingston Valley embraced the challenge of rethinking multicultural education at their school. While maintaining aspects of traditional multiculturalism in the observance of various cultural events and promoting the free expression of cultural difference within the curriculum, they sought to examine what such celebrations might mean in relation to broader conceptions of culture and were one of the few teams to consider the global context. Students were encouraged to think of the range of cultural influences constitutive of identity and the impact of globalization as formative in this process. The team was able to translate into curriculum the ideas from the training devising an effective action research project to evaluate its impact. What these teachers exhibited were capacities commensurate with being a professional combining an intellectual orientation to their work with the ability of a practitioner to apply such understandings in practice resulting in meaningful change within and beyond the classroom. As Ekaterina explained in relation to how the boys could apply what they had learnt, 'They need to know this stuff as part of life and we thought that was a really good finding because it showed that they could apply it to the wider world outside of school as well.'

Conclusion

The five schools examined in this chapter all had a focus on inclusive curriculum in their projects but were very different in approach. Like all the schools discussed in this book, they represented different points along the process of professional development and the RMRME invitation to 'rethink' multicultural education. There were specific factors at each school which led to these different points. Each school had their own specific communities and concerns, team dynamics, organizational and intellectual leadership, differing modes of teacher professionalism, different senses of the nature of the wider project and long-term change, and variable investments in conventional understandings of multiculturalism and contrasting levels of engagement with the training and the idea of action research. Yet, it is clear by grouping these schools that the extent to which they had moved along the path of professional development would shape whether their projects would lead to any substantive change in the school and its approach to multicultural education.

Some schools continued to rely on limited forms of cultural recognition and avoided grappling with the cultural complexities of contemporary Australia reproducing cultural stereotypes in the name of inclusion. At Graham's Point and Hingston Valley things were very different. The teams in both of these schools used the opportunity the training afforded to re-envisage how they approached multicultural education, enrolling students and staff in developing a deeper notion of inclusive curriculum and seeing this project as part of a longer process of change based on solid research and rich data. Both schools were able to engage staff and students in critical discussions of ideas, such as culture and identity and the consequences of this for how multiculturalism is practised in countries like Australia. These schools were embracing the idea of 'cultural intelligence', a beneficial foundation for the development of a robust sociocultural knowledge needed for twenty-first-century schooling. This knowledge involves moving from fixed and essentializing notions of culture to more nuanced understandings that allow for dynamism and complexity that sees global as well as national contexts and replaces reductive emphases on recognition and empathy to more reflexive and critical emphases on the acknowledgement of relations of difference and affinity.

CHAPTER 7

Engaging with Cultural Complexity, Enhancing Professional Practice

In the projects discussed in previous chapters, teachers displayed varying levels of engagement in meeting the challenges of doing diversity differently. This chapter focuses on three very different but highly successful projects where teachers engaged critically with notions of cultural complexity in rethinking how they approached multicultural education. Their work involved innovative practice in the areas of critical literacy, English for Academic Purposes and parent and community engagement. They engaged with diverse logics of multiculturalism without being constrained by reduced forms of these logics, and they also foregrounded critical educational goals. Here, we not only document aspects of each of these projects but examine these teachers' journeys as they came to realize how change was reliant upon the development of their own professional capacities, skills of reflexivity, negotiation with their communities and the importance of viewing teaching as a form of intellectual labour.

Getty Road Public School: Developing Critical Understanding

Getty Road is a large primary school in Sydney's south-western suburbs. The school's LBOTE population was 79 per cent with concentrations of Arabic-speaking students, mainly of Lebanese background, and those of Vietnamese backgrounds with smaller numbers from Chinese, Greek and Italian backgrounds. Getty Road had few students who were recent arrivals.

The school was of a mid-SES, comparable to that of Graham's Point, yet the families at Getty Road tended to be second- and third-generation migrants in contrast to the more recently arrived, skilled migrants at Graham's Point. Veronica, who was the acting principal at the beginning of the year while Isla, the permanent principal, was on leave, referred to the school as 'comfortable' and Getty Road as 'the school of choice in the area'. This was largely due to the school's gifted and talented programme. As Sarah, the deputy who led the school's research team, explained, 'we have enrichment classes from Stage 1 to Stage 3 [this includes Years 1-6], that's why I think the parents really want to get their children into the school.' In her short time at Getty Road, Veronica said she was 'struck by the parents' extremely high expectations for academic achievement'. A similarly strong commitment to the school and students' education was evident among staff, with Veronica remarking: 'It's an incredibly happy school. I've never walked into a staffroom with such a positive energy. The staff appear to be very hardworking and very sincere in wanting to do the very best for students.'

With generations of migrants having attended the school, Getty Road had a long tradition of multicultural education, yet many on staff were weary of the annual multicultural day and felt a fresh approach was needed. Such concerns were raised by Isla on her return from leave. Her remarks critiquing the trivializing emphasis on 'spaghetti and polka' are quoted in the Introduction. She felt an approach with 'more in-depth understanding' was needed. This was a view shared by members of Getty Road's team, such as Fiona, a Year 3 teacher, who felt that

> we already have the multicultural day with the dress-ups and the food, so we want to do something deeper than just surface level. Otherwise, if I was an Aussie, I would be coming to school in my flip-flops and bikini, eating lamingtons and meat pies. So, it is not who we are really, so we want to go a bit deeper.

Sorcha, who taught a Year 5/6 composite class and was also a member of the team, saw little pedagogic value in the traditional multicultural day: 'we all just get all happy on multicultural day? Personally, I don't think that works. I don't think that kids of a young age understand, they just think it's a day of lots of food and it's lovely but in terms of an actual lesson being taught from it . . . nah.' Sorcha felt it was important to continue with the school's multicultural day as it evoked a 'great sense of community', but, within the classroom, she wanted students to develop a better understanding of the nature of Australia's cultural diversity and the patterns of migration that have contributed to it. In particular, she wanted to address the kind of anti-immigrant sentiment evident within the broader community. There seemed little point in simply celebrating diversity if the media and public debates were saturated with antagonistic commentary. A bland celebration of cultural difference masked a range of issues that Sorcha felt students needed to consider:

> The biggest problem I see in the community and in the papers, the media, everything is more of that 'why are you here?', 'why are you in our country?'. You know that, 'go back to where you came from view'. So, I think if we are going to tackle the problem with multiculturalism, it would be perhaps explaining the reason why people need to leave their countries, the circumstances behind it rather than 'let's be warm and fuzzy'.

Multicultural days, as they had been celebrated, had not really captured the cultural experience of many of the students. Most had been born in Australia, and, while it is important to acknowledge their families' cultural heritage, students also need to understand the ways in which this contributes to a complex mix of what constitutes Australia as part of a broader global culture. Peddling stereotypes of 'flip-flops, bikinis, lamingtons and meat pies' does little to assist students understand the complexity of culture in Australia and how it is lived. As Fiona pointed out, 'it is not who we are really.' It was these ideas, with an emphasis on developing students' critical capacities, that the team at Getty Road chose to focus on in their project.

'It's Made Us All Very Buzzing with Interest'

In addition to Sarah, Sorcha and Fiona, the other members of the Getty Road team were Sofia, an assistant principal and Kindergarten teacher, Harriet, also a Kindergarten teacher, and Sally, who taught a composite Year 1/2 class. Many of the team, and also the principals, were of Anglo-Australian background with Veronica indicating she was of 'convict stock'. As with Patrick and Tony at Hingston Valley, Sorcha referred to herself as 'Anglo-Celtic'. Her father was Irish and she had lived there through much of her childhood. The only non-Anglo members of the team were Sofia who, with Macedonian parents, indicated she was 'Australian-Macedonian' and Sally, who was born in Korea and described herself as 'Australian with a Korean background'. It seemed even prior to attending the training that the team at Getty Road had a good sense of how they would approach their project. As Sofia commented, 'The main drive for this project was to use something that was useful for our school. It had a purpose and it was going to be something that we could just take away and bring to the staff, sell it to them and something as a useful resource for the school.'

The team saw the training as providing the conceptual framing for this, the tools with which to evaluate the project and 'sell it' to staff and a chance to survey literature that would guide the direction they took. All but Sofia attended the training, which was capped at five participants per school, but she demonstrated the same level of enthusiasm for what it offered, 'It's given us avenues, it's made us all very buzzing with interest. We have access to the university library to get, you know, to read-up on readings and to get all this background knowledge underway so that's very helpful.' The team also considered numerous other readings that were relevant to the approach they intended to take around critical literacy with their DoE consultant, Camille, providing assistance. Sofia commented on how 'we looked at material that was related to critical literacy, looking at ways that a reading program, however it was delivered, could impact on children, their thinking, so that was the material mostly that we looked at to support our project because we wanted to know if we were going on the right track.' Fiona offered more information on this process:

> I found the readings I did were very useful because it also told you what not to do, and they told you . . . I remember one reading specifically told you not to do surface level things like dress ups and food days, and to do critical literacy. They said that was the best way in and that was research from primary school right up to university, so, I felt I was on the right track.

In addition to engaging in this professional reading, members of the team sought further information on how to conduct action research. Harriet, for example, joked that 'I went and got my Mills' action research textbook off the shelf and was flipping through it and saying, "oh yeah, that's right." So, I was kind of reminding myself of more of the process.' The team saw considerable value in undertaking the project in this way, as Harriet explained: 'We get to find out more about our school, especially if we do it in a systematic way and you can measure it and as action research bring about change, so it forces us to critically look at our school.'

Rising to the Challenge

The team's project, emanating from a logic of incorporation, was to design and implement literature-based units that foregrounded the development of students' critical literacy skills. The units were taught across the classes of four team members: Harriet with Kindergarten, Sally with a Year 1/2 class, Fiona with a Year 3 class and Sorcha with a Year 5/6 class, spanning most of the years of the primary school and connecting to a critical application of the logics of recognition and civility. Each class studied a number of texts with themes relevant to the promotion of intercultural understanding, drawing on a range of other material such as newspaper reports to supplement their examination of the literature under focus and, with the more senior classes, to engage with current debates around immigration and refugees. Despite working with primary school-aged students, the team wanted to challenge them by considering some complex ideas. Sorcha explained that 'the concept of culture is so ambiguous and difficult, so we found that the older grades grasped on to it quite quickly and you know, I mean even adults have trouble defining that, but they were giving it a go and they were really, you know, hitting some good concepts'. Fiona wanted her students to conceive of culture in broad terms rather than its narrow equation with ethnicity:

> Culture encompasses everything you do in your life, not just food or clothes but what you read, what you watch on TV, who your friends are, the choices you make, what you do on the weekend, the sports you play, you know, just everything. That's the way I taught it to my children and they did start to understand it, yeah.

It was this conceptual understanding, and students' development of critical capacities in examining issues around multiculturalism, that the team sought to promote, with Sorcha adding:

> If you take the superficial take on it, like at the beginning of the unit the kids are, especially if they are clever, they are pre-programmed to say what the teachers want to hear. 'Is multiculturalism good? Oh yeah, multiculturalism is great. Oh yes, it's about accepting each other and blah, blah, blah . . .' but, I felt the critical literacy meant people were speaking honestly and it wasn't superficial, 'yes, let's all hold hands and be friendly.'

What Sorcha and the team were aiming for was to move beyond the kind of unreflexive civility that they felt characterized some forms of multicultural education – blandly prizing cultural diversity without interrogating the challenges it poses. Developing skills around critical literacy enabled the students to approach such issues as an analytical exercise rather than one that was emotive and moralizing.

The topics and texts that were chosen for study varied and were very much tailored to the age and ability of the students in each class. With the two younger groups, Harriet and Sally focused mainly on examining cultural similarities and differences, laying the foundations for more complex treatment of topics in later years. Harriet felt that 'If you are exposed to this kind of language and this kind of talk and those kinds of books from Kindy, you know, in our simplistic way that we did it, all the way up to . . . by the time they get to Year 6, I really think it would honestly make a difference'.

With her class of older children, Fiona chose to focus on refugees:

> They weren't really very aware of the notion of boat people, they don't really watch the news at that age but I still felt it important to teach them about refugees because they sure will no doubt hear about refugees in the future and I don't want them having preconceived notions that

other people might have that they are taking over, they are taking all our welfare or whatever. I want them to understand from a young age what a refugee is and the difficulty they have.

Students spent a lot of time examining a range of texts. Sorcha, who also examined the plight of refugees with her Year 5/6 class, referred to how they were 'analysing articles, we were looking for emotive language, what is the aim of this journalist, what are they doing?' Sorcha detailed one lesson with her Year 5/6 class:

> the kids were writing interviews, a media interview where they were interviewing a refugee and they had to make it very clear whether or not they were going to have a negative slant on the interview or a positive slant on the interview and they did it all in the language, like you know, oh in these traumatic circumstances, you know, really loaded words and we looked at different stories, and they started to realize when they were being persuaded and you know, just to take it on facts.

Sorcha's teaching of this unit actually coincided with a riot that occurred in Sydney at this time sparked by a film purporting to depict images of Mohamed. She explained, 'It was great, well it wasn't great, but the riots in Hyde Park happened right then when we were teaching it and I remember I heard it on the weekend "Oh God, oh God, I'm teaching this!"' Rather than avoid classroom discussion of this controversial event, Sorcha decided to make use of it with her class: 'we tried to get as much information as we could about it, we tried to get rid of all the crap and just find out what happened.' To Sorcha's surprise it resulted in some interesting discussions between students and their parents. She recounted how one girl questioned her father's critical take on the event with him suggesting the protestors needed to go back to where they came from, and her mother supporting her daughter's stance. Sorcha reported how 'Mum came to tell me, [I was] talking to parents and Mum thought it was brilliant, especially that kid, [Samantha], because Dad was a Romanian refugee and she said, "I don't get it either, he's a Romanian refugee, but it's different because they are different," and Samantha launched into him about that.' Samantha's mother explained how there was a lively family debate with her daughter able to make a strong argument based on a detailed understanding of the event studied in class. Her father backed down and recognized he needed to take a more measured view of what had transpired at the riot and the reasons for it. While such anecdotes attest to the impact of the work Sorcha and the other teachers were conducting, this was also borne out by the data they collected from focus groups and work samples indicating marked improvement in these students' understanding of these issues.

An additional element of the Getty Road project, for which Sarah and Sofia were responsible, involved ensuring parents were kept abreast of what was occurring in their children's classrooms. Sofia referred to how we got in touch with the parents regularly throughout the term. We outlined each of the units to the parents and we showed them exactly what the children were doing and we invited them to the classrooms and one of the parents who attended Fiona's little workshop said it was just so wonderful being part of the classroom to see how engaged the children were.

The team also sought parent input regarding increasing community involvement with the ensuing result: 'So, their advice for us is to invite more parents and have the project implemented school-wide and involve them in some capacity whether it's telling short stories, short experiences about their livelihood, their backgrounds that would encourage more involvement in some ways.' Given a number of the parents, especially those of Vietnamese backgrounds, had been refugees this provided another source of information that teachers could draw on in their units in the following year and, for older students, it would serve as an important point of contrast between Australia's past and present policies regarding refugees.

Postscript

Both Isla, the principal, and the team were keen to infuse Getty Road's approach to multicultural education with far greater depth than had been the case in the past. While they felt it was important to continue to celebrate the school's ethnic diversity through their annual multicultural day, they realized students lacked understanding about why it was held. They were also concerned about some of the understandings it generated, cultural stereotypes that were unhelpful in assisting students to comprehend culture as lived and the various factors that contribute to this. The team was also cognizant that a celebration of ethnic diversity needed to be coupled with consideration of the challenges diversity poses, hence their examination of public debates around refugees and immigration and how living with difference may involve compromise and a willingness to accept the unfamiliar. Importantly, this was not simply broached as a matter of empathy. In the more senior classes, in particular, the focus was on developing students' critical capacities, interrogating texts to differentiate fact from opinion and the importance of this for students in understanding issues.

As well as depth, the Getty Road project was characterized by its breadth. Despite the complexity of the issues they were dealing with, the team felt students from Kindergarten to Year 6 needed to engage with them. The texts that were studied and the knowledge and skills that were foregrounded may have differed across the four classes, but there was an overarching framework and pedagogic direction informed by the professional reading the team had undertaken ensuring a certain commonality in approach. Even Harriet could remark that 'my Kindergarten children understood more about what multicultural day was about and why we were having it, having done the unit'. Breadth was also evident in the way in which the team kept parents informed about the project and sought their guidance for future iterations of the units, intent on expanding their role within this curriculum initiative so students could develop a better sense of the nature of the diversity of their community. In reflecting on their efforts over the course of the year, the team felt they had achieved much but were aware that it was unfinished business. As Sorcha explained, 'It is more than scratching the surface, and I know it is very difficult with multiculturalism to do something meaningful, and it's awkward and you don't want to offend anybody and it's hard, but I really do think that we've done something quite good.'

Harringvale High School: Breaking Cultural Assumptions

Harringvale HS is a very old school in Sydney's south-west with a long tradition of academic excellence associated with its gifted and talented program. As with other schools with similar programmes, Harringvale had experienced considerable change in its student population over the last twenty years due to increasing numbers of skilled migrants, primarily from Asia, seeking to secure enrolment for their children which is dependent upon performance in competitive entrance exams. From what was once a predominantly Anglo school, Harringvale was 83 per cent LBOTE with most of these students of Chinese, Vietnamese and Indian backgrounds. Not only was its LBOTE population much higher than neighbouring high schools, the ethnic mix of these students was also very different, as was their SES which is comparable to that of Graham's Point. As indicated, students at Harringvale were predominantly of various Asian backgrounds compared to the greater number of Anglo, Pacific Islander and those of Arabic-speaking backgrounds at other non-selective schools in the area. For this reason, Harringvale had the reputation of being an 'Asian' school reflecting the skew in demographics evident in other selective schools (Ho & Bonnor, 2018). This phenomenon of Asian educational success and an associated Anglo anxiety related to it are well documented within Australia (Ho, 2020; Watkins, 2017; Watkins & Noble, 2013) and elsewhere within the Anglosphere (Cui, 2015; Francis et al., 2017; Lee & Zhou, 2015). At Harringvale, tensions around these issues certainly emerged in discussions with teachers, parents and students earlier in the project centring on perceptions of the school within the local area and how this impacted relations between students at the school (Watkins, 2017). Karin, the principal, and members of Harringvale's team, commented on these matters, though they weren't foregrounded. Louise, an English teacher and member of the team, referred to how 'we've got to try and kill that kind of separate, that cultural aspect which separates, or discriminates Asians from non-Asian backgrounds', but all seemed to see this as more of an issue outside the school than within. Rather than giving this their focus in their project, Alice, the head teacher of English and leader of the team, felt that 'Maybe, that's another project'.

Instead, Harringvale's team chose a different aspect of multicultural education to explore related to issues of equity and English language provision. As Karin pointed out,

> we are very strong in maths and science but we do need a lot of support around oral skills and literacy.... Just because you are in a gifted, selective setting doesn't necessarily mean, and you happen to be multicultural, doesn't mean that you are going to sail through the door. So, I mean English, and advanced English, are always challenges for our kids, they really struggle with it.

The team shared this view. As Julie, an executive member on the team, explained, 'It's a massive issue for us' – a perspective borne out by the results of the school's RMRME survey where staff rated this aspect of multicultural education as the most important area of need for LBOTE students. The team used this data to guide how they approached their project, particularly given the broader RMRME project was about addressing issues of multicultural education specific to individual schools. While a focus on English language and literacy may seem an odd choice in such a high performing school, the team felt the stereotypical image of the successful Asian learner masked the fact that many had issues with academic literacy that were not being addressed. They wanted to ensure their LBOTE students moved from what they saw as the limitations of basic interpersonal communication skills to the greater command of English associated with cognitive language academic proficiency (Cummins, 2008). The staff, as a whole, may have recognized this but doing something about it was another matter. As Julie pointed out, they needed 'to break the cultural assumption here that because we are a high performing school, they can just do it and I don't need to teach it'. The team wanted all staff to see academic literacy as their responsibility and felt they could model such an approach given they were, themselves, drawn from various faculties.

The Benefits of Professional Learning

Together with Alice and Louise from the English faculty and Julie who taught history and legal studies, the other members of the team were Sylvia from maths and Eun-Jung who taught Japanese. Alice and Julie were of Anglo-Australian background, though Julie's mother had migrated to Australia as a teenager from Wales. Lauren saw herself as 'Australian', though her father's parents had migrated to Australia from Czechoslovakia, Sandy was born in the former Yugoslavia but identified strongly as 'Australian' and Eun-Jung was born in Korea but had lived in Australia for twenty years, describing herself as, 'I am kind of half-way you know'. The multidisciplinary nature of the team was important for the project they wanted to pursue around academic literacy. Sylvia highlighted this in her comment: 'Even though I'm a maths teacher, I do think it's my responsibility as well to push that side of things because I think it's like a whole community thing to do together.' Sylvia was similarly enthusiastic about the professional learning component of the project, not only that provided in the initial training but what the team itself would organize over the course of the project. She explained how 'I want to do professional learning as well because I've just started in my career and I think the more knowledge I can get the better I can make my classroom teaching'. As there was no EAL/D teaching expertise within the school, which the team considered necessary to inform their project, they sought the advice of Pamela, their DoE consultant. While the team had a broad interest in improving their students' academic literacy, they felt they needed to narrow their focus for the purposes of the project and so decided to concentrate on the texts and grammar of the genre of explaining which they saw as a particular concern. The team engaged in their own professional learning in this area, guided in the process by Pamela. As Alice explained, 'she has certainly given us relevant readings, things that she's found from sort of the National Curriculum in terms of looking at explain texts. Passed on other readings to us, suggested approaches.' The team also made full use of their access to the university library. Alice had 'used the university library to download quite a few readings' and Louise set up a site as a repository for these and others that the team drew on to refine their approach over the course of the year and through cycles of curriculum implementation. Louise explained: 'reading through some of the literature definitely affected the way that I approached it the second time around. It is more critical thinking and how you engage with it that's important.' Julie agreed: 'the academic readings helped you be reflective, and that's what I think, if you didn't do that reading you would be sitting here puzzled and maybe keep trying the same thing over and over again without going, oh well look at the steps this book is telling us to take.'

The team also embraced their initiative as action research. While, as with many other teams, they found it, in Alice's words, 'very challenging' and Julie, 'overwhelming', this did not deter them. In fact, prior to commencing their project, Julie said she was 'excited about the practical application of it'. The team understood they were not simply implementing an initiative but were researching its effectiveness and they needed to think carefully about how they would do this. As Louise explained, 'we keep thinking in the back of our minds, we need to have something that we can analyse because we need to collect data, we want to see a change and how are we going to see that change in the data.' Pamela, who had been involved in a number of action research projects over many years, was impressed with the team at Harringvale:

In all the action research projects that I've been involved in, Harringvale has been the school that has involved themselves in the process the most. I think they really took that on board. They got the whole idea of it being an academic process and in the fact that it didn't matter if not all the kids improved at the end but some kids improved through explicit teaching but that made them happy because that was part of their action research to see how well did we go. Let's evaluate what we do, did it work? No, it didn't work all the time, it worked if we did this, therefore we've learnt something from it.

A Common Goal of Attainment

Drawing on the literature and the principles of action research, the team set about implementing their project. This was undertaken with two Year 8 classes of students (aged thirteen to fourteen years) who were taught units of work concurrently across maths, Japanese, history and English that took a similar approach to teaching explanation but which was geared towards the disciplinary content of the four subject areas. Each team member developed their own teaching resources but pursued a similar curriculum cycle of field-building, deconstructing exemplar texts, jointly constructing and then independently constructing texts. The team members met regularly to share resources, build pedagogic knowledge and monitor the progress of their research. This involved the collection of work samples, lesson reflections and classroom observations of each other's lessons. Each team member implemented the curriculum cycle twice, analysing the student data to gauge improvement but also comparing their results with another Year 8 class that was not involved in the project. There was considerable improvement in the target students' writing and the observational data and teacher reflections contributed to a better understanding as to how this was achieved. Throughout their project, the team kept staff across the school updated on their progress and were pleased with the reception. Sylvia referred to how,

> we have shown the importance of it to staff. We have gone back to them a couple of times now and given them updates of how we are going and a lot of them have come back interested. I think it has opened everyone's eyes up too, that we can't have that idea that yes, they are selective kids and they can do it but there is an area that they are lacking and we need to help them to improve.

Pamela had been so impressed with the team's achievements that she asked Alice and Julie to present their results to a gathering of teachers from high LBOTE schools. Julie described the impact of what transpired in the following way: 'Just because they are LBOTE doesn't mean that they can't be extended. So, we broke that mould, that stereotype, that day and so Pamela, Alice and myself we were quite excited by that.'

To some extent, Harringvale's project aligns with what Banks (2009) terms 'equity pedagogy', ensuring all students no matter what their background in relation to ethnicity, race, class or gender are given every opportunity to succeed. Yet, Harringvale's project differed markedly from what Banks and proponents of similar approaches propose which tend to essentialize students' cultural differences tailoring teaching to an assumed ethnicity and a narrow conception of what a student's 'culture' entails. Banks (2009, p. 16), in discussing his approach, explains that an equity pedagogy 'includes using a variety of teaching styles and approaches that are consistent with the learning characteristics of various cultural and ethnic groups'. Such approaches, however, can be highly problematic. They rely on antiquated notions of culture as fixed and unchanging, long since critiqued (Barth, 1969; Bhabha, 2004; Wimmer, 2013), yet still peddled within education to affirm a direct correspondence between ethnicity, culture and a student's propensity for learning. Taking the lead from alternate perspectives on ethnicity and culture within RMRME and focusing more on the pedagogical needs of the content, the team at Harringvale adopted a different approach. As Julie explained, 'it was sort of this idea of, you know, shift away from looking at their ethnicity and thinking well we all have this common goal of attainment and engagement, let's create a culture that supports that instead of it being about, "what's your background, what's my background?"'

Postscript

The shift in focus that Julie describes is not about erasing difference – what Boler and Zembylas (2003) rightly critique as the Denial/Sameness model, drawn from a liberal humanist philosophy of equality. Such a position, in denying difference, obscures the inequalities that may result. Rather, Julie and the team simply encouraged a different orientation to cultural difference. They distanced themselves from any tendency to essentialize their students' ethnicity and instead emphasized the importance of equity in educational outcomes. They realized their students required a better grasp of writing explanatory texts used in subjects across the curriculum. Equity lay in ensuring they acquired this which Julie summed up in the following way:

> in the end, it didn't feel like there was a focus on ethnicity, it was about there is a need that we all have and then we all engage.... The kids always knew it was a multicultural project and never ever said well why aren't I learning about my cultural background? There was this understanding of, we are going to have a culture of being engaged and attain no matter what our background.

Eun-jung agreed, 'it's moved from the ethnicity, where you were born, that kind of stuff and come to realize your culture is all around you and the different things that you do, yeah.'

Wellington Heights Public School: Understanding Culture/Building Community

Wellington Heights is a large primary school in Sydney's western suburbs, with a LBOTE population of 95 per cent, the highest of any of the RMRME schools. Students were mainly from Indian, Sri Lankan, Chinese and Korean backgrounds with a noticeable concentration of those of South, rather than East, Asian backgrounds. Most of these students were children of skilled migrants: doctors, nurses and other health care professionals, accountants and IT workers. The SES of the school community was therefore relatively high and parents placed considerable emphasis on academic achievement. The school itself seemed imbued with a similar ethos. As Gillian, an executive teacher and member of Wellington Height's team, commented: 'I think high expectations would be the way to explain the ethos we have. We have high expectations of ourselves, the community has high expectations, the students have high expectations, so that's a really big driving force behind a lot of the things that we do here.'

The school was certainly recognized as a top performer, with Axel, the principal, indicating that 'Wellington Heights is a school of first choice in the area'. This was a reputation built on a highly committed staff involved in numerous activities to ensure the success of the school. Axel provided strong leadership and was a very hands-on principal. He insisted on conducting all new enrolments himself to not only acquire a sense of his school community but so parents felt acknowledged and welcome at the school. As he explained, 'The reason why I do all the enrolments, and we have a lot of enrolments, is because I learn, I ask questions about students' culture and I learn about where they have come from.' Despite its success, the school was not without its issues. With such a high LBOTE population, Axel explained how the school had to work hard on maintaining relations with parents and community cohesion remarking: 'It ain't easy in a multicultural school in terms of community involvement. We have done so many things in this school to be proud of but we are still not connecting with everyone.' A concern of both Axel and the staff was what was viewed as an excessive focus on academic achievement by many parents. As Jean, an EAL/D teacher and member of the Wellington Heights team, commented, 'Our kids are quite pressured, the Opportunity Class [OC] and getting into selective [high school] and a lot of that stems from the expectations of parents and the pressure that they put on their kids. We need to help parents realize that it is not all about getting into selective you know.'

These aspirations led to many parents enrolling their children in academic coaching after school and on weekends. This was especially for additional and accelerated maths tuition as many felt it was either not adequately taught at school or simply wanted to advantage their children in the highly competitive entrance exams for places in OC classes and selective schools, creating friction between parents and staff. Despite numerous information sessions with parents aimed at addressing this issue and providing assurance about the school's ability to cater for their children's needs, little had changed. Teachers had ongoing frustrations about dealing with what they saw as parents' unrealistic expectations and the difficulties these created, for many, for their children who received mixed messages about their performance in maths. For Axel, this was a key issue within the school community: 'My main challenge is not the academic. My main challenge is to maintain and improve an emphasis on a balanced curriculum . . . getting parents to understand Australian curriculum and schooling and the difference from where they have come from.' This became the focus of Wellington Heights' project with a desire to not only improve parents' understanding of the maths curriculum and what was expected of their children but relations between parents and teachers.

Engaging with Theory

The team at Wellington Heights was led by Isaac, an assistant principal at the school, who had responsibility for learning in the early years and supervising teachers of Kindergarten to Year 2. In addition to Isaac, Gillian and Jean, the team included Caitlin, a Year 2 teacher, and Phoebe, the school librarian. While Phoebe was of Greek background, the remaining members of the team identified as 'Australian' by which they meant Anglo-Australian. This was also the case with Axel, though he pointed out his mother was originally from Malta. The predominantly Anglo background of the team was, therefore, very different to the student population at Wellington Heights. Axel indicated that while there were two teachers on staff of Indian background and a number of others with a LBOTE, the majority were Anglo-Australian. The team, however, was formed from those expressing an interest to be involved and their commitment to the project was evident from the start. Each displayed a strong interest in the RMRME training and what it offered regarding an alternate perspective on how multicultural education was understood and practised in schools. Jean particularly valued, 'the theoretical insights, I think that there is a need for being aware of theories about multiculturalism. I think that's something that we probably didn't know about until the training and it's been quite helpful in the way that, well, I'm thinking about classroom practice.'

Isaac found the readings and discussion a highlight: 'thinking about what culture is, I found that quite powerful.' This was similarly the case for Gillian who indicated that 'it kind of turned my thinking around'. The team began to reflect on how they had previously understood the term 'culture' with Caitlin declaring: 'we all sort of essentialized before in a way.' The training, therefore, prompted the team to think about culture in more complex terms viewing it as a composite of various factors of which ethnicity, itself a variable category, was simply one of a number.

Doing this then led the team to think differently about the nature of their parent body and how to better inform them of the way maths was taught and the need for a balanced curriculum. In discussing this, Isaac referred to,

> the assumptions that we make as teachers and we talked about the Indian culture in the school where there are a lot more different cultures but sort of saying that the parents are focused on academics because they are Indian but they also have sort of well-paid jobs such as doctors or scientists or engineers. So, is it because they are Indian or is it because they've got the education background themselves?

In seeing culture through a different lens and questioning their assumptions, Gillian explained how it allowed for a clearer focus on equity:

> I am not saying that, you know, people completely box people but we do make generalizations and everyone likes to make generalizations . . . but for me it became really, really important that we look at it through that equity issue because once you start to look at equity then all of those factors melt away because you start seeing all of the different groups that make-up our school and you start seeing factors like socio-economics, gender, all of those things come under that bridge of equity and how we can make things equitable.

Together with the reading in the training, the team took full advantage of access to the university library and conducted literature searches in a number of areas. They investigated research on working with parents through community learning programmes and approaches that had been successful elsewhere. They also felt it was important to gain a better understanding of the education systems in the countries of origin of many of their students, concentrating, on those of India and China which would then give them additional insight into parents' perspectives on schooling. Isaac explained how valuable this reading was for the team, the conversations it provoked and the connections they made between this and discussion of culture within the training:

> It was vital because it made us reflect and the more that we read the more we reflected on . . . this idea of putting people into boxes . . . we talked

about the essentialism and breaking things down, I think we realized these are parents first and foremost . . . each one of those parents sitting there wanted the best for their child. As a school, we make assumptions about why parents were putting their kids in tutoring and why they were making them do extra study, but ultimately it was because they wanted to give their child the best chance they could to have at an education.

Isaac then described the process the team pursued in formulating their project and the importance of reflection in refining their approach:

we sort of started exploring and that was the way that our project was really about, it was about us getting the parents to, to train the parents up. But through the process we began to realize that in a way that was almost similar to what we were doing . . . we were again telling parents and we were expecting them to change to meet what we expected. We began to realize that perhaps it needed to be a halfway, we had to meet them halfway. And what really became apparent that it was more about changing values, well not changing values but understanding how values are really strong and you can't tell people to change something, if it is not necessarily part of their values, and that by building a relationship we began to understand where their values were. The parents began to understand our values as a school and it is a system, and it was much easier then to build that mutual understanding and I think that was, personally, the key.

Strengthening Relationships

The action the team decided upon involved conducting six two-hour workshops with parents, discussing their experiences in learning maths, how the teachers had learnt maths and how things had changed with the current approaches to learning maths experienced by the students. Rather than simply offering 'information evenings', which, while well attended, had been unsuccessful in promoting better understanding, teachers and parents worked through the syllabus together and then participated in a series of different maths-problem-solving activities with 'homework' that they undertook with their children and then reported back on at the next session. Gillian described how,

we showed them the strategies that we use and got the parents to do it and then they could see the difference in understanding between doing a kind of rote type of learning compared to something that required a deeper level of understanding and that was a really big moment for a lot of parents and a big moment for us because we realized that it is not a resistance to the methods, it's just that we haven't really explained things before.

Caitlin referred to how 'the parents had such light bulb moments'. Parents came to understand the curriculum much better; they were able to assist their children with their homework and school relations with parents improved dramatically. In the last of the workshops, which were offered a number of times, the parent participants became the 'teachers' and invited another set of parents to participate in the programme, running the session themselves. Attendance rates at these events formed one data set to measure their effectiveness together with surveys and interviews with parents. The team found collecting and analysing data useful for not only evaluating their practice but to provide evidence to the rest of the staff about the value of their approach. This was an aspect of action research that Gillian felt was particularly useful: 'I really like the action research model because it tends to be the most effective way of getting it filtering into the school.'

In the process of conducting these workshops, teacher–parent relations became systematically dialogic, but it also meant that the teachers themselves were reflexive about their own experiences as learners, as socially situated activities, and their assumptions about the parents. Towards the end of the project, Caitlin once again reflected on how her changed perspective on culture had impacted how she approached working with parents:

> In addressing culture, because it is the political and the right thing to do, I think it had a reverse effect because we were grouping them, so I think in trying to do the right thing and to be multicultural and to address culture we've actually – it's had more of a reverse effect because we did group them into particular groups. . . . OK, they are Indian, [now] we just treat them as people.

Gillian also offered her view:

> I just feel a lot more relaxed about the whole thing. I just don't feel that it is as big deal to tell you the truth. I don't know if that's the right thing but it just doesn't come into the foreground for me at all. When I look at parents now I think I just see parents, you know I don't really see Indian parents, and the baggage that might have come with them beforehand. I just see . . . there is a parent that I am going to communicate with to the best of my ability about their child, and about that building of relationships.

Gillian wasn't saying ethnicity didn't matter in people's lives. What she was suggesting, like the Harrington team, was that educational equity wasn't all about seeing issues reductively in terms of ethnicity. Moreover, rather than see parents' culture as an 'obstacle', the team had come to acknowledge the cultural and social contexts of all knowledge.

Postscript

Through conversation and the building of relationships with parents, the Wellington Heights team worked together to build an effective learning community in their school, moving away from limited forms of cultural recognition to practices of negotiation. Ethnicity was not foregrounded in this exchange, simply a willingness to work together which brought with it a reflexivity about each party's own situatedness which in the end led to common ground around ensuring the best for the students at their school. A powerful effect of the project was the enhanced professional capacities that the team felt they attained through their involvement in RMRME. As Caitlin explained,

> because we have changed, I definitely changed as a professional. I definitely had my pedagogy, like my pedagogy has changed, like I am going to do things differently next year with my parents. I just don't know why I haven't thought of it before. They are such a valuable resource and if we have that shared understanding like we are trying to get through this project, I mean half the battle is won.

Conclusion

The projects in each of the three schools discussed here were very different; tailored to what each team saw as the specific needs of their particular context. Yet, despite their differences, the projects, or at least, what informed them and how they were approached, had much in common. As well as a reflexive and critical approach to the logics of multiculturalism, what was most pronounced was how the teams shared a similar professional vision guided by the importance of reading to enhance understanding. The teachers in each of these teams saw their role as not simply being practitioners but professionals, who needed to update their knowledge to inform their practice. The nature of this knowledge is also significant. It was not that which has a narrow instrumental application, which seems to dominate much of teachers' work, but knowledge with an intellectual orientation which led them to question taken-for-granted categories such as culture, ethnicity and, indeed, multiculturalism. While teachers in some of the schools in previous chapters found engaging with such knowledge 'a chore', outside their role or simply had difficulties enacting it within their projects, those at Getty Road, Harringvale and Wellington Heights seemed to relish the challenge and could see the possibilities it offered. As Caitlin at Wellington Heights remarked,

> I love tapping into another side of education and it is a side that we don't do enough, the intellectual side and the reading and the academic side

and I think it's really kind of put a passion back into teaching because it is easy to just go through the motions and I wish I could do it all the time.

At Getty Road, this intellectual orientation to knowledge prompted their team to rethink their approach to multicultural education. They retained their traditional multicultural day but ensured students had a better grasp of why it was celebrated and the nature of Australia's ethnic diversity. They tempered its celebratory focus with units of work that developed students' critical capacities, knowledge of migration and the challenges that confront those seeking asylum. Harringvale's project took a different tack. With the intent of improving their students' academic literacy, their team pursued multicultural education as a matter of enhancing LBOTE students' educational outcomes and, in the process, countering assumptions about Asian learners. In doing this, the teachers' pedagogy was not about aligning their students' educational needs with narrow conceptions of what their ethnicity or culture may have been but with identified skills that need to be mastered in the study of various disciplines. Engaging with their reading, the team began to conceive of culture in more complex terms, alerting them to the problems of ethnicizing educational achievement which, in the case of Harringvale, had masked the difficulties their students were confronting. The intellectual orientation to the way the Wellington Heights' team approached their project led to a completely different perspective on community engagement. Rather than attributing many parents' use of academic coaching for their children to ethnicity, they began to realize the array of factors such as class, education and migration status that informed their decision. This then allowed teachers to reflect upon the processes of essentializing that had clouded their dealings with parents and to fashion an effective community learning programme where parents, teachers and students could work together to develop a better understanding of the curriculum augmenting community relations within the school.

Together with a shared professional vision that led each of their teams to rethink how they approached multicultural education; these schools had other commonalities. Each had a high LBOTE population, were of a relatively high SES and were high performing schools academically. The first of these factors may have meant teachers were far more sensitized to issues of multicultural education and far more ready to reassess their practices in this area. This was certainly the case at Getty Road where they seemed eager to change what had become tired and superficial ways of recognizing the school's cultural diversity. Schools of a higher SES, that are also top performing, similarly tend to have fewer behavioural issues, a factor Isaac acknowledged at Wellington Heights. Given this, these teams may have had more time and 'headspace' to devote to professional development and to think more deeply about issues of multicultural education confronting their schools. Either way, with the exception of Graham's Point and Hingston Valley, what distinguished these schools from most of the others in previous chapters was the ability of their teams to engage intellectually with how multicultural education is practised. These teams were recalibrating their professional vision, moving away from the perceptual schema of 'older' multiculturalism and embracing a scholarly orientation beyond a pragmatic mode of professionalism. They were able to produce meaningful change as a result, effectively engaging with the cultural complexity of their school communities and the broader Australian society. What these three schools showed more clearly with their projects was that it was possible to productively meld the logic of incorporation with the logic of recognition without resorting to reductive schemas of ethnicity, and that they could embrace a reflexive civility (Kalantzis, 2011) that was well aware of the larger cultural contexts of intercultural relations and educational practice.

CONCLUSION
Diversity Done Differently

This book has documented and analysed the RMRME project and the school-based action research that it fostered. The research we conducted was designed to provide an ethnographic study of the field of multicultural education in Australia and of a process of professional development within that field. But it was also designed to promote change and to provide some conceptual and methodological tools for doing that. We asked fourteen schools to 'rethink' multicultural education with us, foregrounding a number of challenges to assumptions about 'culture' in an increasingly globalized and hyperdiverse world. We were interested to see how teachers, as professionals, would respond to these challenges and deploy their existing and developing expertise to 'do diversity differently'. The comment from Mia in Chapter 5, 'you sort of need to continually learn', reminds us that this 'doing' is not a one-off task but an ongoing process of professional growth without which you 'revert to your old stereotypes'. Her comment also reminds us that teaching is a profession which, by valorizing pragmatics over critical reflection, makes 'doing diversity differently' increasingly difficult.

The book has explored this process but sets it in the context of an examination of multiculturalism and multicultural education. In the opening chapters we presented a series of challenges around the popular and professional discourses around multiculturalism, including the conceptual complexity of the idea of 'culture' at the heart of multiculturalism, arguing that these challenges have consequences for teaching practice. These challenges were central to the professional development we offered to teachers, outlined in Chapter 3, and the ensuing practical and intellectual problems of knowledge translation in professional contexts. The remaining chapters provided empirical accounts of the projects the schools devised, implemented and evaluated, with the support of the DoE; not just the content of those projects, but the ways the schools went about their task of 'grappling with complexity'. The insights from these case studies, and the laudable but uneven efforts of schools to rise to these challenges, provide valuable lessons on how we need to rethink both multicultural education and professional learning. The acknowledgements that open this book thank all the principals, teachers, students and parents who participated in the RMRME research project. In this concluding chapter it is important to acknowledge again the willingness and candour of educators in reflecting not only on the issues we posed around multiculturalism but on professional practice and the degree to which change is required in reimagining multicultural education.

Rethinking Multicultural Education

A frequent criticism of multiculturalism has been that its meaning is unclear. This semantic confusion is in itself a significant issue in public and popular discourse, not least because, without a clear agreement about what is being discussed, public debate and policy enactment can be at cross purposes. Some scholars subsequently argue that there are many multiculturalisms (Colombo, 2015). We suggested that this was in part related to the fact that multiculturalism is constituted by an array of programmes and goals that represent competing logics. The rationales behind teaching migrants the skills they needed to survive in Australia, preventing racial discrimination, encouraging minority groups to retain their languages, enjoining people to 'live in harmony' and to treat each other with respect are all slightly different, even if they connect. We have glossed these as logics of incorporation, recognition and civility and embedded within them are conceptions of social justice, national identity, ethnic diversity and morality. With scarce resources and less time, schools often have to make choices about what they can do, which may mean emphasizing one logic over another, and not seeing the tensions between choices. We would like to think that these decisions are made with professional deliberation, but they are often made expediently and unreflexively.

Our research, initially, demonstrated two things. First, there was substantial variation among participants (teachers, students and parents) in understandings and perceptions of multiculturalism. Second, there was surprisingly little difference between the views expressed by teachers, on the one hand, and by parents and students, on the other. These two trends were also in evidence when we asked people what they understood by the idea of culture, the keyword of multicultural discourse. They pose two distinct challenges. The first is that there isn't a shared public language for discussing multiculturalism, ethnic diversity or multicultural education, despite over four decades of multicultural policies in Australia. This lack of a common language poses real obstacles for developing a basis for dialogue in school communities around these issues. While there was discussion evident in schools, reflecting the investment and passion of teachers, students and parents, it lacked a shared, critical dimension that addressed ideas with nuance and linked them to social contexts. This problem reflects a larger issue regarding the lack of a shared language across society. The second is that we might expect that teachers, as tertiary-trained educators, might have a developed professional language to talk about multiculturalism, especially in relation to educational goals and their school communities. It underlines the question of whether teachers' experience and expertise in multicultural education equip them well enough with knowledge of their school communities to work effectively with forms of diversity.

Common to both challenges is the issue of whether the understandings people have are adequate for grappling with the cultural complexities increasingly typical of Australian society as elsewhere. We found there was a mismatch between the ways people talk about culture and the complex histories and forms of self-identification within school communities. When people talk about 'culture', they typically fall back on what we have called a 'multicultural imaginary', a way of seeing differences that entails specific perceptual schemas of difference. When people talk about 'cultures', they are usually talking about 'ethnicities', forms of identification that derive from migration histories. 'Cultures' as whole ways of life don't migrate, only aspects of language, customs and faith, which often remain as 'backgrounds'. Moreover, 'culture' is often equated with nation, ignoring the diversity in people's homelands, or reduced to a fixed, unchanging essence. This sense of 'culture' is usually framed in terms of Others and their exotic difference. This schema informed not only popular perceptions but the 'professional vision' of teachers, the forms of perception that identify and address educational problems, as well as broader social categories and relations.

In contrast, the ways people identify themselves challenge conventional wisdom about the nature of ethnic diversity embedded in traditional models of multiculturalism and demonstrate a sense of the world as becoming increasingly global and hyperdiverse, where differences proliferate, adapt, mix and evolve into new identities. People had to tell us stories, or qualify their answers, to do justice to the lives of their families. Again this is not a semantic problem, because reduced understandings of culture shaped participants' perceptions of ethnic difference, and how these operated in explaining academic performance, student behaviour and parental participation. These explanations tended towards essentialized categorizations of ethnically defined communities which, in some cases, could endorse stereotypes. These findings indicate that there is a pressing need for developing a shared language across communities and a recalibrated 'professional vision' of teachers that can facilitate the role of schools in addressing the challenges of diversity. Central to this is the interrogation of the idea of culture, to provide the knowledge base and 'intellectual compass' to help teachers and students navigate the 'poorly charted terrain of multicultural education' (Wren, 2012, p. 165). 'Culture' had been a useful term to avoid the pitfalls of the problematic language of race, but it has lost its critical edge in favour of the celebration of difference. This interrogation would include reflection upon where each of us sits within this global complexity, what we would call, following Gramsci (1971, p. 628), critical, cultural self-understanding: 'The starting-point of critical elaboration is the consciousness of what one really is, and is "knowing thyself" as a product of the historical process to date, which has deposited in you an infinity of traces, without leaving an inventory. The first thing to do is to make such an inventory.' This 'self-understanding' is not an inward-looking self-appraisal but an enquiry into the worlds we inhabit, the histories that make us and the social relations and meanings that frame our lives. As we've suggested, the ethnic categories that typically constitute 'diversity' have to be rethought alongside the awareness of intragroup variations, the hybridities brought about through intermarriage and the complexities of living in a global world where transnational flows reshape everyday life. These reconstitute 'identities' in complex and contradictory ways. This should be the basis of a strong sociocultural focus at three levels – school curriculum, initial teacher education and in-service professional development of teachers. This is foundational for what we have defined as an elaborated 'cultural intelligence' that develops critical frameworks for making sense of the complexities of a globalized, dynamic world (Watkins & Noble, 2016).

The encouraging finding that there *was* discussion going on in schools corresponds to another key finding: teachers, students and parents overwhelmingly saw their schools as having an important role in addressing issues around diversity in Australian society. Two Wollami Lakes teachers, for example, talked about 'the school's responsibility' in addressing issues of multiculturalism, but one added that there was a question around 'the manner' in which it's done; it was 'hard to identify exactly' what to do. A parent at Getty Rd insisted, however, that it was for 'the parents and the school' together to address: 'I don't think it is something you can really segregate, I think it has to be part of the school, because we are all here together, they are all here together working together, so everyone needs to get on.' But 'what is to be done' can't happen without critical, collegial discussion (Timperley & Robinson, 2000). There is a tension between some people's emphasis on issues around equity of outcomes and the celebratory focus of multicultural days, for example, which can't be resolved without dialogue. These events are valued in schools, and for understandable reasons (Dewilde et al., 2021), but they emphasize what we have referred to as a moralizing sense of civility, which foregrounds a feel-good dimension sometimes at the expense of the hard work of thinking through the redesign of curriculum and pedagogy. They constitute 'lazy multiculturalism' because they reproduce old, unquestioned ways of 'doing' multiculturalism'. As one parent at Getty Rd argued,

> schools hav[e] to be accountable for what they are actually producing . . . we need to perhaps more than just appeasing everybody . . . the way that the curriculum approaches it now . . . they've got the multicultural

speeches and they've got certain sections that they just sit down and basically drill the kids on. I don't actually think it is fostering the kids' understanding of each other's culture, it is just satisfying a compulsory part of the curriculum . . . it is ticking those boxes. These children don't actually get up and stand there and talk about their own home family environment or anything that actually matters.

What 'actually matters' is, of course, the thing to be decided. Interrogating culture is intellectually demanding and this reminds us that teaching *is* intellectual work, teaching students how to think, write, analyse and create – an expectation sometimes lost in the pragmatic business of managing a school or a classroom (Noble & Watkins, 2014a). Teachers need to have the critical capacities to make sense of complex phenomena, and the professional capacities to help students develop these capacities. This is significant for addressing the difficult relationship between multicultural and Aboriginal education, for example, an issue that participants across schools kept raising. Such an approach, for example, would allow educators to attempt the articulation of these two areas, not through collapsing both under a vague mantra of cultural inclusion or culturally responsive education but through an awareness of the centrality of relations of culture and nation in very specific histories.

Kalantzis and Cope (2008), arguing against a 'superficial multiculturalism', promote a critical and transformative approach which builds on the lessons of many years of educational change and works towards a civic pluralism that acknowledges the multiple identities and belongings of contemporary life. Such an approach foregrounds an emphasis on 'social literacy' – both the analytical skills needed to understand and the social skills to negotiate the complex relations of difference in contemporary life reshaped by diverse histories and processes of globalization. These skills need to be the result of a considered process of educational design at all levels of educational experience (Kalantzis & Cope, 2005) involving a capacity for 'theoretical' consideration of social life, application of conceptual tools to real-life examples and reflexivity among teachers and students which allows them to interrogate their place in the world (May, 2009). Rizvi (2014) makes a similar argument in his conceptualization of 'cosmopolitan learning' needed to make sense of increasing global connectivity and one's own situatedness within it. This is not simply a bland evocation of an old-fashioned 'cosmopolitanism' which savours exotic difference, but a reflexive and critical, global imagination which interrogates what happens to culture in conditions of globalization, and can engage with the new forms of social life enabled by transnational relations, and develop new capacities for action – particularly significant given the political challenges of globalization (Rizvi, 2014). Unlike a view suggested by one of the teachers during the project, multiculturalism *is* 'core business' for schools – not because students may be in a high LBOTE school but because we are all in a world of global connectivity and transnational movement. Such a 'cosmopolitan' approach would, we think, foster a deep and critical cultural intelligence understood not as the ability to recognize and appreciate different cultures but as the ability to understand, negotiate and engage in the cultural complexity of the world, acknowledging the 'traces' which constitute people's lives without reducing them to ethnic boxes. Such capacities comprise the reflexive civility we have argued for here.

This process, however, does not start in the classroom but in teachers' professional training. Australian curriculum has engaged with the challenges of globalization over the last decade but caught up in the tension between approaches which emphasize what students need to know and what kind of people they ought to become (Lingard, 2018), the role of the teacher in grappling with these debates and approaches often drops out. As we argued in Chapter 3, the challenge of policy enactment is not simply to embed the imperatives of putting policy into school practice but to translate ideas, ways of thinking and researching into robust and sustained curriculum. This book does not intend to provide extensive recommendations about what should be done, but the reorientation suggested above stresses the need to address three interrelated levels:

- reinvigorating a critical sociocultural school curriculum in Years K-12;
- fostering a comparable sociocultural focus within initial teacher education;
- extending this sociocultural focus through the ongoing professional learning of teachers.

To achieve these, we need to provide teachers with the conceptual tools required for a critical approach and the methodological tools to translate this into action research which can support the design and evaluation of effective curriculum, pedagogy and wider school programmes. To do this, the teacher has to engage much more with the intellectual demands of teaching, but with the increasing imperative to embed research into professional practice. Yet, as Mills et al. (2021) show, there are divergent orientations to research among the profession, and an uneven distribution of the capacities to undertake this work, producing a 'compliant' pragmatism where teachers develop little agency. This raises another set of concerns about whether schools, and the education system as a whole, can deliver this 'rethinking'. To address this, we want to return to some of our empirical data.

Rethinking Professional Practice

A recurrent theme throughout the discussions with principals and research teams was the time involved in undertaking their projects. As was explained, the DoE provided grants to each school to finance release from teaching for team members if required and, also, through the involvement with BOSTES, the opportunity for team members to register their involvement as professional learning. Despite this, many teams made reference to the project's impact on their busy work schedules – although the degree to which this impeded their involvement and commitment varied, depending on the school, the team and the teachers. Understandably the time commitment the project required seemed more of an issue in low SES schools where the pressures of teaching appeared to be more pronounced. As Lucy, the principal at Thurston, explained,

> initially it was a big challenge to the team because they had to understand the scope of the project . . . so they had to come to terms with that, and they already have high workloads. I know the time was provided, and the money, which was good but I think just the time involved out of their already busy schedules to complete the work on the project.

Anita, from Addington, considered time a factor in terms of her lack of engagement with professional reading, 'I would love to do more professional reading but you are just so tied up. You've got to get going, you have to have stuff ready for these guys before you hit the classroom.' Sorcha, at Getty Rd, had a different view, 'an imposition on our time, absolutely and it wasn't until I started writing the unit and teaching it that I got a bit passionate about it, yeah loved it, absolutely loved it!' Gillian, at Wellington Heights, also acknowledged the heavy commitment the project involved but then considered the issue of time from a broader perspective, 'reflective practice is really, I suppose, something that is often given up because of time constraints and the, you know, like I am thinking, say staff development day, well we've got to get X, Y and Z done, do we have time for reflective practice?' For one principal, this was a problem with the system:

> there isn't the time allocation to professional learning that allows people, the largess, are actually going outside the very narrow job description that we place them in. . . . For me the best change would be to go towards the Finnish model, cut the school face-to-face teaching day down. I think we can still get as much learning done for the kids and give teachers much more time to actually collegially and or professionally develop themselves.

There are real-time constraints in schools, and this is a serious challenge that needs addressing by departments of education everywhere. Teachers need time to read, talk and think. The requirement that all teachers in NSW must now engage in professional learning to remain accredited is an important development (NSW DoE, 2020c), but it doesn't address the differing issues that are raised here regarding structural and cultural change within the profession nor the pressures on teachers that limit willingness to pursue professional learning.

Other participants suggested there was more involved than 'not enough time'. One principal commented on the professional practice of teachers themselves:

> there is this mindset in schools largely that we are so, we are way too busy, we have no time to do that, unless you are going to let me sign up to a little project, get time out to go and learn about it, come back, time out to talk . . . that's where we are at, and look I don't know what it will take for the whole sector or the education circles or practice in schools to adopt a different kind of attitude.

This comment cuts to the distinction we have made between differing cultures of teaching, between a pragmatic professionalism and that involving an intellectual orientation. It would be easy to dismiss some of the case studies as poor teacher professionalism, but 'professional cultures' don't just come from teachers but from teacher training institutions, departments of education and professional learning provision. Moreover, the capacity to undertake change is constrained by the SES and LBOTE contexts of a school, its size and location, its access to resources, its leadership.

Selena, the principal at Beechton, identified ineffective evaluation as a bulwark to change in schools. Isla, the principal at Getty Rd, spoke of the resistance to change among some within the profession:

> When that comes down to the practice of teaching, it comes down to the type of teacher, it comes down to the philosophy and belief system of the teachers because there are teachers who have refused and resisted change in every single area. There are people who would still have us using ink wells if that was possible, and it's that resistance to change because people are afraid of change . . . there are people within the teaching population who don't feel that it's their responsibility, that their responsibility begins and ends with the three Rs, or their content subject in the secondary system, and that nothing else, the rest of it is irrelevant, that people will pick it up as they go along, that it doesn't have to be a structured and focused form of teaching, which it does because if it isn't structured and focused it will get left behind and in the end it won't be taught at all. So, I think that teachers too, find it's just all too hard, they are being asked to do too much, too many things, and where does this fit in? I think there is an attitude that teaching still only refers to reading, writing and arithmetic.

Isla raises important points about the value teachers place on multicultural education. With an overcrowded curriculum (Topsfield, 2014) where they are stretched to perform a range of extracurricular activities, many give multicultural education little emphasis, especially those schools with low LBOTE populations. As Daphne from Barnett explained, some teachers 'are of the mindset that they are trained to teach a syllabus, you know, and that's what they do very well, that they have this content and if all these peripheral things weren't there then perhaps their job would be better and easier'. Yet, no matter what the stage of schooling or their discipline, teachers teach far more than subject content. Whether aware of it or not, they are intellectual workers engaged in the processes of interpretation and their perception of the world influences how, what and who they teach. Schools are sites of socialization with an important role to play in producing a culturally inclusive and equitable society. Multicultural education involves teaching about the complex world we live in, an aspect of schooling with which all teachers need to engage, as well as servicing the needs of LBOTE students. While teachers responding to the RMRME survey acknowledged that multicultural education is a responsibility for all schools, it needs greater prominence. This was the view of Jason, the principal of Barnett, speaking of ethnic diversity:

> Just to get people in some form or another engaged in multiculturalism and the discussion of multiculturalism is really good because you know, you've got to shake-up or otherwise it's just, you know, slips into the background, particularly if you don't see it. If it's not visible in the environment, it just doesn't exist.

But, of course, 'it' does exist. Even if 'it' is not always obvious within a local community, teachers, students and parents need to see themselves as part of a broader community which spans the local, the regional, the national and the global. Whatever their school, students are heading out into a world of enormous diversity. Multicultural education has a role in fostering a preparedness for this, but it is reliant upon teachers possessing the necessary professional capacities to engage critically with these issues and to assist their students to do the same.

Many of the teachers involved in RMRME raised issues around the nature of the profession and aspects of professional learning. Bemoaning the lack of emphasis given to professional reading, Sorcha, from Getty Rd, felt that 'maybe it's because teachers aren't entering the profession thinking of themselves as professionals, it's viewed as a job'. Two teachers from Thurston felt this was the case but eventually realized it required a greater commitment. Lena admitted that 'very few of us do professional development outside of school'. Sybilla added that 'it's one of the reasons why I chose teaching because I thought it would fit in with my lifestyle, that's originally why I went into teaching. Now I enjoy it and I know I have to do stuff outside school because I am still learning and I always will be learning.'

Raoul, from Pentonville, remarked that 'most teachers don't see themselves as academics. We had to do a degree to get the job, but you know that's all in the past and we've got the qualification.' Yet, having a qualification and maintaining professional standards are different matters. Knowing your community, mastering your craft and understanding the world isn't resolved at one point in time. Being a professional requires ongoing professional learning, but this should involve a particular orientation to knowledge and the ability to engage in practices of knowledge translation in working with students and school communities. Some of the teachers in RMRME found this difficult. Richard, from Wollami Lakes, reflecting on the project, commented that 'what I found frustrating . . . is that there were no answers . . . this hasn't provided us with any definitive answers as to the questions that were proposed'. Richard's unease about the uncertainties of knowledge posed difficulties for him: 'I know we need to do it, but how do we do it?' RMRME, however, was not designed to tell teachers how to teach. Its intention was to prepare teachers for undertaking the task of rethinking multicultural education themselves in the context of their school, by reflecting on core assumptions and different ways to think. Many teachers rose to this challenge, but for others it was too hard. Richard would have liked a different approach: 'I would much have preferred you to produce a resource that we went and trialled . . . our primary business here is teaching kids, not doing research, not producing resources, not doing any of that stuff.' While teachers' 'primary business' is 'teaching kids', as professionals they are also required to do the other 'stuff', producing resources to meet the needs of their students and evaluating their effectiveness. Critical thinking and action research provide key tools for doing this. In fact, critical thinking and research are things that teachers are required to teach students, emphasized in the National Curriculum (ACARA, 2020c), but, once again, the enactment of policy and the conceptual tools needed by teachers to do this are rarely elaborated.

Richard's comments, therefore, do raise an ethical question for academics: Is it enough for researchers to ask teachers to 'do things differently', even if they provide useful tools? Before, during and after the project we debated whether we should have been more interventionist in the design stage, helping teachers, along with the DoE consultants, in addressing our challenges. As we outlined in Chapter 3, many teachers didn't always understand those challenges or dismissed them. Yet others embraced what RMRME had to offer. Isaac, from Wellington Heights, had a different view to Richard's:

> [When] you go to professional learning, you are given something because somebody else has done the thinking and solved the problem for you and just gives you something which you then take back and implement . . . you don't own it, where we, because we've gone through the process we recognized the problem . . . we've been stimulated to think deeply about

the problem and then we've come up with our own way to solve it, which for us, I think, has helped us, not just own, but to really understand it. I mean ... you can show people new ways of doing ... you can show them but will they really understand and value it because they haven't gone through that change and that deep understanding?

For teachers like Isaac, RMRME provided the means to rethink how to approach multicultural education. No package would have been able to deliver the benefits that the project at Wellington Heights was able to achieve, not only in terms of the community learning programme the team developed but in the professional capacities the teachers acquired in researching and designing what was needed to meet the specific needs around multicultural education at their school. Others, however, may need more assistance.

While it may be the case, as Veronica at Getty Rd remarked, 'Teaching is a hard gig!', greater emphasis needs to be placed on developing the professional capacities of teachers to effect change. The comments of Richard and others suggest that a key element is the initial training given to teachers. Whatever is happening, the conventional university claim of the importance of critical thinking does not exist evenly throughout the professional culture of teaching. Institutions of higher education have to take a large share of the blame for whatever limitations we have documented here in the professional capacities of teachers.

A Way Forward

Rethinking multicultural education at all three levels – curriculum, initial teacher education and professional learning – requires the development of a richer sociocultural knowledge and a critical, interrogative framework. Many scholars have called for a 'transformative' approach to multicultural education, and we seek to build on that work. But that too has limitations. Banks (2019, p. 146), famously, argued for 'transformative' action that goes beyond 'additive' approaches to multicultural education. Such a transformative approach makes multiple, alternative perspectives central to curriculum to challenge the ethnocentric mainstream and to underline the constructed nature of knowledge. For Banks, this means the inclusion of the 'points of view' of different racial and ethnic 'groups'. This is important – telling the history of colonization from the perspective of the colonized, for example – but it doesn't go far enough because it can lend itself to the kind of 'groupism' Brubaker (2004) warns against, seeing groups as given, not created. If such groups ever existed, they rarely had a singular perspective; but in conditions of hyperdiversity, as we saw in Chapter 2, such an assumption cannot work for large numbers of people. We need to interrogate culture to get at the kind of complexity that now typifies much of the world, question reductive ethnic categories and abandon a language where 'cultures' do things.

This is not to say that cultures don't exist but to acknowledge that the ways a person lived in their homeland is not the same as the way they live when they migrate to Australia or the ways the second generation lives. Culture is more about practices than identities per se, and we need a nuanced sociocultural understanding to make sense of these complexities – in schools as elsewhere. Identities are important, of course, but we can't collapse these important distinctions into singular, homogenizing categories. A more robust multicultural education should be able to address both the needs of the recently arrived migrant, for whom homeland culture may still feel present, and the needs of second-generation students, while fostering a nuanced understanding of the complexities of the world in which they both live. Indeed, without these nuanced understandings, multiculturalism will simply reproduce problematic categories and programmes.

While multiculturalism needs to continue to meet its different logics – there will continue to be great need for EAL/D, anti-racism strategies, community liaison programmes and so on – we need to reframe this with a different orientation to reflect upon the different demands of incorporation, recognition and civility and guard against the simple reproduction of the reductive tendencies of 'lazy' multiculturalism we have found evident in schools. We propose the following as a heuristic to encourage critical discussion about the goals and capacities needed in multicultural education. This framework emerged during the course of the research, through our engagement with schools and with the DoE, working between ideas coming from sociocultural theory and translating them for professional learning (Figure 2).

This alternative perspective on multicultural education is motivated by the need to move beyond the 'reproductive' conventions of the multicultural imaginary that dominates ways of seeing diversity. Thinking and critical discussion are central to the process of reinvigorating multicultural education. The simple reliance on empathetic understanding that assumes and essentializes the 'cultures' of students needs to be replaced by the development of critical understanding informed by a view of knowledge that embraces and interrogates the uncertainties of cultural dynamism and complexity. Such a perspective is alert to reductive forms of celebratory cultural recognition, moving towards processes of 'cultural acknowledgement' that enable people to be seen in the fullness of their humanity and their complex social relationships rather than foreground ethnicity as the defining feature of identity (Noble, 2009b). Against conventional approaches which generally have a narrow national frame, critical understandings should engender a productive engagement with the global, with all its complexity of relations and meanings. Such an approach also eschews the unreflexive civility of the multicultural day and the moral injunction to appreciate exotic difference that offers little meaningful dialogue for grappling with the challenges of increasing cultural complexity. Rather, we promote forms of reflexive civility

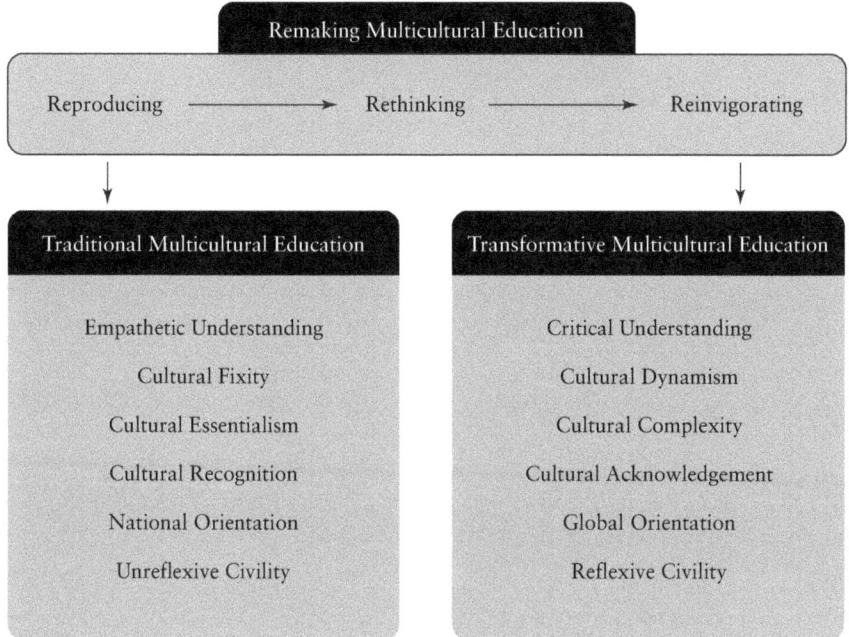

FIGURE 2 *Remaking multicultural education.*

that allow individuals to better make sense of the culturally complex world in which they live. Such a move from traditional multicultural education to one that is potentially transformative, however, is reliant upon extending the professional capacities of teachers. We hope the opportunity RMRME provided for some teachers to undertake this task can inform the ongoing process of rethinking and remaking how multicultural education is practised in schools. It is a task of critical concern in a world racked by division and inequality, and needing a better way of seeing and doing diversity.

NOTES

Introduction

1 The term 'Anglo' is a shorthand form of identification used in Australia that groups together Australians of English-speaking backgrounds, sometimes referred to as Anglo-Saxon or Anglo-Celtic. The vernacular use of the word 'Australian' often equates it with Anglo, but this is obviously a problem, and we retain 'Australian' to refer explicitly to nationality, not ethnicity. In an Australian context 'Anglo' is used more regularly than the racial category 'White', and we retain that preference here too. 'White' makes obvious sense in certain circumstances (especially in relation to 'Black' Australians), but it is not very useful once we factor in the importance of distinctions in waves and sources of migration from various parts of Europe. Sometimes 'Europeans' are lumped together with Anglos to reference 'White' dominance, but it erases the complex positions in relations of power of people from southern and eastern European ancestries. The political and cultural significance of ethnicities resides in their degrees of complexity, not binary oppositions.

2 EAL/D is the term now used in Australian schools to refer to students whose first language is a language or dialect other than English and who require additional support to develop proficiency in Standard Australian English. It was formerly referred to as English as a second language or ESL, a term considered inaccurate as, for many students, English is actually their third or fourth language.

3 Language background other than English or LBOTE is the most common term within the context of Australian schooling to signify ethnic and linguistic difference.

4 CALD is an acronym for 'culturally and linguistically diverse' which we avoid for reasons that are explained in Chapter 2.

5 The research team from Western Sydney included Professor Kevin Dunn and Dr Garth Lean from the School of Social Sciences. Kevin and Garth provided invaluable expertise during the survey stage of the project.

6 This unit no longer exists. Its staff has since been greatly reduced and subsumed within a new Equity Programs division.

7 The NSW Institute of Teachers was combined with the NSW Board of Studies to become the Board of Studies Teaching and Educational Standards which has changed yet again to the NSW Educational Standards Authority.

8 The action research was undertaken in the fourteen schools over the course of the 2012 school year.

9 Sadly, this consultancy team has since been disbanded as a result of the neoliberal move to decentralize support to schools.

Chapter 1

1 As indicated in the Introduction, respondents came from a wide range of schools. The response rate was fairly even across schools and regions, with these exceptions: those in low SES areas were more likely to respond, and especially schools in south-western Sydney, where there are high numbers of LBOTE students and more Multicultural Education consultants. More complete data can be found in Watkins et al. (2013).
2 These categories were not arbitrary but arose from a pilot survey where we asked teachers to provide their own written definitions, which were then distilled into the options available in the electronic survey.
3 Noting that those willing to undertake the survey possibly had greater investment in multicultural education than others, these figures may be generous representations of the overall teaching force.

Chapter 3

1 At the time of the training, this requirement regarding accreditation only applied to teachers who were relatively new to the profession.
2 Ezzy (2002) sees a process of deduction and induction as characteristic of more sophisticated uses of grounded theory.
3 This data could include NAPLAN results, the nationwide testing around literacy and numeracy, the NSW DoE census data on LBOTE numbers in each school together with data schools may have collected themselves around incidences of racism, etc.
4 This requirement dates from 2018 in NSW.

Chapter 4

1 Australia Pride and the Bra Boys are groups associated with anti-immigrant sentiment. The latter originated in the beach-side suburb of Sydney's Maroubra and were influential during the 2005 Cronulla Riots in which White Australian youths tried to ban Middle Eastern youth from what they saw as 'their' beaches.
2 Thong, in this instance, refers to sandal-like footwear worn by many Australians.
3 Vegemite is an Australian sandwich spread much like the English Marmite.

4 Lamingtons are coconut-covered, sponge-like cakes that are considered typically Australian.
5 ANZAC stands for Australian and New Zealand Army Corps, soldiers who fought during the First World War. A slouch hat was part of their uniform.
6 This is a relatively high Aboriginal population given Aboriginal Australians constitute just over 3 per cent of the total Australian population (ABS, 2018).

Chapter 6

1 'Koori' is a collective term for Aboriginal peoples living in what are now the Australian states of NSW and Victoria.
2 NAIDOC originally stood for 'National Aborigines and Islanders Day Observance Committee'. This committee was once responsible for organizing national activities during NAIDOC Week, and its acronym has since become the name of the week itself when festivities are held that celebrate the history, culture and achievements of Aboriginal and Torres Strait Islander peoples in Australia.

REFERENCES

Adelman, C. (1993). Kurt Lewin and the Origins of Action Research. *Educational Action Research*, 1(1), 7–24.
Ahmed, S. (2010). *The Promise of Happiness*. Durham: Duke University Press.
Ahmed, S. (2012). *On Being Included: Racism and Diversity in Institutional Life*. Durham: Duke University Press.
Alismail, H. A. (2016). Multicultural Education: Teachers' Perceptions and Preparation. *Journal of Education and Practice*, 7(11), 139–46.
Allard, C. & Santoro, N. (2006). Troubling Identities: Teacher Education Students' Constructions of Class and Ethnicity. *Cambridge Journal of Education*, 36(1), 115–29.
Allemann-Ghionda, C. (2009). From Intercultural Education to the Inclusion of Diversity. In J. Banks (Ed.), *The Routledge International Companion to Multicultural Education* (pp. 134–45). New York: Routledge.
Ang, I. (2001). *On Not Speaking Chinese*. London: Routledge.
Ang, I. (2011). Navigating Complexity: From Cultural Critique to Cultural Intelligence. *Continuum*, 25(6), 779–94.
Ang, I., Brand, J. E., Noble, G. & Wilding, D. (2002). *Living Diversity: Australia's Multicultural Future*. Artarmon: Special Broadcasting Service Corporation.
Ang, I., Brand, J. E., Noble, G. & Sternberg, J. (2006). *Connecting Diversity*. Artarmon: Special Broadcasting Service Corporation.
Appadurai, A. (1996). *Modernity at Large: The Cultural Dimensions of Globalization*. Minneapolis: University of Minnesota Press.
Appiah, K. (2018). *The Lies that Bind*. London: Profile.
Australian Bureau of Statistics. (2016). *2016 Census QuickStats: Auburn*. https://quickstats.censusdata.abs.gov.au/census_services/getproduct/census/2016/quickstat/SED10002
Australian Bureau of Statistics. (2017, June). *Census of Population and Housing: Reflecting Australia - Stories from the Census, 2016* (No. 2071.0). https://www.abs.gov.au/ausstats/abs@.nsf/Lookup/by%20Subject/2071.0~2016~Main%20Features~Cultural%20Diversity%20Data%20Summary~30
Australian Bureau of Statistics. (2018). Estimates of Aboriginal and Torres Strait Islander Australians. https://www.abs.gov.au/statistics/people/aboriginal-and-torres-strait-islander-peoples/estimates-aboriginal-and-torres-strait-islander-australians/latest-release
Australian Curriculum, Assessment and Reporting Authority. (2013). General Capabilities in the Australian Curriculum. Retrieved February, 2013 from http://www.australiancurriculum.edu.au/GeneralCapabilities/Pdf/Overview

Australian Curriculum, Assessment and Reporting Authority. (2020a). General Capabilities, Australian Curriculum. https://www.australiancurriculum.edu.au/f-10-curriculum/general-capabilities/

Australian Curriculum, Assessment and Reporting Authority. (2020b). Intercultural Understanding, Australian Curriculum. https://www.australiancurriculum.edu.au/f-10-curriculum/general-capabilities/intercultural-understanding/

Australian Curriculum, Assessment and Reporting Authority. (2020c). Critical and Creative Thinking. https://www.australiancurriculum.edu.au/f-10-curriculum/general-capabilities/critical-and-creative-thinking/

Australian Government. (2011). *The People of Australia: Australia's Multicultural Policy*. Canberra: Department of Immigration and Citizenship.

Australian Government. (2017). *Multicultural Australia: United, Strong Successful*. Australia's Multicultural Statement. Canberra: Department of Social Services.

Australian Institute of Multicultural Affairs. (1986). *Future Directions for Multiculturalism–Final Report of the Council of AIMA*. Melbourne: AIMA.

Australian Institute for Teaching and School Leadership. (2011). *Accreditation of Initial Teacher Education Programs in Australia*. Carlton South: Education Services Australia.

Ball, S., Maguire, M., Braun, A. & Hoskins, K. (2011). Policy Actors: Doing Policy Work in Schools. *Discourse: Studies in the Cultural Politics of Education*, 32(4), 625–39.

Banks, J. (1993). Multicultural Education: Development, Dimensions, and Challenges. *Phi Delta Kappan*, 75(1), 22–8.

Banks, J. (2009). Diversity and Citizenship Education in Multicultural Nations. *Multicultural Education Review*, 1(1), 1–28.

Banks, J. (2019). Approaches to Multicultural Curriculum Reform. In J. Banks & C. McGee Banks (Eds), *Multicultural Education: Issues and Perspectives* (10th edn, pp. 137–57). New York: John Wiley & Sons.

Barth, F. (1969). Introduction. In F. Barth (Ed.), *Ethnic Groups and Boundaries* (pp. 9–38). Boston: Little, Brown and Company.

Baumann, G. (1996). *Contesting Culture: Discourses of Identity in Multi-ethnic London*. Cambridge: Cambridge University Press.

Baumann, G. (1999). *The Multicultural Riddle*. London: Routledge.

Bell, J. & Hartmann, D. (2007). Diversity in Everyday Discourse: The Cultural Ambiguities and Consequences of 'Happy Talk'. *American Sociological Review*, 72(6), 895–914.

Berking, H. (2003). 'Ethnicity Is Everywhere': On Globalization and the Transformation of Cultural Identity. *Current Sociology*, 51(3/4), 248–64.

Berry, J. (2013). Research on Multiculturalism in Canada. *International Journal of Intercultural Relations*, 37(6), 663–75.

Bhabha, H. (2004). *The Location of Culture*. Abingdon: Routledge.

Blair, K. (2015). Young Adults' Attitudes Towards Multiculturalism in Australia: Tensions between the Multicultural State and the Intercultural Citizen. *Journal of Intercultural Studies*, 36(4), 431–49.

Boccagni, P. (2015). (Super)diversity and the Migration–Social Work Nexus: A New Lens on the Field of Access and Inclusion? *Ethnic and Racial Studies*, 38(4), 608–20.

Bodovski, K. (2010). Parental Practices and Educational Achievement: Social Class, Race, and Habitus. *British Journal of Sociology of Education*, 31(2), 139–56.

Boler, M. (1999). *Feeling Power: Emotions and Education*. New York: Routledge.

Boler, M. & Zembylas, M. (2003). Discomforting Truths: The Emotional Terrain of Understanding Differences. In P. Trifonas (Ed.), *Pedagogies of Difference* (pp. 110–36). New York: Routledge.

Bottomley, G. (1991). Representing the 'Second Generation'. In G. Bottomley (Ed.), *Intersexions: Gender, Class, Culture, Ethnicity* (pp. 92–109). Sydney: Allen and Unwin.

Bourdieu, P. (1996a). *The Rules of Art* (S. Emanuel, Trans.). Cambridge: Polity Press.

Bourdieu, P. (1996b). *The State Nobility* (L. Clough, Trans.). Cambridge: Polity Press.

Braun, A., Ball, S. J., Maguire, M. & Hoskins, K. (2011). Taking Context Seriously: Towards Explaining Policy Enactments in the Secondary School. *Discourse: Studies in the Cultural Politics of Education*, 32(4), 585–96.

Breidenbach, J. & Nyíri, P. (2009). *Seeing Culture Everywhere*. Washington: University of Washington Press.

Brubaker, R. (2004). *Ethnicity Without Groups*. Cambridge, MA: Harvard University Press.

Brubaker, R., Loveman, M. & Stamatov, P. (2004). Ethnicity as Cognition. *Theory and Society*, 33(1), 31–64.

Bullivant, B. (1981). *The Pluralist Dilemma in Education*. Sydney: George Allen & Unwin.

Burridge, N. & Chodkiewicz, A. (2010). Challenges in Addressing Cultural Diversity: Approaches in Sydney Schools. *International Journal of Diversity in Organizations, Communities and Nations*, 10(3), 281–94.

Byrne, B. & de Tona, C. (2014). Multicultural Desires? Parental Negotiation of Multiculture and Difference in Choosing Secondary Schools for their Children. *The Sociological Review*, 62(3), 475–93.

Caneva, L. (2017, March 22). Teachers Not Equipped for Multicultural Classrooms. *Pro Bono Australia News*. https://probonoaustralia.com.au/news/2017/03/teachers-not-equipped-multicultural-classrooms

Carr, W. & Kemmis, S. (1986). *Becoming Critical: Education, Knowledge and Action Research*. Philadelphia: Falmer Press.

Castles, S., Cope, B., Kalantzis, M. & Morrisey, M. (1990). *Mistaken Identity: Multiculturalism and the Demise of Nationalism in Australia*. Sydney: Pluto Press.

Castro, A. (2010). Themes in the Research on Preservice Teachers' Views of Cultural Diversity: Implications for Researching Millennial Preservice Teachers. *Educational Researcher*, 39(3), 198–210.

Catarci, M. (2015). Interculturalism in Education across Europe. In M. Catarci & F. Massimiliano (Eds), *Intercultural Education in the European Context* (pp. 17–50). London: Routledge.

Chang, B. & Au, W. (2007/2008). You're Asian, How Could You Fail Math? *Rethinking Schools*, 22(2), 15–19. http://rethinkingschools.aidcvt.com/archive/22_02/math222.shtml

Colombo, E. (2015). Multiculturalisms: An Overview of Multicultural Debates in Western Societies. *Current Sociology Review*, 63(6), 800–24.

Colvin, N. (2017). '... diversity is regarded as a strength and an asset': Multiculturalism as Understood, Valued and Lived in Two Regional Australian High Schools (Unpublished doctoral dissertation). Western Sydney University, Parramatta.

Connell, R. (2009). Good Teachers on Dangerous Ground: Towards a New View of Teacher Quality and Professionalism. *Critical Studies in Education*, 50(3), 213–29.

Cope, B. & Kalantzis, M. (2016). Big Data Comes to School: Implications for Learning, Assessment and Research. *AERA Open*, 2(2), 1–19.

Cui, D. (2015). Capital, Distinction and Racialised Habitus: Immigrant Youth in the Educational Field. *Journal of Youth Studies*, 18(9), 1154–69.

Cummins, J. (2008). BICS and CALP: Empirical and Theoretical Status of the Distinction. In B. Street & N. Hornberger (Eds), *Encyclopedia of Language and Education, Vol. 2: Literacy* (2nd edn, pp. 71–83). New York: Springer Science.

DeTurk, S. (2001). Intercultural Empathy: Myth, Competency or Possibility for Alliance Building? *Communication Education*, 50(4), 374–84.

Dewey, J. (1927). The Relation of Theory to Practice in the Education of Teachers. In C. McMurray (Ed.), *The Third Yearbook* (pp. 9–30). Bloomington: Public School Publishing.

Dewilde, J., Kolbjørn Kjørven, O. & Skrefsrud, T. (2021). Multicultural School Festivals as a Creative Space for Identity Construction – the Perspective of Minority Parents. *Intercultural Education*. DOI: 10.1080/14675986.2020.1851173.

Dixson, A. & Rousseau Anderson, C. (2018). Where Are We? Critical Race Theory in Education 20 Years Later. *Peabody Journal of Education*, 93(1), 121–31.

Donald, J. (2007). Internationalization, Diversity and the Humanities Curriculum: Cosmopolitanism and Multiculturalism Revisited. *Journal of Philosophy of Education*, 41(3), 289–308.

Dunn, K. M., Forrest, J., Burnley, I. & McDonald, A. (2004). Constructing Racism in Australia. *Australian Journal of Social Issues*, 39(4), 409–30.

Elliott, J. (2005). Becoming Critical: The Failure to Connect. *Educational Action Research*, 13(3), 359–74.

Ezzy, D. (2002). *Qualitative Analysis*. London: Routledge.

Ferrance, E. (2000). *Action Research*. Providence: Brown University.

Fife-Yeomans, J. (2013). Attacking Sydney's Enclaves of Islam. *The Daily Telegraph*, May 13. http://www.dailytelegraph.com.au/news/attacking-sydneys-enclaves-of-islam/news-story/9e84e79e0a881ae7da805203faaaf848?sv=499c5c258c0b023a7f0dcb6224145e8b

Forrest, J., Lean, G. & Dunn, K. (2016). Challenging Racism Through Schools: Teacher Attitudes to Cultural Diversity and Multicultural Education in Sydney, Australia. *Race Ethnicity and Education*, 19(3), 618–38.

Francis, B., Mau, A. & Archer, L. (2017). The Construction of British Chinese Educational Success. *Journal of Ethnic and Migration Studies*, 43(14), 2331–45.

Gay, G. (2015). The What, Why, and How of Culturally Responsive Teaching: International Mandates, Challenges, and Opportunities. *Multicultural Education Review*, 7(3), 123–39.

Gillborn, D. & Youdell, D. (2009). Critical Perspectives on Race and Schooling. In J. Banks (Ed.), *The Routledge International Companion to Multicultural Education* (pp. 173–85). New York: Routledge.

Giroux, H. (2020). *On Critical Pedagogy* (2nd edn). London: Bloomsbury.
Goodson, I. & Hargreaves, A. (1996). *Teachers' Professional Lives*. London: Routledge.
Goodwin, C. (1994). Professional Vision. *American Anthropologist*, 96(3), 606–33.
Goot, M. & Watson, I. (2005). Immigration, Multiculturalism and Australian Identity. In S. Wilson, G. Meagher, R. Gibson, D. Denemark & M. Western (Eds), *Australian Social Attitudes: The First Report* (pp. 182–203). Sydney: UNSW Press.
Graham, I. D., Logan, J., Harrison, M. B., Straus, S. E., Tetroe, J., Caswell, W. & Robinson, N. (2006). Lost in Translation: Time for a Map? *The Journal of Continuing Education in the Health Professions*, 26(1), 13–24.
Gramsci, A. (1971). Selections from the Prison Notebooks (Q. Hoare & G. Nowell Smith, Eds/Trans.). London: Lawrence & Wishart.
Grint, K. (2005). Problems, Problems, Problems: The Social Construction of 'leadership'. *Human Relations*, 58(11), 1467–94.
Gundara, J. (2000). *Interculturalism, Education and Inclusion*. London: Sage.
Guo, L. (2014). Preparing Teachers to Educate for 21st Century Global Citizenship: Envisioning and Enacting. *Journal of Global Citizenship & Equity Education*, 4(1), 1–23.
Gupta, A. & Ferguson, J. (1997). Culture, Power, Place: Ethnography at the End of an Era. In A. Gupta & J. Ferguson (Eds), *Culture, Power, Place: Explorations in Critical Anthropology*. Durham: Duke University Press.
Gusterson, H. (2017). From Brexit to Trump: Anthropology and the Rise of Nationalist Populism. *American Ethnologist*, 44(2), 209–14.
Hachfeld, A., Hahn, A., Schroeder, S., Anders, Y., Stanat, P. & Kunter, M. (2011). Assessing Teachers' Multicultural and Egalitarian Beliefs: The Teacher Cultural Beliefs Scale. *Teaching and Teacher Education*, 27(6), 986–96.
Hadfield, H. (2012). Becoming Critical Again: Reconnecting Critical Social Theory with the Practice of Action Research. *Educational Action Research*, 20(4), 571–85.
Hage, G. (1998). *White Nation*. Sydney: Pluto Press.
Hage, G. (2003). *Against Paranoid Nationalism*. Sydney: Pluto Press.
Hage G. (2005). A Not so Multi-sited Ethnography of a Not so Imagined Community. *Anthropological Theory*, 5(4), 463–75.
Hall, S. (2000). *Conclusion: The Multicultural Question*. In B. Hesse (Ed.), *Un/settled Multiculturalisms* (pp. 209–41). London: Zed Books.
Harris, A. (2013). *Young People and Everyday Multiculturalism*. New York and London: Routledge.
Harris, S. (2013). Studying the Construction of Social Problems. In J. Best & S. Harris (Eds), *Making Sense of Social Problems* (pp. 1–10). Boulder: Lynne Rienner.
Hickling-Hudson, A. (2004). Educating Teachers for Cultural Diversity and Social Justice. In G. Hernes (Ed.), *Planning for Diversity: Education in Multi-ethnic and Multicultural Societies* (pp. 279–307). Paris: International Institute for Education Planning (UNESCO).
Ho, C. (2013). From Social Justice to Social Cohesion: A History of Australian Multicultural Policy. In A. Jakubowicz & C. Ho (Eds), *For Those Who've Come Across the Seas: Australian Multicultural Theory, Policy and Practice* (pp. 31–41). North Melbourne: Australian Scholarly Publishing.

Ho, C. (2020). *Aspiration and Anxiety Asian Migrants and Australian Schooling*. Melbourne: Melbourne University Press.

Ho, C. & Bonnor, C. (2018). *Institutionalised Separation: The Impact of Selective Schools*. Sydney: Centre for Policy Development.

Horenczyk, G. & Tatar, M. (2002). Teachers' Attitudes Toward Multiculturalism and Their Perceptions of the School Organizational Culture. *Teaching and Teacher Education*, 18(4), 435–45.

Hoyle, E. (1975). Professionality, Professionalism and Control in Teaching. In E. Hoyle, V. Houghton, R. McHugh & C. Morgan (Eds), *Management in Education* (pp. 314–20). London: Ward Lock Educational in association with Open University Press.

Inglis, C. (2009). Multicultural Education in Australia. In J. Banks (Ed.), *The Routledge International Companion to Multicultural Education* (pp. 109–20). New York: Routledge.

Jakubowicz, A., Morrissey, M. & Palser, J. (1984). *Ethnicity, Class and Social Policy in* Australia, *Social Welfare Research Centre Report No. 46*. Sydney: The University of New South Wales.

James, J. (2004). *Teachers' Attitudes and Perceptions of Multicultural and Diversity Awareness in Elementary Schools* (Unpublished doctoral dissertation). University of Tennessee.

Jupp, J. (2011). Politics, Public Policy and Multiculturalism. In M. Clyne & J. Jupp (Eds), *Multiculturalism and Integration: A Harmonious Relationship* (pp. 41–52). Canberra: ANU E Press.

Kailin, J. (2002). *Antiracist Education: From Theory to Practice*. Lanham: Rowman & Littlefield.

Kalantzis, M. (1988). The Cultural Deconstruction of Racism: Education and Multiculturalism. In M. de Lepervanche & G. Bottomley (Eds), *The Cultural Construction of Race* (pp. 90–8). Sydney: Sydney Association for Studies in Society and Culture.

Kalantzis, M. (2011). Some Insights on Australian and US Multiculturalism and Multicultural Education. In M. Kelly, M. Watkins & G. Noble (Eds), *Rethinking Multiculturalism/Reassessing Multicultural Education: International Symposium* (pp. 31–2). Parramatta: Institute for Culture and Society, University of Western Sydney.

Kalantzis, M. & Cope, B. (1981). *Just Spaghetti and Polka? An Introduction to Australian Multicultural Education*. Sydney: Common Ground.

Kalantzis, M. & Cope, B. (2005). *Learning by Design*. Melbourne: Victorian Schools Innovation Commission and Common Ground.

Kalantizs, M. & Cope, B. (2008). *New Learning*. Cambridge: Cambridge University Press.

Keddie, A. (2013). Thriving Amid the Performative Demands of the Contemporary Audit Culture: A Matter of School Context. *Journal of Education Policy*, 28(6), 750–66.

Keddie, A., Gowlett, C., Mills, M., Monk, S. & Renshaw, P. (2013). Beyond Culturalism: Addressing Issues of Indigenous Disadvantage Through Schooling. *Australian Educational Researcher*, 40(1), 91–108.

Kemmis, S. (2008). Exploring the Relevance of Critical Theory for Action Research. In H. Bradbury & P. Reason (Eds), *Handbook of Action Research: Participative Inquiry and Practice* (pp. 91–103). London: Sage.

Kemmis, S., McTaggart, R. & Nixon, R. (2014). *The Action Research Planner: Doing Critical Participatory Action Research*. Singapore: Springer.

Kennedy M. (2016). How Does Professional Development Improve Teaching? *Review of Educational Research*, 86(4), 945–80.

Kenny, S. & Lobo, M. (2014). Addressing Cultural Differences: Whither Multiculturalism? In F. Mansouri & B. Ebanda de B'béri (Eds), *Global Perspectives on the Politics of Multiculturalism in the 21st Century* (pp. 105–23). New York: Routledge.

Kim-Renaud, Y.-K. (2005). Introduction. In Y.-K. Kim-Renaud, R. Grinker & K. Larsen, *Korean Education* (pp. v–vii). Washington: The Sigur Center for Asian Studies, George Washington University.

King, L. & Chandler, P. (2016). From Non-racism to Anti-racism in Social Studies Teacher Education. In A. Crowe & A. Cuenca (Eds), *Rethinking Social Studies Teacher Education in the Twenty-First Century* (pp. 3–21). Singapore: Springer.

Kirylo, J. (2017). An Overview of Multicultural Education in the USA: Grandest Social Experiment. *Social Studies Research and Practice*, 12(3), 354–7.

Koleth, E. (2010). *Multiculturalism: A Review of Australian Policy Statements and Recent Debates in Australia and Overseas*. Research Paper No. 6, Parliamentary Library, Parliament of Australia.

Kymlicka, W. (1995). *Multicultural Citizenship: A Liberal Theory of Minority Rights*. Oxford: Oxford University Press.

Kymlicka, W. (2013). Neoliberal Multiculturalism? In P. Hall & M. Lamont (Eds), *Social Resilience in the Neo-Liberal Era* (pp. 99–125). Cambridge: Cambridge University Press.

Ladson-Billings, G. (1999). Preparing Teachers for Diverse Student Populations: A Critical Race Theory Perspective. *Review of Research in Education*, 24(1), 211–47.

Ladson-Billings, G. & Tate, W. (1995). Toward a Critical Race Theory of Education. *Teachers College Record*, 97(1), 47–68.

Lather, P. (2009). Against Empathy, Voice and Authenticity. In A. Y., Jackson & L. A., Mazzei (Eds), *Voice in Qualitative Inquiry: Challenging Conventional, Interpretive and Critical Conceptions in Qualitative Research* (pp. 17–26). New York: Routledge.

Lee, J. & Zhou, M. (2015). *The Asian American Achievement Paradox*. New York: Russell Sage Foundation.

Leeman, Y. (2008). Education and Diversity in the Netherlands. *European Educational Research Journal*, 7(1), 50–9.

Lentin, A. & Titley, G. (2011). *The Crises of Multiculturalism: Racism in a Neoliberal Age*. London: Zed.

Levin, B. (2011). Mobilizing Research Knowledge in Education. *London Review of Education*, 9(1), 15–26.

Levine-Rasky, C. (2013). *Whiteness Fractured*. Surrey: Ashgate.

Levy, J. (2000). *The Multiculturalism of Fear*. Oxford: Oxford University Press.

Lillico, I. (2004). *Homework and the Homework Grid*. Duncraig: Tranton Enterprises.

Lingard, B. (2018). The Australian Curriculum: A Critical Interrogation of Why, What and Where to? *Curriculum Perspectives*, 38(1), 55–65.

Lingard, B. & Sellar, S. (2013). 'Catalyst Data': Perverse Systemic Effects of Audit and Accountability in Australian Schooling. *Journal of Education Policy*, 28(5), 634–56.

Macintyre, C. (2000). *The Art of Action Research in the Classroom*. London: David Fulton Publishers.
Mamdani, M. (2005). *Good Muslim, Bad Muslim: America, the Cold War, and the Roots of Terror*. New York: Three Rivers Press.
Manfra, M. (2019). Action Research and Systematic, Intentional Change in Teaching Practice. *Review of Research in Education*, 43(1), 163–96.
Mann, J. (2015). Britain Uncovered Survey Results: The Attitudes and Beliefs of Britons in 2015. *The Guardian*, April 19. www.theguardian.com/society/2015/apr/19/britainuncoveredsurveyattitudesbeliefsbritons2015
Markus, M. (2019). *Mapping Social Cohesion: The Scanlon Foundation surveys 2019*. Caulfield: Scanlon Foundation, Monash University.
May, S. (1999). Critical Multiculturalism and Cultural Difference: Avoiding Essentialism. In S. May (Ed.), *Critical Multiculturalism: Rethinking Multicultural and Antiracist Education* (pp. 11–41). London: Falmer.
May, S. (2002). Accommodating Multiculturalism and Biculturalism in Aotearoa New Zealand. *Waikato Journal of Education*, 8, 5–26.
May, S. (2009). Critical Multiculturalism and Education. In J. Banks (Ed.), *The Routledge International Companion to Multicultural Education* (pp. 33–48). New York: Routledge.
May, S. & Sleeter, C. (2010). Introduction. In S. May & Sleeter, C. (Eds), *Critical Multiculturalism: Theory and Praxis* (pp. 1–16). New York: Routledge.
McInerney, V. (2003). Multiculturalism in Today's Schools: Have Teachers' Attitudes Changed Over Two Decades? [Paper presentation]. Annual Meeting of the Australian Association for Research in Education, Auckland, New Zealand. Retrieved 26 June 2017 from http://www.aare.edu.au/data/publications/2003/mci03767.pdf
McKenzie, P., Rowley, G., Weldon, P. & Murphy, M. (2011). *Staff in Australia's Schools 2010: Main Report on the Survey*. Australian Council for Educational Research. Retrieved October, 2014 from http://research.acer.edu.au/tll_misc/14
McLaren, P. (2015). *Life in Schools*. London: Routledge.
Meer, N. & Modood, T. (2012). How Does Interculturalism Contrast With Multiculturalism? *Journal of Intercultural Studies*, 33(2), 175–96.
Meetoo, V. (2020). Negotiating the Diversity of Everyday Multiculturalism. *Race Ethnicity and Education*, 23(2), 261–79.
Megalogenis, G. (2002). New Faces, Old Frictions. *The Australian*. July 13/14, 19, 22.
Mills, C. (2008). 'I Don't Have Much of an Ethnic Background': Exploring Changes in Dispositions towards Diversity in Pre-service Teachers. *International Journal of Pedagogies and Learning*, 4(3), 49–58.
Mills, C. (2013). Developing Pedagogies in Pre-service Teachers to Cater for Diversity. *International Journal of Pedagogies and Learning*, 8(3), 219–28.
Mills, G. (2007). *Action Research: A Guide for the Teacher Researcher*. Upper Saddle River: Pearson/Merrill Prentice Hall.
Mills, M., Mockler, N., Stacey, M. & Taylor, B. (2021). Teachers' Orientations to Educational Research and Data in England and Australia: Implications for Teacher Professionalism. *Teaching Education*, 32(1), 77–98.
Modood, T. (2007). *Multiculturalism*. Cambridge: Polity Press.
Moran, L. (2020). *Belonging and Becoming in a Multicultural World: Refugee Youth and the Pursuit of Identity*. New Brunswick: Rutgers University Press.

Moreton-Robinson, A. (2015). *The White Possessive*. Minneapolis: University of Minnesota Press.

Murji, K. & Solomos, J. (2005). Introduction: Racialization in theory and practice. In K. Murji & J. Solomos (Eds), *Racialization: Studies in Theory and Practice* (pp. 1–27). Oxford: Oxford University Press.

Nelson, J., Dunn, K. & Paradies, Y. (2011). Bystander Anti-Racism: A Review of the Literature. *Analyses of Social Issues and Public Policy*, 11(1), 263–84.

Neuharth-Pritchett, S., Reiff, J. & Pearson, C. A. (2001). Through The Eyes of Preservice Teachers: Implications for The Multicultural. *Journal of Research in Childhood Education*, 15(2), 256–69.

Ngo, B. (2010). Doing 'Diversity' at Dynamic High: Problems and Possibilities of Multicultural Education in Practice. *Education and Urban Society*, 42(4), 473–95.

Nicolaidis, K. (2020). In Praise of Ambivalence – Another Brexit Story. *Journal of European Integration*, 42(4), 465–88.

Nieto, S. (1995). From Brown Holidays and Heroes to Assimilationist Agendas: Reconsidering the Critiques of Multicultural Education. In C. Sleeter & P. McLaren (Eds), *Multicultural education, Critical Pedagogy and the Politics of Difference* (pp. 191–214). Albany: State University of New York Press.

Nieto, S. (2009). Multicultural Education in the United States. In J. Banks (Ed.), *The Routledge International Companion to Multicultural Education* (pp. 79–95). New York: Routledge.

Noble, G. (2009a). Where the Bloody Hell Are We? Multicultural Manners in a World of Hyperdiversity. In G. Noble (Ed.), *Lines in the Sand: The Cronulla Riots, Multiculturalism and National Belonging* (pp. 1–22). Sydney: Sydney Institute of Criminology.

Noble, G. (2009b). Countless Acts of Recognition: Young Men, Ethnicity and the Messiness of Identities in Everyday Life. *Social and Cultural Geography*, 10(8), 875–92.

Noble, G. (2011). 'Bumping into Alterity': Transacting Cultural Complexities. *Continuum*, 25(6), 827–40.

Noble, G. (2012). Where's the Moral in Moral Panic? Islam, Evil and Moral Turbulence. In G. Morgan & S. Poynting (Eds), *Global Islamophobia* (pp. 215–32). Surrey: Ashgate.

Noble, G. (2017). 'Asian Fails' and the Problem of Bad Korean Boys: Multiculturalism and the Construction of an Educational Problem. *Journal of Ethnic and Migration Studies*, 43(14), 2456–71.

Noble, G. & Poynting, S. (1998). 'Weird Science' and 'Common Sense': The Discursive Construction of Accelerative Learning. *Discourse: Studies in the Cultural Politics of Education*, 19(2), 141–56.

Noble, G., Poynting, S. & Tabar, P. (1999). Youth, Ethnicity and the Mapping of Identities: Strategic Essentialism and Strategic Hybridity among Male Arabic-Speaking Youth in South-Western Sydney. *Communal/Plural*, 7(1), 29–44.

Noble, G. & Watkins, M. (2014a). *Rethinking Multiculturalism, Reassessing Multicultural Education. Project Report Number 2: Perspectives on Multicultural Education*. Parramatta: Institute for Culture and Society, University of Western Sydney.

Noble, G. & Watkins, M. (2014b). The Schooled Identities of Australian Multiculturalism: Professional Vision, Reflexive Civility and Education for A

Culturally Complex World. In R. Race & V. Lander (Eds), *Advancing Race, Ethnicity and Education* (pp. 162–77). Houndmills: Palgrave Macmillan.

NSW Department of Education. (2019). *Review of Needs-based Funding Requirements 2019–Public Submission*. https://docs.education.gov.au/sites/default/files/submissions/53417/department_of_education_new:south_wales.pdf

NSW Department of Education. (2020a). *Culturally and Linguistically Diverse People*. https://education.nsw.gov.au/about-us/careers-at-education/why-work-at-education/diversity-and-inclusion/culturally-and-linguistically-diverse-people

NSW Department of Education. (2020b). *Aboriginal Education Policy*. https://policies.education.nsw.gov.au/policy-library/policies/aboriginal-education-and-training-policy

NSW Department of Education. (2020c). *How to Maintain Accreditation*. https://education.nsw.gov.au/teaching-and-learning/professional-learning/teacher-quality-and-accreditation/maintaining-accreditation/how-to-maintain-accreditation

NSW Department of Education. (2020d). *Multicultural Education Policy*. https://policies.education.nsw.gov.au/policy-library/policies/multicultural-education-policy

NSW Department of Education. (2020e). *Multicultural Perspectives Public Speaking Competition*. https://www.artsunit.nsw.edu.au/speaking-competitions/public-speaking/multicultural-perspectives-public-speaking-competition-0

NSW Department of Education and Communities. (2010). *Handbook on Action Research in Education*. NSW DEC Professional Learning and Leadership Directorate.

Osler, A. & Starkey, H. (2018). Extending the Theory and Practice of Education for Cosmopolitan Citizenship. *Educational Review*, 70(1), 31–40.

Park, C. (2002). Crosscultural Differences in Learning Styles of Secondary English Learners. *Bilingual Researcher Journal*, 26(2), 213–29.

Parkhouse, H., Lu, C. & Massaro, V. (2019). Multicultural Education Professional Development: A Review of the Literature. *Review of Educational Research*, 89(3), 416–58.

Phillimore, J. (2015). Delivering Maternity Services in an Era of Superdiversity: The Challenges of Novelty and Newness. *Ethnic and Racial Studies*, 38(4), 568–82.

Pine, G. (2008). *Teacher Action Research: Building Knowledge Democracies*. Thousand Oaks: Sage.

Posch, P. (2019). Action Research – Conceptual Distinctions and Confronting the Theory-Practice Divide in Lesson and Learning Studies. *Educational Action Research*, 27(4), 496–510.

Poushter, J. (2017, February 6). *Diversity Welcomed in Australia, U.S. Despite Uncertainty over Muslim Integration*. Pew Research Center. http://www.pewresearch.org/fact-tank/2017/02/06/diversity-welcomed-in-australia-u-s-despite-uncertainty-over-muslim-integration/

Premier, J. & Miller, J. (2010). Preparing Pre-Service Teachers for Multicultural Classrooms. *Australian Journal of Teacher Education*, 35(2), 35–48.

Priest, N., Walton, J., White, F., Kowal, E., Baker, A. & Paradies, Y. (2014). Understanding the Complexities of Ethnic-racial Socialization Processes for both Minority and Majority Groups. *International Journal of Intercultural Relations*, 43(B), 139–55.

Race, R. (2014). The Multicultural Dilemma, the Integrationist Consensus and the Consequences for Advancing Race and Ethnicity within Education. In R. Race

& V. Lander (Eds), *Advancing Race, Ethnicity and Education* (pp. 210–29). Houndmills: Palgrave Macmillan.

Raible, R. & Irizarry, J. (2007). Transracialized Selves and the Emergence of Post-white Teacher Identities. *Race Ethnicity and Education*, 10(2), 177–98.

Reid, C., Collins, J. & Singh, M. (2014). *Global Teachers, Australian Perspectives: Goodbye Mr Chips, Hello Ms Banerjee*. Singapore: Springer.

Reid, C. & Sriprakash, A. (2012). The Possibility of Cosmopolitan Learning: Reflecting on Future Directions for Diversity Teacher Education in Australia. *Asia-Pacific Journal of Teacher Education*, 40(1), 15–29.

Ripley, A. (2013). *The Smartest Kids in the World*. New York: Simon and Schuster.

Rizvi, F. (2014). *Encountering Education in the Global*. Abingdon: Routledge.

Roxas, K., Cho, J., Rios, F., Jaime, A. & Becker, K. (2015). Critical Cosmopolitan Multicultural Education. *Multicultural Education Review*, 7(4), 230–48.

Rychly, R. & Graves, E. (2012). Teacher Characteristics for Culturally Responsive Pedagogy. *Multicultural Perspectives*, 14(1), 44–9.

Said, E. (1978). *Orientalism*. New York: Pantheon.

Santoro, N. (2013a). The Making of Teachers for the Twenty-First Century. In X. Zhu & K. Zeichner (Eds), *Preparing Teachers for the 21st Century* (pp. 309–21). Singapore: Springer.

Santoro, N. (2013b). The Drive to Diversify the Teaching Profession. *Race Ethnicity and Education*, 18(6), 858–76.

Santoro, N. (2014). 'If I'm Going to Teach about the World, I Need to Know the World': Developing Australian Pre-service Teachers' Intercultural Competence through International Trips. *Race Ethnicity and Education*, 17(3), 429–44.

Schmeichel, M. (2012). Good Teaching? An Examination of Culturally Relevant Pedagogy as an Equity Practice. *Journal of Curriculum Studies*, 44(2), 211–31.

Schwarz, A. (2007). Strategic Uses of Multiculturalism in Germany and Australia. In A. Schwarz & R. West-Pavlov (Eds), *Polyculturalism and Discourse* (pp. 67–90). Amsterdam: Rodopi.

Shankar, S. (2008). *Desiland: Teen Culture, Class, and Success in Silicon Valley*. Durham: Duke University Press.

Sherin, M. (2001). Developing a Professional Vision of Classroom Events. In T. Wood, B. Nelson & J. Warfield (Eds), *Beyond Classical Pedagogy* (pp. 75–93). Hillsdale: Erlbaum.

Sidhu, R. & Dall'Alba, G. (2012). International Education and (Dis)embodied Cosmopolitanisms. *Educational Philosophy and Theory*, 44(4), 413–31.

Silver, H. & Silver, P. (1991). *An Educational War on Poverty*. Cambridge: Cambridge University Press.

Sleeter, C. (2012). Confronting the Marginalization of Culturally Responsive Pedagogy. *Urban Education*, 47(3), 562–84.

Sleeter, C. (2018). Multicultural Education Past, Present, and Future. *International Journal of Multicultural Education*, 20(1), 5–20.

Starkey, H. (2018). Fundamental British Values and Citizenship Education: Tensions between National and Global Perspectives. *Geografiska Annaler: Series B, Human Geography*, 100(2), 149–62.

Stratton, J. (1998). *Race Daze: Australia in Identity Crisis*. Sydney: Pluto Press.

Tellez, K. (2007). Have Conceptual Reforms (and One Anti-reform) in Preservice Teacher Education Improved the Education of Multicultural, Multilingual Children and Youth? *Teachers and Teaching*, 13(6), 543–64.
Third, A. (2016). The Tactical Researcher: Cultural Studies Research as Pedagogy. In A. Hickey (Ed.), *The Pedagogies of Cultural Studies* (pp. 93–115). London: Routledge.
Thomas, S. & Kearney, J. (2008). Teachers Working in Culturally Diverse Classrooms: Implications for the Development of Professional Standards and for Teacher Education. *Asia-Pacific Journal of Teacher Education*, 36(2), 105–20.
Timperley, H. & Robinson, V. (2000). Workload and the Professional Culture of Teachers. *Educational Management and Administration*, 28(1), 47–62.
Tomlinson, S. (2009). Multicultural Education in the United Kingdom. In J. Banks (Ed.), *The Routledge International Companion to Multicultural Education* (pp. 121–33). New York: Routledge.
Topsfield, J. (2014). Abbott Government to Overhaul Crowded Curriculum. *The Age*, October 12. http://www.smh.com.au/federal-politics/political-news/abbott-government-to-overhaul-crowded-curriculum-20141012-114vrg.html#ixzz3HE2elClh
Triandafyllidou, A., Modood, T. & Meer, N. (2012). Diversity, Integration, Secularism and Multiculturalism. In A. Triandafyllidou, T. Modood & N. Meer (Eds), *European Multiculturalisms* (pp. 1–29). London: Palgrave.
Troyna, B. (1987). *Racial Inequality in Education*. London: Tavistock.
Troyna, B. (1993). *Racism and Education*. Buckingham: Open University Press.
UNESCO. (2009). *World Report No. 2: Investing in Cultural Diversity and Intercultural Dialogue*. Paris: UNESCO.
United Nations. (2019). The Number of International Migrants Reaches 272 Million, Continuing an Upward Trend in all World Regions, Says UN. Department of Economic and Social Affairs. https://www.un.org/development/desa/en/news/population/international-migrant-stock-2019.html
Vertovec, S. (2006). The Emergence of Super-diversity in Britain. Working Paper No. 25. Centre on Migration, Policy and Society, University of Oxford.
Vertovec, S. (2007). Super-diversity and Its Implications. *Ethnic and Racial Studies*, 30(6), 1024–54.
Vertovec, S. (2010). Toward Post-multiculturalism? Changing Communities, Conditions and Contexts of Diversity. *International Social Science Journal*, 61(199), 83–95.
Veugelers, W., de Groot, I. & Stolk, V. (2017). *Research for CULT Committee – Teaching Common Values in Europe*. Brussels: European Parliament, Policy Department for Structural and Cohesion Policies.
Voyer, A. (2011). Disciplined to Diversity: Learning the Language of Multiculturalism. *Ethnic and Racial Studies*, 34(11), 1874–93.
Watkins, M. (2011). Complexity Reduction, Regularities and Rules: Trying to Make Sense of Cultural Diversity in Schooling. *Continuum*, 25(6), 841–55.
Watkins, M. (2014). Multicultural Education: Contemporary Heresy or Simply another Doxa. In H. Proctor, P. Freebody & P. Brownlee (Eds), *New and Enduring Controversies in Education: Orthodoxy and Heresy in Policy and Practice* (pp. 129–38). New York: Springer.
Watkins, M. (2017). 'We Are all Asian here': Multiculturalism, Selective Schooling and Responses to Asian Success. *Journal of Ethnic and Migration Studies*, 43(14), 2300–15.

Watkins, M., Lean, G. & Noble, G. (2016). Multicultural Education: The State of Play from an Australian Perspective. *Race, Ethnicity and Education*, 19(1), 46–66.

Watkins, M., Lean, G., Noble, G. & Dunn, K. (2013). *Rethinking Multiculturalism/ Reassessing Multicultural Education Project Report Number 1: Surveying NSW Public School Teachers*. Parramatta: Institute for Culture and Society, University of Western Sydney.

Watkins, M. & Noble, G. (2008). *Cultural Practices and Learning: Diversity, Discipline and Dispositions of Schooling*. Centre for Cultural Research, University of Western Sydney.

Watkins, M. & Noble, G. (2013). *Disposed to Learn: Schooling, Ethnicity and the Scholarly Habitus*. London: Bloomsbury.

Watkins, M. & Noble, G. (2014). *Rethinking Multiculturalism, Reassessing Multicultural Education. Project Report Number 3: Knowledge Translation and Action Research*. Parramatta: Institute for Culture and Society, University of Western Sydney.

Watkins, M. & Noble, G. (2016). Thinking Beyond Recognition: Multiculturalism, Cultural Intelligence, and the Professional Capacities of Teachers. *Review of Education, Pedagogy and Cultural Studies*, 38(1), 42–57.

Watkins, M. & Noble, G. (2019). Lazy Multiculturalism: Cultural Essentialism and the Persistence of the Multicultural Day in Australian Schools. *Ethnography and Education*, 14(3), 295–310.

Watkins, M., Noble, G. & Wong, A. (2019). *It's Complex: Working With Students of Refugee Backgrounds and their Families in New South Wales Public Schools*. Sydney: New South Wales Teachers Federation.

Weinberg, J. & Flinders, M. (2018). Learning for Democracy: The Politics and Practice of Citizenship Education. *British Educational Research Journal*, 44(4), 573–92.

Wenger, E. (2000). Communities of Practice and Social Learning Systems. *Organization Articles*, 7(2), 225–46.

Williams, R. (1976). *Keywords*. Glasgow: Fontana.

Wimmer, A. (2013). *Ethnic Boundary Making*. Oxford: Oxford University Press.

Wren, T. (2012). *Conceptions of Culture*. Lanham: Rowman and Littlefield.

Wright, H. (2011). Between Global Demise and National Complacent Hegemony: Canadian Multiculturalism and Multicultural Education in a Moment of Danger. In M. Kelly, M. Watkins & G. Noble (Eds), *Rethinking Multiculturalism/Reassessing Multicultural Education: International Symposium* (pp. 34–6). Parramatta: Institute for Culture and Society, University of Western Sydney.

Yúdice, G. (2003). *The Expediency of Culture: Uses of Culture in the Global Era*. Durham: Duke University Press.

Zembylas, M. & Papamichael, E. (2017). Pedagogies of Discomfort and Empathy in Multicultural Teacher Education. *Intercultural Education*, 28(1), 1–19.

INDEX

Aboriginal Australians/Peoples 6, 26, 39, 47–8, 50, 55, 57, 60, 64–8, 90, 97, 100, 104–5, 121, 128–31, 134–5, 140–1, 145, 147–8, 160–1, 163
Ahmed, S. 3
Anglo-Australian 1, 6, 44–5, 81, 97, 100, 104–6, 113, 121, 135–6, 139–41, 143, 147, 150, 152, 157, 159, 164, 173, 205 n.1
anti-intellectualism 147–8
anti-racism 5
  education 13
  training 40
Anti-Racism Contact Officer (ARCO) training 39–40
Australia 5, 20
  cultural diversity 3, 5–6, 43–4
  ethnic diversity 3–6, 9, 17, 20–5, 28–9, 30–4, 41, 43, 45, 57, 67, 70, 78, 81, 86, 89, 90, 95, 98, 104, 113, 128–33, 145, 163, 177, 189, 192–3, 199
  First Peoples of 5–6
  Indigenous population 6, 20–1
  migrants 5
  migration programmes in 5
  as multicultural country 5, 52
  multiculturalism education in 6–10 (*see also specific school case studies*)
  multicultural policy 10
Australian and New Zealand Army Corps (ANZAC) 207 n.5
Australia Pride 206 n.1

Banks, J. 7–8, 166–7, 182, 201
Baumann, G. 41

Board of Studies, Teaching and Educational Standards (BOSTES) 14
Boccagni, P. 11
Boler, M. 182
Bra Boys 206 n.1
Bullivant, B. 10
bullying 90–1

Canada, multiculturalism education in 6–7
Castro, A. 3
Chinese students 1–2, 97–8, 100, 114, 118
citizenship education 13
civility 36
  logic of 21–2, 96
  moral 24, 32–4, 90, 96, 111, 194
  reflexive 190, 196, 202–3
  unreflexive 42, 175
communities engagement 113
Connell, R. 17
Cope, B. 2, 195
cosmopolitanism 13
cosmopolitan learning 13–14
critical pedagogy 13
cultural complexity 2–4, 11, 14, 17–19, 41–5, 57–9, 67–87, 171–90
cultural identities 44–51
  of parents 48–9
  of students 46–8
  of teachers 44–5
  unpacking 49–51
cultural intelligence 12, 139–69, 194, 196
Culturally and Linguistically Diverse (CALD) 4, 52–3, 205 n.4
cultural maintenance 9

INDEX

culture 2, 11–12, 29, 43, 139
  Australian 55–8
  categorizations of 55–6
  with country 55–7
  as difference 58–9, 139
  dynamism 4, 169, 202
  essentialism 4, 8, 42, 86, 99–102, 112, 118, 120, 122, 126, 158–9, 186
  vs. ethnicity 57–8
  as explanation 59–61
  flows 13, 109
  fluidity of 154
  and identity 44–51
  meanings of 54–8
  pedagogy 11–12
  of professional teaching 75–80
  and racism 61–4
  social constructedness of 4
  talk 43, 61–4

Dall'Alba, G. 13
Denial/Sameness model 182
diversity 20, 24–5
  cultural 3, 43–4
  ethnic 3–6, 9, 17, 20–5, 28–9, 30–4, 41, 43, 45, 57, 67, 70, 78, 81, 86, 89, 90, 95, 98, 104, 113, 128–33, 145, 163, 177, 189, 192–3, 199
  as exotic difference 139
  lip-service model of 3
dynamism, cultural 4, 169, 202

empathy 4, 37, 93, 96–7, 143–4, 169, 177
enactment 106–9
English as Additional Language/Dialect (EAL/D) 2, 39–40, 68, 205 n.2
  pedagogy 4
essentialism, cultural 4, 8, 42, 86, 99–102, 112, 118, 120, 122, 126, 158–9, 186
ethnic community 21–2, 55–6, 124, 126–7
ethnic diversity 3–6, 9, 17, 20–5, 28–9, 30–4, 41, 43, 45, 57, 67, 70, 78, 81, 86, 89, 90, 95, 98, 104, 113, 128–33, 145, 163, 177, 189, 192–3, 199
ethnicity 1–2, 4–5, 8, 11–13
  vs. culture 57–8
  and identities 8, 10–11, 17, 80, 159
ethnicized schemas 127, 158; *see also* perceptual schemas
ethnography 15–16
exotic Other 133–5

flows
  cultural 13, 109
  dynamic 59
  migrant/people 20, 56, 139
fluidity of culture 154
freedom 22

Gay, G. 11–12
globalization 10–12, 14, 17–18, 31, 43, 57, 61, 66, 72, 77–8, 102, 107–8, 111, 139, 149
Graves, E. 11
Guo, L. 13

Hage, G. 9–10, 16, 53, 102
Handbook on Action Research in Education (NSW) 72
Harmony Day 37, 114, 159, 164
hybridity, cultural 12, 47, 56, 72, 77, 86, 100
hyperdiversity 10, 50, 201

identities 8, 13, 44
  cultural 44–51
    of parents 48–9
    of students 46–8
    of teachers 44–5
  ethnic 8, 10–11, 17, 80, 159
  multicultural 51–4
  politics 8
  unpacking 49–51
inclusion 21, 121–8
  by empathy 143–4
inclusive curriculum
  Barnett High School approach to 139–45
  Graham's Point High School approach to 160–2

Hingston Valley High School
 approach to   166–8
Smithton Public School approach
 to   153–6
Wollami Lakes Public School
 approach to   145–51
incorporation, logic of   21, 41, 65,
 127, 174, 190, 192
intercultural education   8–9
interculturalism   22
intercultural understanding   37–8
intolerance   145
Islamic fundamentalism   9

Kalantzis, M.   2, 195
Kemmis, S.   72
knowledge translation   73–5
Koori   207 n.1
Kymlicka, W.   21

Ladson-Billings, G.   4
language background other than
 English (LBOTE)   2, 205 n.3
 students   2, 4, 16–17, 23, 39–40,
  67, 86, 89–90, 99, 104, 113,
  135, 145–7, 151, 154, 179,
  189, 199
lazy multiculturalism, case studies on
 89–112
 in Addington High School   90–7
 in Beechton Public School   104–11
 in Binto Valley Public School
  97–103
lip-service model of diversity   3
logics of multiculturalism   10, 18,
 20–3
 civility   21–2
 competing   21–3
 inclusion   21
 incorporation   21, 127
 recognition   21, 127

Manfra, M.   72
Māori language   7
May, S.   12–13
metalanguage   166
migration, economic role of   22
Miller, J.   4
monoculture   128, 139–45

moral civility   24, 32–4, 90, 96, 111,
 194
Multicultural Cafés   100
multicultural day   13, 28–9, 35–7,
 51, 89–90, 99–102, 106–7,
 111–12, 133, 149, 154,
 172–3, 177–8, 189, 194
multicultural education   1–3, 14–17,
 19–20, 41–2, 98–9, 192–6;
  see also specific case studies
 Aboriginal Peoples and   64–6
 in age of superdiversity   10–12
 alternative perspectives on   12–14
 in Australia   6–10
 in Canada   6–7
 challenges   4–5
 communities engagement and
  113–37
 critiques   2–3, 6, 8–10
 cultural maintenance and   9
 dimensions   8
 diversity   17–18
 expansion of   5
 identity politics in   8
 inclusive curriculum   139–69
 in New South Wales   2
 in New Zealand   6–7
 parents' perspectives on   36–7
 perceptual schemas and   19, 53–4,
  58–9, 78, 81, 86, 110, 120,
  136
 perspectives   5–10
 remaking   201–3
 social class groupings in   11–12
 students' perspectives on   36
 teacher expertise in   38–41
 teachers' perspectives on   34–5
 within teacher training   3–5
 teaching   3–5
 in UK   8–9
 in United States   7–8
Multicultural Education Policy,
 NSW   24, 80, 140, 142,
 152–3
multicultural identities   51–4
multiculturalism   1–3, 14–17, 19–20,
 41–2
 as compromise formation   22
 critical   12–13

critiques 6, 8–10, 13
dominant/institutionalized vs.
 demotic discourses of 41–2
ethnic diversity 20–2
lazy 3, 35, 89–112, 139, 144–5,
 147, 194, 202
liberal 13
logics of 10, 18, 20–3
parents' understandings of 31–4
policies, coherence of 21
students' understandings of 27–31
surveying teachers on 23–5
teachers' understandings of 25–7
transformative 195, 201–3
Muslims 27

NAIDOC week 164
National Aborigines and Islanders
 Day Observance Committee
 (NAIDOC) 207 n.2
New South Wales 2
 Multicultural Education Policy 24,
 80, 140, 142, 152–3
 multiculturalism education in 2
 (*see also specific case studies*)
 state education system in 15
New Zealand, multiculturalism
 education in 6–7
Nieto, S. 2–3
NSW Department of Education
 (DoE) 1, 14–17, 40, 68–71,
 73, 80, 82, 86, 92–3, 98, 101,
 114, 117, 120, 122, 124, 140,
 142, 146, 152, 155, 174, 191,
 197
NSW Institute of Teachers 14,
 205 n.7

Osler, A. 13

Pacific Islander students 1–2, 80, 90,
 121, 123–6, 129, 178
parents
 complexity in 48–9
 cultural identities of 48–9
 perspectives on multiculturalism
 education 36–7
 understandings of
 multiculturalism 31–4

perceptual schemas 19, 53–4, 58–9,
 78, 81, 86, 110, 120, 136
Phillimore, J. 11
pragmatism/pragmatic culture of
 teaching 91–4, 196
Premier, J. 4
professional cultures of teaching
 75–80
professional practice 196–201
professional vision 25

Quebec 7

Race, R. 9
race/racism 4, 8, 13, 90, 95, 130, 146
 and culture 61–4
 within school 96–7
recognition, logic of 21, 127
reflexive civility 190, 196, 202–3
refugee students 146–51
Refugee Week 37
Rethinking Multiculturalism,
 Reassessing Multicultural
 Education (RMRME)
 14–17, 23–5, 68–87
 action research phase of 68–9,
 82–5, 94–6
 applied, engaged, and action-oriented
 research phase of 69–72
 data analysis 80–2
 knowledge translation 73–5
 professional cultures of
 teaching 75–80
 projects (*see school-based specific
 case studies*)
 school-based action research phase
 of 69–72
 teachers training 75–80
Rizvi, F. 13, 27, 195
Rychly, R. 11

'saris, samosas and steel band' (three
 Ss) approaches 2–3
schemas of difference 54, 58–9, 81,
 136, 193; *see also* perceptual
 schemas
schemas of perception 19, 53–4,
 58–9, 78, 81, 86, 110, 120,
 136, 158

Sidhu, R. 13
Sleeter, C. 12–13
social class groupings, in education 11–12
social cohesion 9, 14, 20, 22, 53
socio-economic status (SES) 1, 16, 33, 60, 97, 104, 114, 116, 121, 128, 139, 146, 157, 163, 172, 178, 183, 189, 197
Starkey, H. 13
students
   cultural identities of 46–8
   LBOTE 2, 4, 16–17, 23, 39–40, 67, 86, 89–90, 99, 104, 113, 135, 145–7, 151, 154, 179, 189, 199
   multiculturalism, understandings of 27–31
   Pacific Islander 1–2, 80, 90, 121, 123–6, 129, 178
   perspectives on multiculturalism education 36
superdiversity 10
   classrooms and 12
   multiculturalism education in age of 10–12
   in social work 11

teachers 1–18, 23–7, 34–5, 38–41, 44–5, 75–80, 91–4, 98, 101–3, 105–37, 171–90
   cultural complexity, engagement with notions of 171–90
   cultural identities of 44–5
   knowledge
      in EAL/D pedagogy 4

      of ethnicity 4–5, 11
      gaps in 3–5
   in multicultural education 14–17
      expertise 38–41
      perspectives on 34–5
   multiculturalism
      surveying on 23–5
      understandings of 25–7
   perceptual schemas and 19, 53–4, 58–9, 78, 81, 86, 110, 120, 136
   perspectives 25
   as pragmatists 91–4
   professional cultures of teaching 75–80
   professional vision 25
   training 75–80
Teaching English Language Learners training 39–40
Tomlinson, S. 8–9
transformative multiculturalism 195, 201–3
Triandafyllidou, A. 22
Troyna, B. 2–3

United States, multiculturalism education in 7–8
unreflexive civility 42, 175

Vertovec, S. 11

White Australians 10, 141, 160, 164
World Refugee Day 94

Zembylas, M. 182